Transformed into God's Glory

Walking in the High Place

Theresa Ann Reyna

Starfish Press
LLC

Transformed into God's Glory: Walking in the High Place
Copyright © 2021 Theresa Ann Reyna

All rights reserved. No part of this book may be used or reproduced by any means, graphic, electronic, or mechanical, including photocopying, recording, taping or by any information storage retrieval system without the written permission of the publisher except in the case of brief quotations embodied in critical articles and reviews.

This book is a work of non-fiction. Unless otherwise noted, the author and the publisher make no explicit guarantees as to the accuracy of the information contained in this book and in some cases, names of people and places have been altered to protect their privacy.

Starfish Press, LLC books may be ordered through booksellers or by contacting:

Starfish Press, LLC
289 Sutton Lane
Franklin, NC 28734
www.starfish-press.com

Cover Art by: Christina Hallmark
Book Design by: Jessica Hallmark
www.jessicahallmark.com

ISBN: 978-1-953129-06-2 (Paperback)
ISBN: 978-1-953129-07-9 (Hardcover)
ISBN: 978-1-953129-08-6 (EPUB)

Library of Congress Control Number: 2022930141

Scripture quotations marked NKJV are taken from the New King James Version®. Copyright © 1982 by Thomas Nelson. Used by permission. All rights reserved.

Scripture quotations marked NASB® are taken from the New American Standard Bible®, Copyright © 1960, 1971, 1977, 1995, 2020 by The Lockman Foundation. Used by permission. All rights reserved. www.Lockman.org.

Scripture quotations marked TPT are from The Passion Translation®. Copyright © 2017, 2018, 2020 by Passion & Fire Ministries, Inc. Used by permission. All rights reserved. www.ThePassionTranslation.com.

Scripture quotations marked (NLT) are taken from the Holy Bible, New Living Translation, copyright ©1996, 2004, 2015 by Tyndale House Foundation. Used by permission of Tyndale House Publishers, Carol Stream, Illinois 60188. All rights reserved.

Scripture quotations marked AMP are taken from the Amplified® Bible, Copyright © 2015 by The Lockman Foundation. Used by permission. www.Lockman.org.

Scripture quotations marked (TLB) are taken from The Living Bible copyright © 1971. Used by permission of Tyndale House Publishers, Carol Stream, Illinois 60188. All rights reserved.

Scripture quotations marked (ESV) are from The ESV® Bible (The Holy Bible, English Standard Version®), copyright © 2001 by Crossway, a publishing ministry of Good News Publishers. Used by permission. All rights reserved.

Scripture quotations marked NIV are taken from The Holy Bible, New International Version® NIV® Copyright © 1973 1978 1984 2011 by Biblica, Inc.™ Used by permission. All rights reserved worldwide.

Scripture quotations marked MSG are taken from THE MESSAGE, copyright © 1993, 2002, 2018 by Eugene H. Peterson. Used by permission of NavPress, represented by Tyndale House Publishers. All rights reserved.

Scripture quotations marked HCSB are taken from the Holman Christian Standard Bible®, Used by Permission HCSB ©1999, 2000, 2002, 2003, 2009 Holman Bible Publishers. Holman Christian Standard Bible®, Holman CSB®, and HCSB® are federally registered trademarks of Holman Bible Publishers.

Scripture quotations marked CSB have been taken from the Christian Standard Bible®, Copyright © 2017 by Holman Bible Publishers. Used by permission. Christian Standard Bible® and CSB® are federally registered trademarks of Holman Bible Publishers.

Scripture quotations marked JUB are taken from the Jubilee Bible, copyright © 2000, 2001, 2010, 2013 by Life Sentence Publishing, Inc. Used by permission of Life Sentence Publishing, Inc., Abbotsford, Wisconsin. All rights reserved.

Scripture quotations marked (ERV) are taken from the HOLY BIBLE: EASY-TO-READ VERSION™ © 2006 by Bible League International and used by permission.

Scripture quotations marked KJV are taken from the King James Version of the Bible.

Scripture quotations markd VOICE are taken from The Voice™. Copyright © 2012 by Ecclesia Bible Society. Used by permission. All rights reserved.

Scripture quotations marked ASV are taken from the American Standard Version of the Bible.

Scripture quotations marked BLB are taken from The Holy Bible, Berean Literal Bible, Copyright ©2016, 2020 by Bible Hub. Used by Permission. All Rights Reserved Worldwide.

Scripture quotations marked EXB are taken from The Expanded Bible. Copyright ©2011 by Thomas Nelson. Used by permission. All rights reserved.

Scripture quotations marked CEV are from the Contemporary English Version Copyright © 1991, 1992, 1995 by American Bible Society. Used by Permission.

Scripture quotations marked GW is taken from GOD'S WORD®. © 1995, 2003, 2013, 2014, 2019, 2020 by God's Word to the Nations Mission Society. Used by permission.

Contents

Dedication..ix
Introduction..xi

Chapter 1   The Trip to the Top..1
            Natural and Spiritual Mountain Climbing........................2
            God's Mountain of Transfiguration...............................14

Chapter 2   Guardian of the Ark: Part 1..................................24
            The Ark of the Covenant..26
            Carriers of His Gloy...31
            It is Finished..33
            The Veil is Torn..37
            God's Holiness...38
            Victory Over the Enemy..46

Chapter 3   Guardian of the Ark: Part 2..................................53
            The High Calling of a Guardian..................................53
            Nehemiah's Wall...56
            Noah as God's Watchman..68
            The Children's Teeth are Set on Edge..........................73

Chapter 4   My Personal Testimony..82
            My Childhood Memories..84
            Troublesome Years of Grief......................................90

Years of Warfare, Grace, & God's Purifying Fire..............91
The Healing Power of God's Word................................99
In His Glory – Transformed!..103
The Transforming Power of Forgiveness.....................107

Chapter 5 Divine Reversal..116
Joseph – From the Pit to the Palace.................................122
The Number 40 – A Time of Testing..............................125
The Changing of the Guards..130
Mordecai and Esther – A New Breed & Anointing........141
Jesus Reversed the Curse..146

Chapter 6 Walking in the High Place of Sacrifice & Victory............151
The High Place of Sacrifice..155
Mount Moriah – Our Hearts, God's Altar......................163
Warring from the High Place...173
The Power of Praise and Worship..................................177
The Keys of the Kingdom..180

Chapter 7 God's Chariot Throne...195
God's End-Time Horsemen..207
The Jehu Company – The Zeal of God..........................216
God's Final Showdown – The Fall of Jezebel................223

Conclusion..234
Bibliography...243
Acknowledgments..248
About the Author..249

DEDICATION

With heartfelt love I want to dedicate this book to all who have paid the price to walk in the High Place with Jesus. To those who have allowed the Spirit to transform them: I bless you and pray God's richest blessings and miracle power to explode in your lives. May the Lord strengthen every one of you that are climbing His Holy Hill and that are in the process of being transformed from "glory to glory" in His presence.

I want to dedicate this book to Pastor Calvince Osongo and his family in Africa, God's faithful warrior and a pioneer in God's Kingdom. You have been faithful in a few things; now watch and see what your God will do in the days ahead! You are loved and cherished.

To:

All my beloved friends in Erie, Pennsylvania, and to Jane Blank and Anita McCoy: You are loved deeply, and I pray this book will bless you deeply as you climb into God's chariot of fire and move with Him into all that He has for your lives! I love both of you deeply.

To:

My husband Ron, children, grandchildren, and to all of my loved ones: You are called to be champions in the faith. Keep climbing

God's Holy Hill; Jesus has so much more for your lives. Know that you are loved and cherished deeply.

Denise, Ken, Isabel, Alanna, John K, and Ron: You are God's special warriors and intercessors. It has been an honor and a privilege to pray and to worship with you for so many years. You have enriched my life greatly, and I love you more deeply than you know.

Above all, I dedicate this book to you: Father, Jesus, and Holy Spirit. You are my Inspiration and my Life. I pray this book will bring glory, honor, and praise to You, and may many souls be set free as they embrace the Truths in this book.

INTRODUCTION

As we entered the Hebrew year of 5780 during the year 2020, God released us into a *new era*, a *new decade of glory*. The word for 80 in Hebrew is "Peh" and means *"mouth."*[i] In this new era we are called to *open our mouth* and to *declare the glory of our King, Jesus*. The Spirit is calling us to open our mouths and to proclaim the Truth, but there has been great resistance. Many of God's people have been confused over the intensity of warfare that they have gone through these past years such as wearing of masks, social distancing, personal tragedies, and governmental upheaval.

Little did I realize when I published my book **"The God of War: Breaking Through the Barriers"** in 2020 that we would enter into such an intense time of spiritual warfare and resistance from the powers of hell, but none of what we have gone through has been in vain. God has a purpose in all of these "seeming" setbacks. God's desire is to draw us close to Him in times of upheaval in order for us to experience His love in a deeper measure and to embrace His transforming power and glory. His desire is to refine us with His Holy Fire and to transform us more fully into the image of His dear Son, Jesus.

Millions of God's children are walking in a *cloud of confusion* and *pain* during this time of great darkness, not realizing what God is after. God's "Kingdom rules over all" (Psalm 103:19 – New International Version), and what the enemy has meant for evil God is turning around for our good and for His glory!

(See Genesis 50:20.) Some of God's people have embraced the change in their lives and have allowed the Spirit to transform them more deeply on the inside. On the other hand many have not embraced the "fire" and have even been "offended" in this past season. This book will expound on the importance of being transformed in God's glory, not only the HOW but the WHY.

The Spirit showed me recently a couple of reasons for this intense warfare and persecution from the adversary. It came in order to bring judgment against the enemy and to make us worthy of inheriting the Kingdom of God. It is during our deepest struggles and persecutions that we are being changed internally and made ready for the next glory that Jesus desires to bring us into.

> We point to you as an example of unwavering faith for all the churches of God. We boast about how you continue to demonstrate unflinching endurance through all the persecutions and painful trials you are experiencing. All of this proves that God's judgment is always perfect and is intended to make you worthy of inheriting the kingdom of God, which is why you are going through these troubles.
>
> –2 Thessalonians 1:4–5 – The Passion Translation

In the Merriam-Webster Dictionary it states that transformed means: (a) **to change in composition or structure,** (b) **to change the outward form or appearance of,** (c) **to change in character or condition: CONVERT.**[ii]

Why is transformation so important in a Believer's life? Is it really necessary to go through a spiritual process, the process of the cross and the resurrection, in order to become Christ-like? Isn't it enough to just go to church, do a few good works, and then go home to Heaven?

These are just a few questions that you might be thinking as you begin to read this book. I believe by the time you finish this book you will be convinced that it is necessary to be transformed in God's presence in order to walk in the High Place that you long for so deeply. We are called to be "carriers of His presence," and this emptying of all that is not of Jesus is a necessary course that we must take.

Many of God's people feel a deep internal emptiness...a deep yearning for something more, to find purpose and significance in this life. They may have read the verse that says: *"The thief does not come except to steal, and to kill, and to destroy. I have come that they may have life, and that they may have it more abundantly"* (John 10:10 – New King James Version). They read this verse and believe the first part of it, but they wonder: "Where is the abundant life that Jesus promised me?"

The Word of God tells us that in order to climb His Holy Hill we need to have "clean hands and a pure heart, who has not lifted up his soul to an idol, nor swear deceitfully" (Psalm 24:4b). We see here that in order to walk in the High Place, His Holy Hill, we need to have a clean heart, and this can only come through repentance and the washing of the water of God's Word. (See Ephesians 5:26.)

There is no satisfaction greater than that of walking in the fullness of the Father's will, no matter what we have to go through in order to get there. God will never give us more than we can bear, and His grace will always be sufficient for us.

When the storms of life come, we can either run from our problems and try to fix them in our own strength, or we can run to the "secret place," open our hearts to the Holy Spirit, and allow Him deep access into every past wound and trauma that we may have endured. There are some children of God who do not struggle as deeply as others because they had stable upbringings. They may not have known the trauma or the abuse that others have, but millions of God's children are suffering silently in shame because of past abuse and generational iniquities.

According to the _**National Sexual Assault Hotline**_, 1 out of every 6 American women has been the victim of an attempted or completed rape in her lifetime (14.8% completed, 2.8% attempted). Younger people are at the highest risk of sexual violence: 15% age 12–17, 54% age 18–34, 28% age 35–64, 3% age 65+. Males ages 18–24 who are college students are approximately 5 times more likely than non-students of the same age to be a victim of rape or sexual assault.[iiivx]

In addition to sexual abuse there are many other forms of abuse that millions have suffered as children and as adults. Coming from a past of sexual, emotional, and physical abuse, I know the trauma and the suffering that is involved in this. There are many that have come to Jesus with their pain and have known His healing love, but deep inside there still lingers feelings of pain, rejection, fear, unbelief in His promises, and a lack of love. I know many personally who are struggling, and I'm sure that you do to.

I was not healed overnight; it took years for me to come to know the deep love of Jesus and my heavenly Father. Iniquities in the bloodline such as suicidal spirits, perversion, cancer, religious spirits, and many other "bloodline" strongholds were passed down from my parents, grandparents, and great-grandparents.

Multitudes are looking for answers, and the answer is JESUS! His healing love alone is what transforms us and sets us free. Many people want instant wholeness, but the sanctification process is progressive as they walk with the Lord in full surrender and obedience to His will; such was my case. There is a lack of understanding concerning the ways of the Lord, and because of this many have turned back into a worldly lifestyle. Millions of God's children do not understand why it is "taking so long" to be made whole, but God has a plan and a purpose in every delay.

> I will not drive them out before you in a single year, so that the land does not become desolate [due to lack of attention] and the [wild] animals of the field

do not become too numerous for you. I will drive them out before you little by little, until you have increased and are strong enough to take possession of the land.

–Exodus 23:29–30 – Amplified Bible

God has called us to sacrifice our lives completely to Him, to walk in His footsteps, and to experience the "abundant life" that He has promised us. (See John 10:10.) God has a Biblical pattern in His Word, and it must not only be *read* but *applied* to our lives in order to experience the fullness of His glory and love. God is calling us in this hour to COME UP HIGHER and to ride His WAVE OF GLORY over every storm in this life. Jesus is beckoning us to pick up our cross and to follow Him every day. This requires a total commitment to His will and a full surrender to all that He would ask of us. On this path of surrender we will find *"fullness of joy"* (Psalm 16:11b – NKJV) and *a peace that passes all understanding.* (See Philippians 4:7.)

Now is the time to cut the ties that are binding us to the things of this world and to go "all the way" with Jesus. Compromising with this world and a half-hearted commitment to Jesus will never work. With Jesus it is *all or nothing;* lukewarm love for Him will never do but will only lead us to frustration and grief. If compromise and idolatry are not dealt with, it will lead us to a dead end, and we will wonder why our hearts are cold and our prayers are not answered. Wholehearted commitment will lead us into a "crucible of suffering," but we will find that our Savior is with us, purifying us, and leading us up to the High Place of glory in Him. We will *know* that we have been crucified with Jesus and that our life is now hid in Christ. We will say with Paul: *"For to me, to live is Christ, and to die is gain"* (Philippians 1:21). We will rejoice that Jesus is now living His life of faith and love in and through our lives. (See Galatians 2:20.)

God is calling His children to step into His fire *seven times hotter* in order to experience His transforming power and to have every stronghold burned up and forever removed from their lives. Jesus is calling us to walk with Him on His Holy Hill, that High Place of power, where we will see miracles, signs, and wonders such as this world has never known. We have entered into a *new era of glory* and *power* and are at the beginning of a 3rd Great Awakening. As we allow God to transform our lives, it will qualify us to be a part of His end-time Gideon army. God is looking for a *prepared people* who are fully surrendered to His will...willing vessels who have paid the price to go to the ends of the earth as His ambassadors. God is calling you! Can you hear His voice? Will you respond to the wooing of the Spirit in this hour? If your answer is "yes," Jesus will not disappoint you, and you will walk in the High Place with Him!

Jesus says:

> *"When I come this time, it will not be in a 'light' way... the way it has always been, for I will break through the barriers with great power and authority. Man has tried to control My presence, and many ministers have tried to control My 'intrusion' in their midst. This time it will be different, for I am taking the reins of My Church into My hands, and I will bring forth My heavenly order, NOT the order of man. Trust Me as I move in ways that will astound you. I am coming in great strength and power to bring divine order in the midst of My people, and I will display My glory and power in a way that My people have never seen or known before.*
>
> *"There is a release of glory more wonderful, more exuberant, more life-changing than the Church has ever known. This heavenly fire will purify many souls and release inside of them a hunger and a desire to do My will alone. No more will they 'fancy' the things of this world, for their one desire will be to love Me, honor Me, and serve Me above all. They will live to*

please Me daily, and I will orchestrate the steps of My people and My Church fully in this hour.

"No more control of man! No more control of religious spirits that are trying to shut down My voice, the voice of the prophets, and the move of My Spirit. I will tolerate this no more.

"Watch now as I 'invade' your services in new and powerful ways...in ways that will move out the flesh and soulish designs of man as I set up a new standard of holiness and submission to My will in your midst. This is not a light, small fire but an all-consuming, life-changing fire that will obliterate the dark deeds of man...the motives and intents of the heart that do not line up with My Word and the 'hidden' iniquities that man has tried so hard to conceal. They will no longer be hidden, and as they come to the Light, many will repent of 'demonic patterns' in their lives, and they will, at last, be set free by the power of My Spirit.

"This move of My Spirit is now at hand, and millions will have life-changing encounters with My Spirit. All will see and know that the Church, My people, My chosen ones, belong to Me above all! This is the time and the season for this to come forth. Get ready for this next, glorious move of My Spirit—says your God!"

CHAPTER 1

The Trip to the Top

Even as a young Christian my heart's passion was to know Him intimately and to learn His *ways* not only to see His *acts*. (See Psalm 103:7.) This desire led me down a path "less traveled" as I picked up my cross daily to follow Him in full abandonment to His will.

When the Holy Spirit led me to His Holy Hill, I began to climb upwards with the Lord as My Guide, and I have found Him to be faithful. Little by little as I climbed to reach the Heights that He ordained for me to reach, I have experienced transformation in my soul. This process did not happen overnight but day after day, week after week, month after month, and year after year. Many of God's children want a "quick fix," but this is not the way of the Lord. The transformation process will always lead us through the cross of self-denial and into the power of His resurrection. This is God's way, His pattern, for His children, and you will find the Truth of this in His Word.

> For He knew all about us before we were born and He destined us from the beginning to share the likeness of His Son. This means the Son is the oldest among a vast family of brothers and sisters who will become just like Him.
>
> –Romans 8:29 – TPT

God's passion is to take us from glory to glory and to see His Son's image formed within our souls. (See 2 Corinthians 3:18.) Concerning his own life the Apostle Paul said that *he had not arrived* and that he was *pressing on to lay hold of all that God had for him.* (See Philippians 3:12.) So, too, we can press on, yield to the Spirit's work in us, and lay hold of the fullness that God has for our lives. It is an *upward* climb, and the Lord never told us that this would be easy. As we climb to the top of His "Holy Hill," "Mount Zion," the city of the living God, the heavenly Jerusalem, we will experience what many mountain climbers experience in the natural realm. (See Hebrews 12:22.)

Natural and Spiritual Mountain Climbing

Let's take a tour now and compare natural mountain climbing with our spiritual journey. There are many comparisons and examples of what we will experience as we are "transformed into the image of Christ." (See 2 Corinthians 3:18.)

As I studied the effects of mountain climbing, I found that some of the symptoms people experience can be acute *mountain sickness, headaches, insomnia, fatigue, nausea, dizziness, faster heart rate, and vomiting.*[iv] Some say that mountain climbing can kill brain cells and cause a high-altitude sickness called *cerebral edema (brain-swelling)* which is potentially fatal.[iv] *Lack of oxygen* can directly damage brain cells and can cause dangerous swelling.[iv]

Mountain climbing can be a dangerous sport, and the risks of injuries are great. Experts tell us that the number one danger of mountain climbing is *lack of awareness.*[iv] Dangers caused by careless human action can lead to disastrous results. The same is true in the spiritual realm; climbing the "Mountain of the Lord" can be filled with pitfalls and dangers, and we need to make sure that we are covered with the presence of the Spirit of God and that we are well-equipped with His Word of Truth. At times we may fall, but the Lord will always protect us and will pick us up as we cry out to Him. We need to be aware that there is an enemy that is out to trip us up and even destroy us. We must abide in the Lord and stay in His "safety zone" by staying close to Him in prayer and praise.

Mountain climbers must always follow the directions of their leader,[iv] and in humility we must always follow the leading of the Spirit as we begin to climb to greater heights in Him. We must listen to the voice of the Spirit and follow His directions always or we will find ourselves in dangerous situations that will require His help and deliverance. We must humble ourselves before the Lord and lean on Him through our journey uphill. Our goal is total transformation in His glory, and we must keep our eyes on the prize! How desperately we need His manual, the Bible, on our journey upward, for if we lean on our own understanding, we will fail. (See Proverbs 3:5.)

A climber is told to **focus** on where they are **at the moment.**[iv] Mountain climbing is about enduring pain and exhaustion,[iv] and this is true for all those who journey with Jesus. He is taking us to great heights, and we must never look back only straight ahead, even in the darkness, knowing that glory awaits us. We have need of endurance so that we may receive what He has promised. (See Hebrews 10:36.) We must always focus on the face of Jesus as we climb the "mountain of difficulty," for if we **focus on Him** we will have the grace and strength to make it to the top.

We are climbing into **HIGH ALTITUDES,** and we must daily breathe in the Breath of Life, the Holy Spirit, into our lungs. We do not want to experience altitude sickness or to faint on the way. Our minds need to be **renewed daily** in the Bible as we journey on in order to experience **constant renewal in our thought life.** (See Romans 12:2.) This will keep us from fear and from the lies of the enemy. The Word will strengthen our inner-man and bring deep spiritual growth. Many have fallen, even at the beginning of their climb, because of a lack of knowledge of God's Word. They do not understand that the "way is hard" and that the "gate is narrow." (See Matthew 7:14.)

As God's children continue on their journey, many experience *spiritual insomnia*, for they are troubled and depressed concerning their circumstances and feel abandoned in their time of need. Little do they realize that their Guide, the Holy Spirit, is right beside them leading them upward into a glorious, broad place of spiritual fulfillment in Christ. They experience a loss of appetite and energy, and they wonder if God has left them. They are in a *time of growth and expansion*, but they feel as if they are going backward in their spiritual journey. Jesus never said it would be easy, but He promised to never leave us or forsake us, and He never will! (See Hebrews 13:5.)

It is in our weakness that God reveals His strength to us. It is in our weakness that His very Life is filling us and transforming us into the overcomers that He has destined us to be. It is in our *troubles* that this transformation is being worked out deep in our hearts, souls, and minds. God is patient with us and will not hurry the process in our souls in order to make us comfortable, for He will take us through the deepest valley in order to spiritually strengthen us. In the midst of our mountain climbing, the Spirit will come with His "oil of joy" and His deep love in order to encourage us on our journey, and we will know that He is with us.

Confusion and lethargy are also symptoms of mountain climbers[iv] and are also what many of God's people have experienced, or are experiencing now, as they climb His "Hill of Glory"! I remember long ago when I started my journey in Jesus there were times of anger, pain, and confusion. I felt as if the Lord was *destroying* me when in reality He was freeing me from my sin and iniquity. There is a lack of understanding concerning the *ways of the Lord* in the Body of Christ because many ministers do not teach the whole counsel of God's Word. (See Acts 20:27.) Many of God's people are in a state of *spiritual lethargy* because they have stopped moving with the Spirit, and because of this they are in a *spiritual slumber*. God is calling His people to arise and to take this "High Place of Glory." Some of

God's people are nearing the top, and others are just starting their journey or are midway up this mountain. We must continue to climb God's "Mountain" until we reach the *mountain peak of glory!*

If climbers experience mild *altitude sickness,* they need to rest and to sleep until their bodies acclimate to the altitude.[iv] The experts advise that they rest in the shade and that they drink cold water.[iv] It is the same spiritually; when weariness sets in, we need to drink the refreshing waters of the Spirit and to spend extra time with the Lord waiting in His presence in order to renew our strength. Then we will mount up with "wings as an eagle" and soar with Him into the heights of glory that He has prepared for us. (See Isaiah 40:31.) God is calling us into His rest, and this can only come as we spend time in the "quiet zone" with Him. The experts also advise mountain climbers to *remove all excess clothing* and to use *sponges filled with water* to cool their bodies to help alleviate altitude sickness.[iv] In the same way *spiritual climbers* need to "lay aside every weight, and the sin which so easily ensnares us" (Hebrews 12:1b – NKJV).

Sometimes mountain climbers experience loss of body heat, a weak heartbeat, and even suffer loss of consciousness.[iv] There may be times, spiritually, when a child of God just wants to give up. They feel spiritually weak and are at the point of losing the *consciousness* of Jesus and His presence *with* them. They find themselves at a crossroads to either turn back into the world or to continue on in their journey in the Spirit. Many of God's children have turned back to the world for help. Their hearts are no longer on fire for Jesus but have "cooled" and become "lukewarm." They no longer feel a passion for the lost or care for the things of God. Their church attendance has waned, and they have slipped into a lifestyle of compromise and idolatry. In spite of all this I believe that we have entered into a 3rd Great Awakening... a great shaking that will bring millions of God's prodigals back home to His heart, and they will continue their climb upward into the fullness of glory that their hearts truly long for.

Frostbite is another symptom that many natural climbers will experience, and they advise the climbers to move to a dry and warm area to warm up their bodies.[iv] I believe there is a *spiritual frostbite* that many have experienced these past years and that they may still be experiencing, even now, because of *seeming* delays in the answers to their prayers. Coldness and a *spiritual stiffness* have entered into the hearts of many through this *frostbite*. God's desire has been to empty our souls of the things of this world and to do a deep transforming work inside of us through these troubling times. Some of God's children have allowed this work of the Spirit to be accomplished in their souls while many others have felt *on ice* as they have been waiting upon the Lord and seeking Him with their whole heart, not understanding what the Spirit is after. God has been teaching us to stand on His Word, no matter what we feel or see, and to not allow our emotions to rule over our lives or to dictate our actions. I go into detail concerning this in my **God of War** book. Others have run to the false comforts of this world through earthly pleasures, addictive drugs, perversion, and alcohol. Their hearts have turned *cold* to the things of the Lord, and they feel that it is too late for them. Nothing could be further from the Truth! The enemy is a liar and the "father of lies" (see John 8:44), and we must learn to control our thought life. We have to take our thoughts captive to the obedience of Christ. (See 2 Corinthians 10:5.) Jesus is about to melt the ice and remove the *numbness* that has formed around the hearts of millions with the fire of His love.

Climbers need to pack the appropriate climbing attire,[iv] and in the same way God's people need to wear the *spiritual armor* that He has provided for them. (See Ephesians 6:11–17.) If you don't know what this armor is, I encourage you to read these Scriptures and to make sure that you have on the proper *clothing* as you journey with Jesus. God's people need proper *wet weather clothing,* and then we can be sure that when we go through deep waters, Jesus will be with us, and we will not drown. (See Isaiah

43:2.) We must be covered from head to toe in order to be protected against the "wiles" of the enemy on our journey upward. There will be many distractions and lies that we will have to overcome as He takes us to His "Mount of Glory"!

There are potential natural disasters for mountain climbers such as avalanches, hurricanes, volcanic eruptions, and earthquakes.[iv] Serious injuries, or even death, can happen to the climbers if they are caught in these disasters.[iv] During seasons in our lives when we experience great upheaval and intense spiritual warfare, it is important to be deeply rooted in the heart of Jesus and His love. If our spiritual roots are shallow, it will be easy for the enemy to uproot our faith and to bring great despair into our souls. Many who have shallow soil have "withered" as the "parable of the sower" reveals to us. (See Matthew 13:6.)

Mountain guides also stress the importance of *staying in groups*,[iv] and spiritually, this is most important. Those who isolate themselves are in great danger because they are more likely to fall into fear and temptation without a support group. I am a strong believer in *home groups* as well as *church attendance* where you can meet with those who are of *like faith*. I have met some of my best friends at church through the leading of the Spirit, and I wouldn't trade these friends for the world! Gathering in small groups is also important, for you can open your heart and share intimately with those you have come to trust.

One of the hazards a mountain climber might encounter are *falling objects* such as rocks.[iv] They must be *fully awake* and aware of any potential danger.[iv] In the Spirit we need to be alert and to make sure that our "shield of faith" is up to protect us from the "fiery darts" of the evil one. (See Ephesians 6:16.) We need to be as Habakkuk who stood his watch on the tower waiting to hear what God would say. (See Habakkuk 2:1.) It is during our daily *quiet time* with the Lord that the Lord will warn us of impending danger and draw us close to Him.

Climbers may encounter and disturb *wildlife* in an area where human activity is low.[iv] You can be sure that when you follow the Lord fully you will stir up the wrath of the enemy, but we never have anything to fear, for the Lord is our "Shelter" and our "Rock of Refuge." (See Psalm 31:2.) God will allow warfare for a season to build us up spiritually and to teach us how to bring down evil empires of darkness. He will give us courage to face our "giants" and to never back down from them. The Lord will waste nothing that we go through. Everything that we overcome will be for the glory of His name and for our good. Those who are encountering spiritual warfare can know for a fact that they are on the Lord's path of glory; they are on a path where there is *little human activity*. You are *disturbing* the enemy because you are a threat to the devil's kingdom of darkness. Rejoice, those of you who are fighting spiritual battles, for God is strengthening you and positioning you in His end-time army. In my last book, **The God of War,** I go into great depth explaining how the Lord had me resist the enemy and break through barriers of darkness when I was diagnosed with cancer. God could have healed me immediately, but His plan was to strengthen me and to draw me closer to Him and deeper into His heart of love. God showed me that the cancer was a "viper" from hell, and that like the Apostle Paul, I had to shake it off into the fire, the fire of His presence.

Mountain climbers have been taught to make loud noises in order to avoid encountering wildlife,[iv] and I can tell you from experience that there is nothing greater than praise and shouts of victory when you are in spiritual warfare. Praise and worship will cause your enemy to run as far as he can from you, for God inhabits our praise. (See Psalm 22:3.) Confront the enemy with the Word of God, and never, never turn your back to him and run. Never allow the "spirit of fear" to control your life. Step out in faith no matter what confronts you, and God will give you the victory every time.

We have been told to never "feed" any wildlife, for they become dependent on us for food.[iv] This is a good principal for us spiritually. In a dream that I had during my *fiery trial of faith*,

I saw a wolf *behind a screen,* and the wolf said, *"Give me some vitamins."* In the next scene the wolf was right next to me, and I was holding his *mouth shut.* The Lord showed me that when we speak words of unbelief and fear it feeds the enemy and makes him *stronger* in our lives. Negative words are *vitamins* to the enemy, and that is why I had to hold his mouth shut and to not listen to any of his lies. Believe me, it was quite a battle! The enemy hides behind a *smokescreen* and tries to cover up what he is doing in our lives. He tries to "trip us up" through his lies and demonic schemes, but we are not ignorant of his schemes. (See 2 Corinthians 2:11.)

In mountain climbing school they teach you to get to *higher ground* if you think you are in danger.[iv] This is a great lesson for all who are under attack and going through the fires of affliction. We must keep climbing and get to higher ground in the Spirit, for this is our place of safety. The higher you climb in the Lord the harder it will be for the enemy to attack you and the safer you will be.

There can be deadly, poisonous plants where people climb, and these climbers must be able to identify them.[iv] If they come in contact with these plants, they must wash the infected area and seek medical attention if the area worsens.[iv] Some of these poisonous plants can be deadly if ingested.[iv] In the same way we must avoid eating the poison of the enemy: bitterness, fear, unbelief, rebellion, willfulness, greed, pride, idolatry, compromise, lust, jealousy, and a host of other sins that will hinder and weaken our walk in Jesus. We must avoid these, but if we do sin, we can run to Jesus and repent, and He will be faithful and just to forgive and to cleanse us. (See 1 John 1:9.)

Without proper *preparation* and training, mountain climbing can be extremely dangerous.[iv] You will never be fully equipped to mountain climb in just a few weeks. It is so important to have an experienced guide and to learn all that you can about climbing.[iv] It is wise to take courses, to read books, and to watch videos about mountain climbing. Climbers should never start out climbing a high mountain but practice on easier climbs.[iv] This can take months or even years in the natural. And how much more important is it to study the Word, to pray, to spend hours with Jesus in the "secret place," to go to church, to fellowship with other Believers, to be mentored by matured Christians on how to walk with the Lord, and to learn how to resist the enemy in spiritual warfare? Climber's risk getting injuries when they have insufficient training, and these injuries could be catastrophic.[iv] In the same manner, immature Christians who are not built up in the Lord can injure themselves spiritually, and even others, if they step into areas where they are not properly trained and anointed by the Lord to go into.

Mountain climbers are taught to never rely *fully* on others or to be overconfident.[iv] If they follow others blindly they could endanger their lives.[iv] Likewise, we must never *fully* trust another, though their intentions may be good. Our full trust, reliance, and confidence should be in the Holy Spirit to lead and to guide us on our path of Truth. We should never blindly listen to or follow another Christian if what they are telling us does not line up with the Word of God. We must always go to the Lord in prayer when we have a question about ministry or about our personal lives. The Lord promises us that His "sheep hear His voice" (see John 10:27), and we can develop a "hearing ear" early in our Christian walk. (See Matthew 11:15.) We must never just *go with the flow* when the Lord gives you a *check* in your spirit. Always, always seek the Lord and His will **first** in all things. Go to the Word, for Jesus will speak to you and give you a "Living Word" as you read and study the Bible.

Sometimes climbers *lose visibility* because of heavy rain, snow, or a lack of lighting.[iv] The ground they are walking on may become icy and slippery, and there is a risk of falling.[iv] Also, *snow blindness*, a temporary blindness, is not uncommon.[iv] The Lord will, at times, lead us through "slippery places," and we will need the help of the Spirit of God and others to pray and to bear us up. When we walk through the "valley of the shadow of death" (see Psalm 23:4), it can be very, very dark, and we will need the Light of the Spirit of God to lead and to guide us through our times of testing. Jesus will give us *spiritual sight,* and His Word will be a "light unto our path." (See Psalm 119:105.)

Many climbers have died because they did not listen to their expedition leader or did not follow the rules that they were taught.[iv] My husband hiked the Grand Canyon, and on arriving home he heard of several deaths that had recently happened there. Some ignored warning signs and closed zones and went off the designated path. This carelessness led to their demise. We must always follow our Leader, Jesus, as He leads and guides us into our destiny. We must never ignore the warnings of the Holy Spirit, and we must stay close to the Lord always. There are so many pits that the enemy has placed in our path, but as we follow Jesus He will warn us, protect us, and keep us safe.

Some climbers have lost their way because they took a wrong turn or because they wandered away from the person they were hiking with.[iv] Guides tell the climbers to stay in pairs for safety reasons,[iv] and in the Gospels we read that Jesus sent them out two by two. (See Mark 6:7.) We need one another in the Body of Christ, for there is safety in numbers. Climbers are told to retrace their steps if they get lost, and many souls that have wandered off the path of righteousness have had to retrace their steps and return to the Lord. True repentance will always bring us back into fellowship with the Lord. If we fall Jesus will always take us back, wash our wounds, and forgive us.

The symptom of *resistance* is big in climbers when attempting overly difficult routes,[iv] and this is true for us as well. When we see a "giant" before us, a *mountain of difficulty,* it is very common for a Believer to pull back spiritually and to not want to move forward in the Spirit. We will also experience resistance from an angry foe, but our "Guide" will see us through to the end. We must continue to walk in faith no matter what we feel or see. For the true Believer there is no turning back!

Climbers must never allow themselves to become *dehydrated*, or they could experience headaches, fatigue, carelessness, and loss of appetite.[iv] In the same way we must never allow our souls to dry out. As we drink daily from the "Well" that never runs dry, we will be like a "well-watered spring." (See Isaiah 58:11.) This will keep us strong and spiritually healthy.

Pray with me: "Father, hear our cry! Strengthen and guide us as we continue to climb Your 'Mountain of Holiness.' Purify us as we go through our fiery trials. Help us to pray and to praise You with our whole heart as we go through the 'valley of the shadow of death' (Psalm 23:4). Fill us to overflowing with Your Living Water, and may we never grow weary in well-doing. May we desire Your will above all as we seek You and passionately pursue Your presence daily. As we climb Your Holy Mountain, may there be no resistance in our hearts and may we trust You implicitly. You are our Guide and will lead us to 'still waters' (see Psalm 23:2) and into the deep rest that You have promised us. In our weakness be our Strength. In our pain be our Solace. Purify our hearts as we press forward...as we press on into all that You have for our lives. When our hearts are cold, warm them with the fire of Your love. Ever protect us from the onslaughts of the evil one, for You are our Hiding Place. In Jesus' name we pray."

Hear the Lord say:

> *"What is in your 'hand,' children? What is on your heart in this hour? Are you desperate for My presence? Is there a deep desire for Me and My will for your life?*
>
> *"I am drawing My people into the 'secret place' and am revealing to them My 'blueprint' for their lives. I am downloading My heart and My plans to many of My people in this hour, for the hour is late. I am raising up laborers to go into the harvest field and to reap precious souls. (See Luke 10:2.)*

"Do you feel this stirring? Do you sense in My Spirit that I have so much more for your life? What you are feeling and sensing in the Spirit is My love call...My call for you to enter into the fullness of your destiny in this new era. There are new things, new plans, new experiences for you now. Take these things that I am placing in your heart and pray and praise Me; seek Me with your whole heart, and they will manifest in this natural realm. Doors of ministry will begin to open that have never opened up before. You will walk in a new dimension of my Spirit, and the Spirit-realm will be more real to you than the physical, natural realm.

"I am moving mightily in this hour, and as you step into your destiny in obedience, you will begin to flow with My Spirit as you never have before. My 'Wind' is blowing upon you and moving you into this new place of glory. As you line up perfectly with My will, you will sense My rest and an ease of My Spirit unlike anything you have sensed before. This is My place of rest and ease; this is My place of abundance, the place that I have promised to bring you into. Do not fear to take this step of faith, for this is from Me. It may be new; it may be different from anything you have ever experienced in the past but know that this is of Me. Step out of the boat and into the wild, and you will find Me there. You will ride this 'wild wave' with the Lord your God. This is of Me, and for some of you this word is a confirmation of the things that I have been speaking to you! This is your confirmation!

"'Arise, shine; for your Light has come!' (Isaiah 60:1a). This is your time to shine for Me in a way and in a manner that is new and exciting! This is the season of glory that you have long been waiting for. This is what your heart has been longing for, pounding for; it has arrived! Some of you have been

on a long spiritual journey, and you thought it would never change. You have wept; you have longed for something deeper, something new and exciting in My Spirit. You knew there was more, and how right you have been! You have not given up, and now, My reward is in My hand, and I am ready to release it into your life. Move forward now, for I am holding your hand, and I promise you: You will not fall, for I am holding you in the palm of My hand—says your God!"

God's Mountain of Transfiguration

God is calling us up to a "High Mountain," a place where we will experience a passionate encounter with our Savior. Jesus is calling out to us, to a prepared people, to come up higher and to receive the glory that He has prepared for us. A fiery "pillar of glory" is about to enter into our beings that will transform us from the inside out. This is a deep work, a pulling up of the deep roots of iniquity that have troubled many souls and have kept them in fear and unbelief. These 2 pillars, these 2 strongholds, will now be uprooted out of millions of souls that have been in bondage for years. It will be through the power and the passionate love of Jesus that these strongholds, and many other demonic "chains," will be removed from the hearts of God's children.

Because of a lack of teaching and a lack of understanding concerning the ways of the Lord, many believe that every sin and every iniquity is instantly removed when they say a simple *sinner's prayer*, but the Word teaches us that we must confess our sin first. This is not just a general *"forgive me for sinning"* prayer. There is a great difference between God *forgiving* us of our sin when we come to Him and truly repenting and being *cleansed internally* from all unrighteousness, including generational iniquities. Every child of God must go through the *process of the cross* and *then* into the *power of His resurrection.* This is where many ministers have failed to teach and to preach the *whole counsel* of God. (See Act 20:27.) We will go into this in more detail in the chapters ahead.

This is a new day, and a glorious "Whirlwind" is about to lift us up to new heights where we will encounter the Lord in ways that will astound us.

> About eight days after these sayings, He took along Peter, John, and James, and went up on the mountain to pray. And while He was praying, the appearance of His face became different, and His clothing became white and gleaming. And behold, two men were talking with Him; and they were Moses and Elijah, who, appearing in glory, were speaking of His departure, which He was about to accomplish at Jerusalem. Now Peter and his companions had been overcome with sleep; but when they were fully awake, they saw His glory and the two men who were standing with Him. And as these two men were leaving Him, Peter said to Jesus, "Master, it is good that we are here; and let's make three tabernacles: one for You, one for Moses, and one for Elijah"—not realizing what he was saying. But while he was saying this, a cloud formed and began to overshadow them; and they were afraid as they entered the cloud. And then a voice came from the cloud, saying, "This is My Son, My Chosen One; listen to Him!" And when the voice had spoken, Jesus was found alone. And they kept silent, and reported to no one in those days any of the things which they had seen.
>
> –Luke 9:28–36 – New American Standard Bible

Luke 9:28 starts by saying, "About **8** days." This number 8 means **new beginnings,**[v] and we have now entered into the "new things" that the Lord has prepared for us. These are days when we will have "God-encounters" as we enter into His "Cloud of Glory." We will be empowered to do the "greater works" that the Spirit has prepared for us to walk in. In His "Cloud" we will experience powerful *explosions of glory* that will *prepare* and *position* us to bring in this final harvest.

God is not only calling His remnant to encounter Him but Jesus is calling all of His children in this hour to meet with Him in the "secret place" and to know Him more deeply and intimately than ever before. He is calling **all** of His children to encounter Him so that they can be made whole: spirit, soul, and body. He is calling us to come up higher, to come up into the next glory, and enter into the "portal of power" that He has prepared for us to enter into. This is a call to rise up on "Jacob's ladder" (see Genesis 28:10–22) and to enter into the heavenly sphere where we will encounter an innumerable company of angels and walk in the High Place, even Mount Zion.

> But you have come to Mount Zion and to the city of the living God, the heavenly Jerusalem, and to myriads of angels, to the general assembly and church of the firstborn who are enrolled in heaven, and to God, the Judge of all, and to the spirits of the righteous made perfect, and to Jesus, the mediator of a new covenant, and to the sprinkled blood, which speaks better than the blood of Abel.
>
> –Hebrews 12:22–24

Jesus was calling Peter, James, and John up to the Mountain of Prayer where they would encounter Him in a new and dramatic way! *While they were praying* indicates that we will encounter Jesus when we seek Him with our whole heart in prayer and in worship. Prayer and praise will prepare our hearts for heavenly encounters, and in our "secret place" Jesus will reveal Himself to us in ways that will overwhelm us. As we behold His glory we will experience an inner transformation, a holy fire, that will consume everything in our souls and our bodies that have held us captive. I've had many dreams lately about *roots* being pulled up and out of the deep hearts of believers, and I know that this is God's desire for each one of His children. In 2 Corinthians 3:18 (New Living Translation) it states: *"So all of us who have had that veil removed can see and reflect the glory of the Lord. And the Lord—who is the Spirit—makes us more and more like Him as we are changed into His glorious image."*

God's desire is to take us "behind the veil" through the "circumcision of our hearts." (See Romans 2:28–29; Jeremiah 4:4.) As we gaze on the Lord's beautiful face, we are changed and transformed more fully into His image. This comes as we spend much time in His presence listening to His voice and receiving daily infillings of the Spirit. As we seek Him "the appearance of His face will change," and we will encounter the Lord in new and glorious ways, in ways we have never seen Him before. Some of God's children will be shocked as they encounter Jesus as the "Lion of Judah." Others will encounter the Lord as their "Bridegroom" as He sweeps them off of their feet. Still others will meet their King as a gentle "Lamb" because of their deep grief and pain. God's people will experience His love and His compassion in a way they never have before. To the weak He will show Himself strong, and to the timid He will infuse them with the power of the Holy Spirit and with boldness. Get ready to encounter your King in ways that will startle you, in ways that will amaze you! Jesus is holy, and millions will encounter Him as a "Consuming Fire." When John encountered Jesus on the Isle of Patmos, he fell down at the feet of Jesus as "dead."

> Then I turned to see the voice that spoke with me. And having turned I saw seven golden lampstands, and in the midst of the seven lampstands One like the Son of Man, clothed with a garment down to the feet and girded about the chest with a golden band.

His head and hair were white like wool, as white as snow, and His eyes like a flame of fire; His feet were like fine brass, as if refined in a furnace, and His voice as the sound of many waters; He had in His right hand seven stars, out of His mouth went a sharp two-edged sword, and His countenance was like the sun shining in its strength. **And when I saw Him, I fell at His feet as dead.** But He laid His right hand on me, saying to me, "Do not be afraid; I am the First and the Last. I am He who lives, and was dead, and behold, I am alive forevermore. Amen. And I have the keys of Hades and of Death.

–Revelation 1:12–18 – NKJV, emphasis added

Jesus is about to visit His Church in a way that will cause many to "fall at His feet as dead." Those who have tried to cover their sin and their iniquity will know the uncovering and exposure of the Spirit. Ministers and preachers who have lived a hypocritical lifestyle of compromise and idolatry will now cry out as the Lord comes in a power and a fire they have never known. This *shaking* from the Lord will uncover all that is false and dark.

Some years back I had a dream, and in this dream I was on my face before the Lord with other people around me. I remember seeing the glory of God descending from on High, and all those who were on the floor with me started crawling out of the room as His glory drew closer and closer. I stayed on my face before the Lord, for My desire was to encounter Him in a greater way. I believe this is what we will see in this hour, for as deep, hidden sin is uncovered, we will hear heart-wrenching cries from many who thought their sin would never find them out. Those who stay in the presence of God and allow the Spirit to uncover their sin and to cleanse them will know God's greatest love and glory! They will be placed and positioned in God's end-time army, and they will go to the ends of the earth as the Spirit leads them. God's fire is meant to *burn off* our chains, *not to destroy us*. He will look at His people with eyes of fire and eyes of love, not condemnation.

In Luke 9:30 Jesus was talking to Moses and Elijah which I believe represents *plagues and judgment* and His *miracle working power* in our generation. Moses represents the judgments of God...the plagues that were manifested in Egypt so long ago. During these plagues God kept His people safe in the land of Goshen. (See Exodus 7:1–13:22.) In the same way God is keeping us safe in the midst of the *plagues and viruses* that have invaded the world and the ones that are yet to come. Moses also represents the power of God that will be displayed as God judges our enemies and opens the "Red Sea" of difficulty for us. We will be protected and kept safe in the midst of coming disasters. Much destruction is on the horizon, but we will experience and walk in Psalm 91 through it all.

Elijah represents God's *miraculous power*, the *rain* of the coming *revival*, and the 3rd Great Awakening. It has already begun as I write this, but it will grow stronger and stronger in the years ahead. No man, no devil will be able to stop this worldwide revival and awakening. The Lord told me years ago that this *outpouring of His Spirit* will not stop until He comes back. In former revivals the interference of man and of the devil blocked the move of the Spirit from continuing but not this time, not in this new era!

God's intercessors, like Elijah, have prayed for the rain of the Spirit for years, and the Lord has heard our cries. We will witness the dead raised and creative miracles such as this world has never seen. In this very hour God is raising up His Elijah's and Elisha's who will stand against devils and "giants" that have tried to destroy our nation and the nations of this world! They will fear nothing that the devil or man throws against them. They will be as *immovable mountains* in this era of glory, and we will see God sweep across this entire earth! The "spirit of Jezebel" that has controlled this earth, and even the Church, this "spirit of perversion and compromise" will now be dealt with by the Living God. His fire will tear down evil empires and release millions of captive souls in this hour. We will live to see it and shout and praise our God as we never have before!

Peter and his companions had been *overcome with sleep,* but when they were *fully awake* they *saw* the glory of Jesus and Moses and Elijah who were standing with Him. Many of God's children have been overcome with *spiritual lethargy* and are *sleepy* because of the tremendous trials and sufferings they have endured in this past season. Many have grown weary, but the Lord is about to come with His refreshing rain and revive His battle-weary warriors. The souls of those who have *medicated* themselves with the pleasures of this world and idolatry will be awakened through the greater shakings that are coming and will return to the Lord. The Church has grown *sleepy,* but God is about to awaken Her (the Church) with His great fiery love and with miracles, signs, and wonders.

Peter asked if he could make 3 tabernacles: one for Jesus, one for Moses, and one for Elijah. While Peter was saying this *a cloud formed and overshadowed them,* and they were afraid as they entered the cloud. Jesus comes to us many times in a cloud, even a "dark cloud."

> He bowed the heavens also, and came down with darkness under His feet. And He rode upon a cherub, and flew; He flew upon the wings of the wind. He made darkness His secret place; His canopy around Him was dark waters and thick clouds of the skies. From the brightness before Him, His thick clouds passed with hailstones and coals of fire.
>
> —Psalm 18:9–12

The Lord is calling us into His "Cloud of Glory," and some of His children, His remnant, have already experienced this glory, at least to some degree. God's true children have found that Jesus reveals Himself to them in *greater ways* during times of darkness and great sorrow and in fiery testings and temptations. This dark cloud is a *cloud of protection,* for Jesus is pure and radiant Light, more powerful than the rays of the sun.

As Peter and his companions entered this cloud, they were afraid. They were experiencing something new and frightening. Jesus is coming to His people as the "Lion of Judah." He is coming in ways they have never seen or known Him, and for many this experience will cause their hearts to tremble in fear. I believe that the *fear of God* is returning to the Church. The encounters that are coming will fill the hearts of God's people with a reverential fear, but for the rebellious it will be terrifying! I believe that when Jesus comes in His greater glory everyone will fall on their faces before Him, and not one will be left standing! Most "church people" have not encountered Jesus in this way yet, but I know this revelation of His holiness is coming very soon.

We are His "temples," His "tabernacles" (see 1 Corinthians 6:19), and I believe that Peter wanting to make 3 tabernacles signifies wholeness: spirit, soul, and body. God wants to inhabit our lives fully. He desires to possess every part of our being. Many have given Jesus a part of their hearts but not the deep places within the core of their being. The Word tells us to love the Lord our God with **all** our heart, with **all** our soul, with **all** our strength, and with **all** our mind (see Luke 10:27), but many have held back major parts of their heart from the Spirit of God.

God spoke from the cloud and confirmed that Jesus was His "Chosen One," His Son. When the voice finished speaking, "Jesus was found alone" (Luke 9:36). The Spirit of God is drawing His people to become one with Jesus. The Father longs to see the image of His Son formed inside of our souls and filling our bodies. This generation will see the fulfillment of John chapter 17 in ways no other generation has. Jesus prayed for oneness with His Church and for His Church to become one with each other. Many times in the past I wondered how this could be accomplished because of all the differences I saw between brothers and sisters in Christ. God has given me an understanding concerning this, and now I see what His plan is. Through great fiery trials and the love of God as each individual member in the Body of Christ become one with Jesus, it is then, and only then, that we will be one with each other. As we experience deep purification in our hearts through the Spirit of God, this mighty work of "unity" will be accomplished, and in spite of differences we will love each other with the love of Jesus. This love will transcend all differences, and it will not matter what race or color we are or whether we are male or female, for His love will bind us together in unity. God's fiery love will bring down denominational walls and the traditions of men. Every wall of division is coming down in this hour, and we will truly be one in the Spirit. In this unity and oneness the Lord will command His blessing, and we will see this 3rd Great Awakening come in fullness. (See Psalm 133:1–3.)

Hear what the Spirit would say:

> *"Now you will see; now you will know My purpose and what I have been after. Make no mistake, all is in order, and as you climb My 'Mountain of Holiness,' all that is not of Me will fall to the ground. It is not an easy climb, but I have equipped you with My strength, My Holy Spirit, and He will lead and guide you to the top of My 'Mountain' where you will meet with Me and know Me as a 'Blazing Pillar of Fire.' You have known Me as a 'Cloud,' a dark 'Cloud' at times, and you have wondered: 'Where are you God?' (See Psalm 18:7–12.) But now your eyes will see your 'Teacher,' and you will know that I have never left you, not even for a moment.*
>
> *"These are days of glory for you, and I am lifting you up to a High Place, a place where miracles, signs, and wonders will be commonplace. This place will be under an 'open Heaven,' and you will know Me and My presence in a dimension you never have before.*

I am pouring out My glory in this hour; you only need to have an open heart and receive it.

"Let My Spirit remove all the clutter and all the distractions of this earth, and allow My Spirit to fill your heart with My glory as your heart empties out fully. Cry out to Me for this 'emptying' of your heart. Let me heal every hurt and cut away every stronghold from your past and free you completely. It is then that you will join My 'freedom fighters' and will bring in this final harvest.

"I am on the move, and I will not stop until every soul has heard the 'Good News' of My great salvation. This is 'harvest time,' and I am bringing in My 'sheaves,' millions of souls who will praise Me throughout the eternal ages. You have heard it said that I am bringing in a billion souls. I say: 'More than a billion, for My heart has enlarged to take in countless souls, souls without number, who will know Me, love Me, and praise Me for what I have accomplished for them through the cross and through the power of My resurrection.' Let Me enlarge your heart to see the glorious harvest before you, for truly it is 'white,' and now is the time to bring these precious souls in. (See John 4:35.)

"Let Me flow through you and use you as My end-time vessel, as My 'harvester,' for now is the time—NOW—says your God!"

CHAPTER 2

Guardian of the Ark
Part 1

Hear what the Lord says:

> *"'For I have called you to be a "blazing fire" in Me,' says your God. Come to Me, and I will ignite your soul, and you will know that you have been called to be My end-time 'mouthpiece.' Don't look at others; don't look to the right or to the left but look straight ahead, and you will walk through the open door that I have for you.*
>
> *"I have called you to be a 'watchman on the wall.' (See Ezekiel 3:17–21.) I have called you to be a 'guardian,' not only of your own soul and body but to care for the souls of others, to those that I would send you to. I have called you in this hour to carry My presence to your nation and to the nations of this earth. Do not hesitate. Do not delay when you hear My voice say: 'Go!' For I am sending you near and far. Now is the time. Now is the season that I am sending you to fulfill your calling and your destiny in Me.*
>
> *"You have waited; you have longed to hear My voice telling you where to go and what to do. Now*

you will hear and see Me clearly, and you will run with Me, for I have called you to be a 'guardian' for many souls, in prayer, in Truth, and in obedience to My will. You are My Joseph; you are My David, and even as they struggled for years so have you, My children, but it has not been in vain. You have been in a 'pit of despair and depression' long enough! Get ready for your breakthrough. Get ready for your 'suddenly,' for I am lifting you up out of your 'pit,' out of your 'dungeon,' and I am lifting you up to the **High Place** *now, in this very season of glory.*

"You thought these days would never come, days of freedom and delight in Me, but now they have arrived! You will be released quickly now, and your prison garments are being removed. I will now place on you a 'garment of righteousness' and a 'garment of praise for the spirit of heaviness!' (See Isaiah 61:3.)

"New adventures...the new life of glory that I have prepared for you will be fulfilled quickly before I come to receive you unto Myself. The time is short, and now is the time to move. You will no longer stand still and wait for Me, for I say: 'Move now! Pick up your cross and follow Me. Accomplish My will and My purpose in this generation, for you have been called for "such a time as this"'—says your God!"

Before I wrote this chapter, the Lord *downloaded* the words "guardian of the ark" to me in a dream. I prayed about the meaning of this for days, and I knew that it was going to be an integral part of this book. God showed me that He has called us to be "guardians of the ark" in a very special way.

According to the Family Law Self-Help Center, **"guardianship means:** *obtaining the legal authority to make decisions for another person. A 'guardian' is the person appointed by the court to make* *decisions on behalf of someone else. The person over whom the guardianship is granted (the child or the adult) is referred to as the 'protected person.'"*[vi]

Dictionary.com defines a guardian as *"a person who guards, protects, or preserves."*[vii]

All parents are legal guardians of their child until that child attains 18 years of age.

The Online Etymology Dictionary says that a guardian is *"one who guards...keeper, custodian."*[viii]

Some synonyms from the Merriam-Webster Dictionary are *"keeper, lookout, minder, sentinel, warden, watch, watcher, and watchman."*[ix]

God has called His "watchers" to guard and to protect His presence inside of their own hearts and lives and to warn and to speak the whole counsel of His Word to God's children. God is calling us to be "guardians" of His presence, and for this to happen there needs to be an internal transformation in our lives. As His "guardians" we must always **guard our hearts** from evil and darkness and be filled with the righteousness of Jesus.

> Above all else, **guard your heart,** for everything you do flows from it. Keep your mouth free of perversity; keep corrupt talk far from your lips. Let your eyes look straight ahead; fix your gaze directly before you. Give careful thought to the paths for your feet and be steadfast in all your ways. Do not turn to the right or the left; keep your foot from evil.
>
> –Proverbs 4:23–27 – NIV, emphasis added

The Ark of the Covenant

> According to all that I am going **to show you as the pattern of the tabernacle** and the pattern of all its furniture, so you shall construct it. Now they shall

construct an ark of acacia wood two and a half cubits long, one and a half cubits wide, and one and a half cubits high. You shall **overlay it with pure gold, inside and out you shall overlay it,** and you shall make a gold molding around it. You shall also cast four gold rings for it and fasten them on its four feet; two rings shall be on one side of it, and two rings on the other side of it. And you shall make poles of acacia wood and overlay them with gold. **You shall put the poles into the rings on the sides of the ark, to carry the ark with them.** The poles shall remain in the rings of the ark; they shall not be removed from it. You shall **put into the ark the testimony which I shall give you.** And you shall make an atoning cover of pure gold, two and a half cubits long and one and a half cubits wide. You shall make two cherubim of gold; make them of hammered work at the two ends of the atoning cover. Make one cherub at one end and one cherub at the other end; you shall make the cherubim of one piece with the atoning cover at its two ends. And the cherubim shall have their wings spread upward, covering the atoning cover with their wings and facing one another; the faces of the cherubim are to be turned toward the atoning cover. Then you shall put the atoning cover on top of the ark, and in the ark you shall put the testimony which I will give to you. **There I will meet with you;** and from above the atoning cover, from between the two cherubim which are upon the ark of the testimony, **I will speak to you** about every commandment that I will give you for the sons of Israel.

–Exodus 25:9–22 – NASB, emphasis added

> The priests on earth serve in a temple that is but a copy modeled after the heavenly sanctuary; a shadow of the reality. For when Moses began to construct the tabernacle God warned him and said, "You must precisely follow the pattern I revealed to you on Mount Sinai."
>
> –Hebrews 8:5 – TPT

Moses constructed a tabernacle in the wilderness "according to the pattern" that God showed him on the mountain. God also has a *pattern* for our lives, and we are to follow His Word and to pattern our lives after Jesus through the power of the Holy Spirit.

> **For [as a believer] you have been called for this purpose, since Christ suffered for you, leaving you an example, so that you may follow in His footsteps.** HE COMMITTED NO SIN, NOR WAS DECEIT EVER FOUND IN HIS MOUTH. While being reviled and insulted, He did not revile or insult in return; while suffering, He made no threats [of vengeance], but kept entrusting Himself to Him who judges fairly.
>
> –1 Peter 2:21–23 – AMP, emphasis added

The Ark has a lid on it that is called the Mercy Seat. The Mercy Seat has two Cherubim on each end that are stretching their wings toward and touching the center. It was on this lid that God was supposed to sit. **The Ark *was* the Throne.** The mercy seat was the *actual seat* where God dwelt among His people. From there He would judge, and therefore they called it the Mercy Seat.

The Shekinah, the Glory of God, the cloud and fire of His presence, sat or rested on the mercy seat. And that's why the ark and the Shekinah are associated with one another. The Shekinah Glory is God's *visible presence* sitting between the

Cherubim in the Holy of Holies. The Shekinah, God's visible presence, rested above the Mercy Seat between the Cherubim.

God wants to meet with us as He did with Moses and to reveal His manifest glory to us and through us to this generation, but we must build our lives according to His standard of holiness, not ours. We are now God's "ark," His "temple," and He desires to fill us to overflowing with His presence, but we will only experience His "Shekinah Glory" as we yield to the work of the Spirit and allow Him to cleanse us on the inside, deep in our souls. There is a greater glory that the Lord wants to reveal to this generation, and He has a prepared people who will walk in the High Place with Him. During these past few years I've had quite a few dreams of gigantic tsunami waves and floods coming, and I know that God is giving me a glimpse of the glory and the judgment that is on the way. God's desire is to manifest Himself to this generation through His "arks," and as His glory fills us we will become true *carriers of glory and of power* to millions of souls.

Inside the Ark of the Covenant were the Ten Commandments, Aaron's rod that budded, and a jar of manna. (See Hebrews 9:4.) In the New Covenant that was ratified through the blood of Jesus, His law is now *written in our hearts.* (See Hebrews 8:10.) As Believer's God has given to us His *rod of authority* and His "manna," the *Living Bread,* which is the Word of God, Jesus. His divine power has given us everything we need to live a godly life. (See 2 Peter 1:3.)

> Behold, the days are coming, says the LORD, when I will make a new covenant with the house of Israel and with the house of Judah—not according to the covenant that I made with their fathers in the day that I took them by the hand to lead them out of the land of Egypt, My covenant which they broke, though I was a husband to them, says the LORD. But this is the covenant that I will make with the house

of Israel after those days, says the LORD: **I will put My law in their minds, and write it on their hearts; and I will be their God, and they shall be My people.**
—Jeremiah 31:31–33 – NKJV, emphasis added

Thank God for the New Covenant, for now the *living presence* of God abides within us, His "ark." His very Life, His law, is now written on our hearts. Jesus now flows through us and gives us the power to walk in His righteousness. During the Old Covenant when God's people did not have the infilling of the Holy Spirit, they did not have the power to walk in God's law. Outward works, laws, and ordinances were kept, but there was no internal change deep in their hearts. A good example of this is when God's people wandered in the wilderness for 40 years. There were only a few who followed the Lord wholeheartedly and believed in His promises. They desperately needed their hearts to be "circumcised" and to be given a new heart, a heart of "flesh."

> Moreover, I will give you a new heart and put a new spirit within you; and I will remove the heart of stone from your flesh and give you a heart of flesh.
> —Ezekiel 36:26 – NASB

Though the "ark" was made of wood (symbolic of us as *trees of righteousness*—see Isaiah 61:3), it was overlayed with pure gold *inside* and *out*. God is calling us to an *inner transformation* of holiness. It is not enough to do good works; there must be a deep, inner cleansing in our souls. In a dream I had some time ago, I saw someone painting a wall with white paint. I then saw someone else digging feverishly into a wall until a bedroom was exposed. This person represented going deep into the heart...into that place of intimacy with Jesus. The one who was painting the wall *white* had no intention of going any deeper into Christ. Like the Pharisees of old this person represented outward works being done for the approval of man, an outward show of righteousness. No wonder Jesus called the Pharisees "whitewashed tombs!" (See Matthew 23:27.)

> The king's daughter is all glorious within: her clothing is of wrought gold.
>
> —Psalm 45:13 – Jubilee Bible 2000

> But when the goodness and kindness of God our Savior and His love for mankind appeared [in human form as the Man, Jesus Christ], He saved us, not because of any works of righteousness that we have done, but because of His own compassion and mercy, by the cleansing of the new birth (spiritual transformation, regeneration) and renewing by the Holy Spirit, whom He poured out richly upon us through Jesus Christ our Savior.
>
> —Titus 3:4–6 – AMP

Thank God for His goodness and His kindness in sending us His only Son to save us through the blood of Jesus. God's mercy and grace not only saves us when we truly surrender our lives to Him, but it also cleanses us and transforms our lives as we pick up our cross daily and follow Jesus. We can now be cleansed of all unrighteousness, not through our own good works of righteousness which are as "filthy rags" (see Isaiah 64:6) but by His great mercy and love!

Carriers of His Glory

The Father is calling us into His holiness; He is calling us to worship Him in Spirit and in Truth. (See John 4:24.) We, the true Church, are called to be "carriers of the ark" in this hour...

to carry His glory and His presence to this generation just as the priests of old carried the Ark with poles on their shoulders. (See 1 Chronicles 15:15.) I believe that the "poles" represent the cross that we are called to pick up daily. (See Luke 9:23.) Jesus is calling us to live a life of self-denial and obedience to our Heavenly Father. The "yoke" of Jesus is easy and His burden is light (see Matthew 11:30), but if we resist this work in our lives, it will bring great heartache.

Many in the Church do not understand the transforming work of the cross in their lives, and when trials come they are offended. Many even turn away from the Lord, not understanding what He is after. Only through the work of the cross in our lives will we become an "ark" empty enough to carry the glory of God inside of our spirit, soul, and even our bodies. The transforming power of the cross will accomplish this work, and only then will rivers of "Living Water" will be released through us. (See John 7:38.)

> Now then arise, O LORD God, [and come] to Your resting place, You and the ark of Your strength and power. Let Your priests, O LORD God, be clothed with salvation and let Your godly ones rejoice in [Your] goodness.
>
> –2 Chronicles 6:41

> Or do you not know that your body is the temple of the Holy Spirit who is in you, whom you have from God, and you are not your own?
>
> –1 Corinthians 6:19 – NKJV

> Don't you realize that together you have become God's inner sanctuary and that the Spirit of God makes His permanent home in you? Now, if someone desecrates God's inner sanctuary, God will desecrate

him, for God's inner sanctuary is holy, and that is exactly who you are.

-1 Corinthians 3:16–17 – TPT

When we truly repent we become God's "ark," His "inner sanctuary," and our hearts become His throne. The Spirit of God comes to make His home in us, but this is only the beginning. As we hunger and thirst for more of the Lord and ask for the "Baptism of the Spirit," Jesus comes and fills us to overflowing, and it is then that we truly realize that we are His "temples." Jesus desires to be the Center of our lives, not just a part of it. His passion is to fill our "temples" full of His glory and His presence and then for us to be *carriers of His presence* and to be His witnesses to our families, friends, neighbors, and even to the ends of the earth.

It is Finished

After this, Jesus, knowing that all things were now accomplished, that the Scripture might be fulfilled, said, "I thirst!" Now a vessel full of sour wine was sitting there; and they filled a sponge with sour wine, put it on hyssop, and put it to His mouth. So when Jesus had received the sour wine, He said, "It is finished!" And bowing His head, He gave up His spirit.

–John 19:28–30 – NKJV

When I was young in the Lord, I knew that I had many strongholds and "issues" that I was still struggling with. After a church service I went to the front and laid before the Lord on my face and cried out to Him. I heard the words: *"It is finished,"* and a profound peace filled my soul. Jesus showed me that though I was struggling He had already paid the price for my freedom. I realized that

Jesus had completed the work on the cross and that I was to stand on this solid Truth no matter what He would take me through in the days ahead. It was not a matter of feeling but of fact. This foundational Truth strengthened me through years of suffering as I went through many fiery trials. I knew from that day forward that I could never *earn* His great salvation and freedom. I was to surrender and to trust Jesus fully to deliver me from every "evil work" of the enemy. My debt was paid, and in Christ I was free no matter what I felt or saw in the natural or in my flesh and soul.

Recently, I had a dream, and in this dream I saw a minister. He said: *"It is finished!"* I was in a circle with a few others, and I shouted in agreement with this Scripture. We went around the circle, and others shared what was in their hearts. When they came back to me, I told them that I was not finished speaking. I immediately spoke the Scripture from Philippians about "working out our salvation with fear and trembling."

> So then, my dear friends, just as you have always obeyed, not only in my presence, but now even more in my absence, work out your own salvation with fear and trembling. For it is God who is working in you, enabling you both to desire and to work out His good purpose.
>
> –Philippians 2:12–13 – Holman Christian Standard Bible

We must "work out" what was "worked into" our lives through the power of the Holy Spirit when we surrendered to Jesus. Jesus is the *propitiation* for our sin and for the sins of the whole world (see 1 John 2:2); we are called to *propagate*, to spread and to promote, this Good News to all people. We *work out* our salvation through *surrender, obedience to the Father's will, daily prayer,* and *Bible study*. God is enabling us and giving us the grace and the strength that we need to walk with Him and to fulfill His purposes in the earth. Salvation is only the very beginning of our walk in Jesus. There is so much more that God desires to work in and through our lives.

> You rejoice in this, though now for a short time you have had to struggle in various trials so that the genuineness of your faith—more valuable than gold, which perishes though refined by fire—may result in praise, glory, and honor at the revelation of Jesus Christ.
>
> —1 Peter 1:6–7

Part of this "working out our salvation" will require going through various trials in order to free us and to prepare us for our destiny in Christ. Our fiery furnace experiences will only "burn off our bands" and transform us more fully into the image of Jesus. Only as we go through trials and suffering can our faith be made "genuine." It is easy to *talk* about having faith, but in order to make it *real* in our lives, we must be tested and tried. God is out to deepen our faith and trust in Him as we work out our salvation.

> Therefore, since Christ suffered in the flesh, equip yourselves also with the same resolve—because the One who suffered in the flesh has finished with sin— in order to live the remaining time in the flesh, no longer for human desires, but for God's will.
>
> —1 Peter 4:1–2

When we praise God in our trials and understand that He is purifying us deeply through them, we then know that our suffering is not in vain. He is equipping us to be His warriors and overcomers, to be His ambassadors who will go forth into this world to preach and to teach the Good News. Through all that the Lord takes us through, we will find that doing the will of the Father is our highest priority.

> Therefore we do not give up. Even though our outer person is being destroyed, our inner person is being renewed day by day.
>
> —2 Corinthians 4:16

> Share in suffering as a good soldier of Christ Jesus... This saying is trustworthy: For if we have died with Him, we will also live with Him; if we endure, we will also reign with Him; if we deny Him, He will also deny us.
>
> —2 Timothy 2:3, 11–12

We never give up as children of God; we press on and trust the One who died for us. Jesus has called us to persevere through every trial and temptation, and believe me, there are many. Because Jesus has overcome this world, we can, too, in the power of His Spirit. We are not called to be cowards and to turn back in the face of evil but to stand strong and to know that our Savior will see us through every difficulty. Our "outer person," our fleshy desires and corrupt habits, are being destroyed, but our "inner man" is being renewed and transformed daily. Jesus has called us to "share in suffering as a good soldier" and to "fellowship with Him in His sufferings." It is here, in the very crucible of suffering, that we will "work out our salvation" and come to know Jesus in a depth we never dreamed we could. If we have "died with Him," we will live in Him and know the "abundant life" that He has promised us. If we embrace the suffering of the cross in our lives, Jesus promises us that we will reign with Him. Glory to God for His promises; all of them are "Yes and Amen" in Jesus! (See 2 Corinthians 1:20.)

> I am sure of this, that He who started a good work in you will carry it on to completion until the day of Christ Jesus.
>
> –Philippians 1:6

> His generation yet to be born will glorify Him. And they will all declare, "It is finished!"
>
> –Psalm 22:31 – TPT

I believe that we are this generation! God's work in our lives will be completed as we yield fully to the Spirit and allow Him to lead and to guide us through every circumstance we encounter. We will find that no suffering, no trial, no pain, no loss is in vain, for as we trust Jesus fully we will awaken in His likeness and praise Him throughout the eternal ages!

> As for me, I will see Your face in righteousness; I shall be satisfied when I awake in Your likeness.
>
> -Psalm 17:15 – NKJV

The Veil is Torn

The Word of God tells us that the Ark of the Covenant was behind the veil in the Holy of Holies, and the high priest could only enter once a year to offer the blood of lambs and of goats. The blood of these animals was a "shadow and type" of the blood sacrifice of Jesus, the Lamb of God, the atoning sacrifice for our sin.

> But into the second part the high priest went alone once a year, not without blood, which he offered for himself and for the people's sins committed in ignorance; the Holy Spirit indicating this, that the

way into the Holiest of All was not yet made manifest while the first tabernacle was still standing.

–Hebrews 9:7–8

The blood of the cross has given us access into the Holy of Holies, and it is here, behind the "veil," that His very presence fills us as we open our hearts and our lives to Him in full surrender. The "curtain" that once separated us from His presence has been torn through the sacrifice of Jesus, and now we can draw near to His heart and be flooded with His glory and His love. As the "veil" in our hearts is torn through a spiritual "circumcision," we can then know deepest intimacy with our Savior. Because of the blood of Jesus our communion with our heavenly Father is now without fear or condemnation. We can enter the "Courts of Heaven" and lay our *case* before the Lord, knowing that He hears us and that He will bring justice and mercy into our lives.

> Jesus passionately cried out, took his last breath, and gave up His spirit. At that moment the veil in the Holy of Holies was torn in two from the top to the bottom. The earth shook violently, rocks were violently split apart.
>
> –Matthew 27:50–51 – TPT

As we allow the Spirit of God to rend our hearts through repentance, we will enter more fully into His Shekinah glory, His manifest presence, as He fills us with His glory and His love. (See Joel 2:13.) As we are "shaken violently" our hearts will be "split apart" and opened through repentance, and we will find ourselves standing behind the veil and in the very Holy of Holies!

I remember a dream I had years ago, and in this dream, I was standing before a large purple veil. I looked around and saw one of the "Four Living Creatures." (See Ezekiel 1:5–28; Revelation

5:6–14.) As I stood before this veil, all of a sudden it came off, wrapped around me like a "Whirlwind," and took me into the High Place. I remember seeing myself with some others at a table. I believe this dream shows the *power of the cross* in our lives; its power to remove the "veil" from our hearts so that we can enter into the Holy of Holies. He is coming to us as a mighty "Whirlwind of Glory" in this hour, and we will see and know Him in a greater fullness than we ever have before!

> And now we are brothers and sisters in God's family because of the blood of Jesus, and He welcomes us to come into the most holy sanctuary in the heavenly realm—boldly and without hesitation. For He has dedicated a new, life-giving way for us to approach God. For just as the veil was torn in two, Jesus' body was torn open to give us free and fresh access to Him!
>
> –Hebrews 10:19–20

May this be our prayer from the song **"Take Me In"** by Dave Browning.[x]

> Take me past the outer courts, into the Holy Place. Past the brazen altar. Lord, I want to see Your face. Take me past the crowds of people, the priests who sing Your praise. I hunger and thirst for Your righteousness. And it's only found one place. Take me into the Holy of Holies. Take me in by the blood of the Lamb. Take me into the Holy of Holies. Take the coal, cleanse my lips, here I am.

God's Holiness

As I was praying about this chapter, I asked the Lord what part He wanted me to emphasis, and He spoke to me loud and clear and said: *"My Holiness."* Our God is a "Consuming Fire," and Jesus comes to us with His "baptism of fire" in order to purify and to consume all the sin and all the iniquity within us.

Many of God's people have taken His Holy presence and power lightly, and there is little fear of God in the modern Church. The Lord has a pattern, an order, and a way that He works His will in our lives, and that pattern is found in His Word. When Moses built the tabernacle he fashioned it according to God's pattern, not his, and he got this pattern on God's Holy Mountain. (See Exodus 25:40.) In the same way we must fashion our lives, our "tabernacles," our "temples," after the pattern of God's Word as we become doers of the Word and not hearers only. (See James 1:22.) This change will come as we spend time with Jesus on His Holy Mountain and are transformed from the inside out.

Millions of God's children do not realize, appreciate, or understand what Jesus has purchased for them. They come to the Lord and say a prayer then continue to live their own lives according to their carnal reasoning and the pattern that *they* have designed for themselves. They believe that because they are in the New Covenant, they can now live as they please and as they desire.

> So they set the ark of God on a new cart, and brought it out of the house of Abinadab, which was on the hill; and Uzzah and Ahio, the sons of Abinadab, drove the new cart. And they brought it out of the house of Abinadab, which was on the hill, accompanying the ark of God; and Ahio went before the ark. Then David and all the house of Israel played music before the LORD on all kinds of instruments of fir wood, on harps, on stringed instruments, on tambourines, on sistrums, and on cymbals. And when they came to Nachon's threshing floor, Uzzah put out his hand to the ark of God and took hold of it, for the oxen

> stumbled. Then the anger of the LORD was aroused against Uzzah, and God struck him there for his error; and he died there by the ark of God. And David became angry because of the LORD's outbreak against Uzzah; and he called the name of the place Perez Uzzah to this day. David was afraid of the LORD that day; and he said, "How can the ark of the LORD come to me?"
>
> –2 Samuel 6:3–9 – NKJV

There are many *new things* in the Church that man has devised according to their own design and carnal reasoning. They have put in place *techniques* to draw in the lost according to the standards of this world that are not in God's pattern or design. This is man's "new cart," but God will have nothing to do with it. It may sound pleasing to the natural ear and understanding, and many may accept this *new way* of doing things, but without God's approval, it will fall to the ground. In the eyes of God it is "wood, hay, and stubble." (See 1 Corinthians 3:12–13.)

Uzzah was called to be a "guardian of the ark," and he touched the Ark in ignorance, not following the *pattern* and the *way* that God had shown them through Moses. According to 1 Chronicles 15:15, the priests were to carry the Ark on their shoulders with it's carrying poles as the Lord had instructed Moses. As we see here: Ignorance is *not* bliss! Our God is Holy, and we cannot *touch* His Holy Presence in ignorance. We must serve Him according to His will and His pattern for our lives. We need to seek Him as Moses did on the Lord's Holy Mountain, in our "secret place," in order to hear what the Lord would say and to get our guidance and instruction from His Holy Spirit.

> Do not think that I have come to abolish the Law or the Prophets; **I have not come to abolish them but to fulfill them.** For truly, I say to you, until heaven and earth pass away, not an iota, not a dot,

will pass from the Law until all is accomplished. Therefore **whoever relaxes one of the least of these commandments and teaches others to do the same will be called least in the kingdom of heaven, but whoever does them and teaches them will be called great in the kingdom of heaven.** For I tell you, **unless your righteousness exceeds that of the scribes and Pharisees, you will never enter the kingdom of heaven.**

–Matthew 5:17–20 – English Standard Version, emphasis added

Jesus did not come to abolish the Law or the Prophets but to fulfill them. His Law and His Word which was spoken through the prophets is His pattern for our lives. What does this mean for us, personally? Millions believe that there is no way that they can keep the Commandments of God in their own power, and this is true. Jesus came, lived a sinless life, and paid the penalty for our sin and our iniquity through the cross so that now, in the *power of the Holy Spirit*, Jesus can live His life through us, purify us from sin, and heal all our wounds. Only in the power of the Holy Spirit can we live a life that is pleasing to the Father.

We are called to walk in the footsteps of Jesus, but millions do not believe this Truth even though it is in God's Word. They live in fear, unbelief, compromise, and idolatry. They live a self-consumed life of rebellion against the will of God for their lives. This is not completely the fault of individuals even though they are responsible to search out the Word of God for themselves and to apply His Truths to their lives. Many teachers and pastors do not teach the truth of living a holy life, and if they do, they do not tell their flock how to accomplish this in their lives. They have people pray a *sinner's prayer* but then neglect to teach them the deeper truths of God's Word such as how to pick up their cross daily and follow Jesus.

> Yet how much more will the sacred blood of the Messiah thoroughly cleanse our consciences! For by the power of the eternal Spirit He has offered Himself to God as the perfect Sacrifice that now frees us from our dead works to worship and serve the living God.
>
> –Hebrews 9:14 – TPT

We can now be freed from our dead works so that we can worship the Lord in Spirit and in Truth in the Holy Spirit's power. Without the "Baptism of the Spirit," we will not have the power to be the *witnesses* that Jesus desires us to be. We must wait in the "upper room" and pray until we are endued with power from on High. (See Acts 1:12–14; Luke 24:49.) We can never walk out God's will and purpose for our lives or be filled with His power and righteousness apart from the Holy Spirit.

> If we say that we have fellowship with Him and yet walk in the darkness [of sin], we lie and do not practice the truth; but if we [really] walk in the Light [that is, live each and every day in conformity with the precepts of God], as He Himself is in the Light, we have [true, unbroken] fellowship with one another [He with us, and we with Him], and the blood of Jesus His Son cleanses us from all sin [by erasing the stain of sin, keeping us cleansed from sin in all its forms and manifestations].
>
> –1 John 1:6–7 – AMP

> Because it is written, Be ye holy; for I am holy.
>
> –1 Peter 1:16 – King James Version

Our God is Holy, and He desires to come into our hearts, reveal Himself more fully to us, and bring us into full maturity in His Son. This will not be accomplished unless we open our hearts to the Spirit and allow Him to purify us deeply with His Holy Fire. God desires deep and intimate fellowship with us, and He is grieved when we close off our hearts to Him in fear and in shame. He died to free us, not to condemn us or to keep us in bondage. This is not the heart of God for His people. When we close off our hearts to Him and live according to our own plans and purposes, He cannot move in and through us as He desires. His deep desire is to draw us close to Him and to reveal His passionate love to us. Jesus desires to fill us with the fruit of His Spirit and to ignite His love in us so that we will love Him above all.

> Work at living in peace with everyone, and work at living a holy life, for those who are not holy will not see the Lord.
>
> —Hebrews 12:14 – NLT

"Look! I'm sending My messenger on ahead to clear the way for Me. Suddenly, out of the blue, the Leader you've been looking for will enter His Temple—yes, the Messenger of the Covenant, the One you've been waiting for. Look! He's on His way!" A Message from the mouth of GOD-of-the-Angel-Armies. But who will be able to stand up to that coming? Who can survive His appearance? He'll be like white-hot fire from the smelter's furnace. He'll be like the strongest lye soap at the laundry. He'll take His place as a refiner of silver, as a cleanser of dirty clothes. He'll scrub the Levite priests clean, refine them like gold and silver, until they're fit for GOD, fit to present offerings of righteousness. Then, and only then, will Judah and Jerusalem be fit and pleasing to GOD, as they used to be in the years long ago. "Yes, I'm on

My way to visit you with Judgment. I'll present compelling evidence against sorcerers, adulterers, liars, those who exploit workers, those who take advantage of widows and orphans, those who are inhospitable to the homeless—anyone and everyone who doesn't honor Me." A Message from GOD-of-the-Angel-Armies.

–Malachi 3:1–5 – The Message

Our God is coming with a Holy Fire that few in this generation have experienced. Jesus is about to visit the Church with a white-hot Fire that will expose and consume hidden sin and iniquity. He is about to expose in the hearts of His people deep, hidden motives and iniquities that they may not even be aware of. The Holy Spirit is coming to purify the people of God in a way that will cause many to fall to the ground in deepest repentance. I believe this work has already started, but it will intensify in the days ahead. The Holy Spirit will "scrub" and "wash" His people in the deepest recesses of their hearts. Jesus is out to cleanse His people and to make them ready for His coming. His true bride will be without spot or wrinkle, and she will shine with His glory for the whole world to see! (See Ephesians 5:25–27.)

It came to pass, when the trumpeters and singers were as one, to make one sound to be heard in praising and thanking Jehovah; and when they lifted up their voice with the trumpets and cymbals and instruments of music, and praised Jehovah, saying, For He is good; for His lovingkindness endureth for ever; that **then the house was filled with a cloud, even the house of Jehovah, so that the priests could not stand to minister by reason of the cloud: for the glory of Jehovah filled the house of God.**

–2 Chronicles 5:13–14 – American Standard Version, emphasis added

In the days ahead when the "Cloud of His Glory" enters the Church, the fear of God will return, and His Holy Name will once again be revered as it was in past generations. God's desire is to fill His "temple" with His glory, and *we* are His "temple." God will not only fill physical buildings with His presence but His very glory will be seen in and upon us, His "arks," as His Shekinah glory comes in a way that the Church and this world has never seen before. I believe that in this 3rd Great Awakening, when the Lord visits His Church in Fire and Glory, not one of His children will be left standing, for everyone will fall before Him in awe and wonder. His Fire and Presence will fill and change hearts, internally, and we will never be the same again. God is about to ignite His Holy Fire in a measure that will transform lives from the inside out. God is calling us to be the "guardians" of His presence, both for our lives and for others, and for this to happen there needs to be a deep, internal transformation in our lives.

Victory Over the Enemy

When the Philistines captured the ark of God, they brought it from Ebenezer to Ashdod. Then the Philistines took the ark of God and brought it into the house of Dagon and set it up beside Dagon. And when the people of Ashdod rose early the next day, behold, Dagon had fallen face downward on the ground before the ark of the Lord. So they took Dagon and put him back in his place. But when they rose early on the next morning, behold, Dagon had fallen face downward on the ground before the ark of the Lord, and the head of Dagon and both his hands were lying cut off on the threshold.

–1 Samuel 5:1–5a – ESV

As "guardians of the ark" God has given us power and authority over the enemy. With the presence and holiness of the Lord inside of us, we can face any "giant" and bring them down. The enemy does not fear *us* but the *presence of God inside of us*. It is "Christ in us, the hope of glory" that the enemy fears. (See Colossians 1:27). Dagon's head was cut off just as David cut off the head of Goliath. In the same way we defeat the enemy as we **face our enemies.** Both of Dagon's hands were cut off signifying that in the power of the Spirit we can bring down the works of the enemy in our lives, in the lives of others, and even in our nation and this world. Remember: **Purity brings power,** and as we allow the transforming work of the Spirit to be accomplished in our lives, we will become more than conquerors!

> He divided the three hundred men into three companies. **He gave each man a trumpet and an empty jar, with a torch in the jar.** He said, "Watch me and do what I do. When I get to the edge of the camp, do exactly what I do. When I and those with me blow the trumpets, you also, all around the camp, blow your trumpets and shout, 'For God and for Gideon!'" Gideon and his hundred men got to the edge of the camp at the beginning of the middle watch, just after the sentries had been posted. They blew the trumpets, at the same time smashing the jars they carried. All three companies blew the trumpets and broke the jars. They held the torches in their left hands and the trumpets in their right hands, ready to blow, and shouted, "A sword for God and for Gideon!" They were stationed all around the camp, each man at his post. The whole Midianite camp jumped to its feet. They yelled and fled. When the three hundred blew the trumpets, God aimed each Midianite's sword against his companion, all

over the camp. They ran for their lives—to Beth Shittah, toward Zererah, to the border of Abel Meholah near Tabbath.

> –Judges 7:16–22 – MSG, emphasis added

In this new era God is bringing together His *Gideon army* to move forward and to shout His praise! He is asking His people to "smash the jars" they are carrying. We are called to be those empty "jars" with the Light of Christ shining within us. We must realize that the "jars," our hearts and lives, need to be broken open in order for the Light of Christ to shine forth through us. If we are filled with "self," the Light of Jesus in us will be dim or may even become non-existent. When we are "broken" the enemy no longer sees us but Jesus inside of us, and he runs from us in great fear. This is our victory over the enemy! In this very hour God is calling His Gideon army, His remnant, to rise up, to empty our lives before Him, and to allow the Spirit to break us open in the recesses of our hearts. When we allow this work to be done, His "Living Water" will then flow through us freely and bring life and healing to many.

> We are like common clay jars that carry this glorious treasure within, so that this immeasurable power will be seen as God's, not ours.
>
> –2 Corinthians 4:7 – TPT

God is transforming our hearts and lives so that we can see the place and position we have in Jesus. The Lord has given us power and authority over darkness and the "Keys of His Kingdom," but many of God's children are not walking in this power. We are "seated in heavenly places" with Jesus, and He has made us to be "kings and priests" before Him. (See Ephesians 2:6; Revelation 5:10.) I believe this authority in Christ will be embraced as His people allow this transforming work in their lives and as they see who they truly are in Him.

Recently, I had a "night vision" of Jesus on His throne, and I saw myself sitting beside Him with my hand on His thigh. The thigh represents *strength and a place of trust*.[xi] It also represents *a place that you rely on to stand.*[xi] This is the place of *power and authority* in Christ. Our thighs support our legs, and in Jesus we can walk in strength and in His ability and power.

In another dream I saw a man walk into my kitchen. He was formally dressed in a top hat and a tuxedo. There was a *carriage* outside, and there were other *attendants* that came into my house with him. As I walked into my kitchen, he took my hand, kissed it, and said: *"Your majesty."*

Little do we realize the High Place that Jesus has called us to and who we are in His grace. God has called us to be His "kings and priests"; He has called us to be His bride, His queen, but few have realized their high position in Christ. I believe that many revelations through His Word are going to be released to His true children, and they will see who they are in Christ. Too many of God's people live in the lowlands of fear and unbelief, but in this very hour we will see who we truly are in Christ through powerful revelations of His love and power. We will rise up to be the glorious Church without spot or wrinkle, and we will walk in His overcoming power and victory in this very generation. Without these revelations of His love and the power that resides within us, we will not be victorious over the enemy. We must realize, without a doubt, that He has given us the "Keys of His Kingdom." (See Matthew 16:19.)

> See that you do not refuse Him who speaks. For if they did not escape who refused Him who spoke on earth, much more shall we not escape if we turn away from Him who speaks from heaven, whose voice then shook the earth; but now He has promised, saying, "Yet once more I shake not only the earth, but also heaven." Now this, "Yet once more," indicates the removal of those things that are being shaken,

as of things that are made, that the things which cannot be shaken may remain. Therefore, since we are receiving a kingdom which cannot be shaken, let us have grace, by which we may serve God acceptably with reverence and godly fear. For our God is a consuming fire.

–Hebrews 12:25–29 – NKJV

God desires to shake us, His Church, in order to release us from chains of bondage, the bondage of our past, and to bring us into His glorious resurrection power. His desire is to make us *as strong as a mountain,* immovable in the face of danger and trouble. He has called us to be "giants" in the land and to never tremble before any devil or adversity. God wants to remove from our lives the things that are hindering our walk with Him. We must allow the Spirit to remove the "fig leaves" that we try to hide under and to cover us with His "robe of righteousness" through the blood sacrifice of Jesus. It will cost us our own will and way; it will cost us the "cutting away" of our sin, iniquity, and selfish ways, but it will be worth it when we see His glory and experience His love and power in a measure we never have before!

Let us not refuse this powerful work of transformation in our lives, no matter how painful it may be. Let us not resist change in our lives, for it will only bring heartache and rebellion. Let us embrace the cross and the discipline that our loving Father has for us. Surrendering our will for *His* will brings deepest peace and rest in our souls. If we resist His will it will only delay this process of transformation in our lives.

Now is the time, saints of God, to rise up into the place and the position that Jesus has ordained for your life. No more demonic fear; no more feeling "less than" and like the underdog. This is your time, your season of change and transformation in the presence of the Lord. Through the power of the Holy Spirit, you will undergo a transformation so life-changing that you will not even recognize yourself when you look into your mirror! Get ready to ride the *wild wave of change and transformation*. Step into His whirlwind and let Him spin you, transform you, and create in you a clean heart filled with His glory and righteousness!

Hear the Spirit speak:

> *"There is a new thing that I am about to release in your midst. I am coming as a 'Whirlwind' to remove from your midst what the enemy has planted so long ago, both in your personal life and also in the Church worldwide.*
>
> *"This next move of My Spirit will cause the enemy to 'vacate' the premises, in your hearts and in the Church. For too long the enemy has had his way, but now the Winds are changing, and new things are on the horizon for My people. I am blowing My Trumpet; can't you hear it? This is NOT the 'last trump,' but it is a call for My army to gather together in unity and oneness. This is a call to step into the fullness that I have for your life. This 'trumpet blast' will awaken My children to their calling and destiny. Many are waiting for this; they are watching for this next move of My Spirit. Realize that I have already begun to move. This is not something that is far in the future, but it is here, now, in your very midst.*
>
> *"Listen for the Wind of My Spirit; listen for His sound, for you will hear Him calling you, drawing you, inviting you into this next move of glory. 'What of the night? What of the night?' I hear many saying in this hour. (See Isaiah 21:11–12.) They are wondering and asking Me: 'When are You going to move; when are You going to give us this great turn-around that we have been praying and interceding for?' I say to you: 'Do not grow weary in well-doing, for you will reap if you do not faint in this hour.' (See Galatians 6:9.)*

"Some of My children have been in 'hard labor' concerning the state of your nation and government. But I have promised: 'In My appointed time I will uncover all and show this entire earth that I am God. I will uncover the evil schemes of the devil, and you will see him flee before you. You will see many captives freed and the glory of your King come forth in power and majesty!' (See 1 Corinthians 4:5.)

"Wait in praise and patience, and do not allow the enemy to discourage you. I am lining up everything in perfect alignment with My will. I am setting up My 'dominoes' in perfect order according to My pattern and My purpose for your nation and this world.

"Look now and wonder. Look now and come out of the shadows of depression and discouragement and praise Me. Praise is the answer, for it releases My faith in and through your life, and it scatters the enemy! A fire goes before Me and burns up all My enemies and yours. (See Psalm 97:3.) Praise releases My fire and My glory, and this is what I have been waiting for in this 'delay.'

"So, come to Me. Love Me and praise Me. Let My Spirit equip you fully for the next stage of glory that you are entering into. Now is the time. Rise up; take the Land. Let Me hear your shout of victory, for even now the 'walls' are beginning to come down—says your God!"

CHAPTER 3

Guardian of the Ark
Part 2

The High Calling of a Guardian

The words "guardian of the ark" came to me in a dream, and in this dream I was at my parent's house *standing* in front of the *garbage can* in their kitchen. We are called as intercessors to stand between the clean and the unclean, to stand in the "gap" for others. The Spirit of God began showing me that He has called His children to be "guardians," to be "watchmen on the wall," and to *stand in the gap* before Him for our family, the Church, our nation, and even the nations of this world. But not all of His children respond to this call.

> And I sought for a man among them who should build up the wall and stand in the breach before Me for the land, that I should not destroy it, but I found none. Therefore I have poured out My indignation upon them. I have consumed them with the fire of My wrath. I have returned their way upon their heads, declares the Lord God.
>
> —Ezekiel 22:30–31 – ESV

According to Merriam-Webster.com a watchman is: **a person who keeps watch: GUARD.**[xii] On Dictionary.com it says that a watchman is: **a person who keeps guard over a building at night, to protect it from fire, vandals, or thieves.**[xiii] I see the watchman as one who keeps watch over the Church and warns of coming attacks from the enemy, who we know is the *thief* and the *vandal.*

I believe that God has called every one of His children to pray and to intercede, but God has called the *prophet* to be His *watchman* in a special way, a way that not all of His children are called. The *prophet* is a gift to the Church and is one of the 5-fold ministers in the Church according to Ephesians 4:11.

Ezekiel was one of these men. He was faithful to his calling and completed the mission that God had entrusted to him.

> Son of man, I have appointed you as a watchman for the house of Israel; whenever you hear a word from My mouth, warn them from Me. When I say to the wicked, "You will certainly die," and you do not warn him or speak out to warn the wicked from his wicked way so that he may live, that wicked person shall die for wrongdoing, but his blood I will require from your hand. However if you have warned the wicked and he does not turn from his wickedness or from his wicked way, he shall die for wrongdoing, but you have saved yourself.
>
> –Ezekiel 3:17–19 – NASB

God has called His prophets to *watch* and to *warn* His people to repent of their sin and their iniquity and to *warn the wicked* to turn from their evil ways. They are not a timid group of warriors but have been set apart to fulfill God's calling in their lives. The prophet, or watchman, is also called to warn God's people of coming judgments and of the coming of the Spirit's glorious outpourings.

When Jesus gave me the dream about standing in my parent's kitchen in front of the garbage can, He was calling me to be a "guardian of the ark," to stand in the gap between His holiness and the *garbage* of sin and darkness, not only for my family against the sin and the iniquity in our bloodline but for the Church, my city, and my nation.

What does it mean to stand in the "gap" for others? A gap, according to Merriam-Webster.com, means: **a) a break in a barrier (such as a wall, hedge, or line of military defense) and b) an assailable position.**[xiv] The Apostle Paul said:

> Now I rejoice in the sufferings for you, and I am filling up in my flesh that which is lacking of the tribulations of Christ for His body, which is the church.
>
> —Colossians 1:24 – Berean Literal Bible

Because of sin there was a **breach,** a separation, between God and man. The cross of Jesus has closed that breach, and now we can receive His great salvation and enjoy intimacy and fellowship with God. Paul was a true "watchman on the wall" and intercessor. He stood in the "gap" for the souls of men and participated in the sufferings of Jesus so that others could come to know Him. Being a true minister of Christ will *always* involve suffering. We are called to "fellowship with the sufferings of Christ" as we pick up our cross daily and follow Him. (See Philippians 3:10.) This is the call of a true *watchman*. We "fill up in our flesh" and stand in the gap as we surrender to the will of the Father in obedience and intercede on behalf of others. This will require a life of self-sacrifice that will bring *fullness of joy* and a deep satisfaction in our souls. We lay our lives down for Jesus and for His Church and do all that He commands us to do, no matter the cost. We *lay across the brokenness* in the lives of others as we bring them to Jesus. This comes through our union with Jesus: abiding in Him and His Word abiding in us. (See John 15:7.)

Nehemiah's Wall

One of the greatest examples I can give to you about a watchman is from the Book of Nehemiah. As a true watchman Nehemiah heard the voice of the Lord telling him to go and to rebuild the temple walls. He not only listened but obeyed the Lord in what he was told to do. In the same way when we go to the Lord in prayer, we need to ask: *"Father, what is on Your heart this day for my life, my family, the Church, this nation, and the world?"* The Lord will always respond to us when we pray this way just as God revealed to Nehemiah what was on His heart. As we listen and obey in the *secret chamber* of prayer, we will find our hearts transformed and our lives fruitful.

> Then I said to them, "You see the distress that we are in, how Jerusalem lies waste, and its gates are burned with fire. Come and let us build the wall of Jerusalem, that we may no longer be a reproach." And I told them of the hand of my God which had been good upon me, and also of the king's words that he had spoken to me. So they said, "Let us rise up and build." Then they set their hands to this good work.
>
> –Nehemiah 2:17–18 – NKJV

Many *walls* and *gates* of protection have been burned down, and the enemy has had access into the hearts of millions of souls and even in the lives of many of God's children. This includes our government and our nation as a whole. God is out to rebuild His *walls of protection* through His power and His holiness as His people come back to Him, turn from their wicked ways, pray, and seek His Holy Face. (See 2 Chronicles 7:14.)

> When Sanballat the Horonite, Tobiah the Ammonite official, and Geshem the Arab heard of it, **they laughed**

at us and despised us, and said, "What is this thing that you are doing? Will you rebel against the king?"

–Nehemiah 2:19b, emphasis added

Now Tobiah the Ammonite was beside him, and he said, "Whatever they build, if even a fox goes up on it, he will break down their stone wall."

–Nehemiah 4:3

Now it happened, when Sanballat, Tobiah, the Arabs, the Ammonites, and the Ashdodites heard that *the walls of Jerusalem were being restored and the gaps were beginning to be closed,* that they became very angry, and all of them conspired together to come and attack Jerusalem and create confusion. Nevertheless we made our prayer to our God, and because of them we set a watch against them day and night.

–Nehemiah 4:7–9, emphasis added

Through the years the enemy has come against God's prophets and has mocked and ridiculed God's people as they have determined to rebuild a foundation of holiness in the Church. There has been great resistance from the powers of Hell through intense warfare and demonic intrusion. A "Jezebel spirit" of compromise has invaded many churches, but God is rebuilding the Church through His true prophets and releasing a *spirit of repentance* throughout the land. The "gap" is closing in this new era, for God's remnant is rising up in greater faith, trust, and obedience to the will of the Father. God's true watchmen have stood firm in Truth in this hour against the powers of hell, and the building of the *wall* is almost complete.

I remember years ago when God called me to *build a wall* through intercession, obedience, and full surrender to His will and how the enemy tried to get me off the *wall* and to stop building. The adversary was constantly calling me a fool and telling me that I was "cursed." God encouraged me and led me to these Scriptures in Nehemiah:

> Now it happened when Sanballat, Tobiah, Geshem the Arab, and the rest of our enemies heard that I had rebuilt the wall, **and that there were no breaks left in it** (though at that time I had not hung the doors in the gates), **that Sanballat and Geshem sent to me, saying, "Come, let us meet together among the villages in the plain of Ono." But they thought to do me harm.** So I sent messengers to them, saying, **"I am doing a great work, so that I cannot come down.** Why should the work cease while I leave it and go down to you?" But they sent me this message four times, and I answered them in the same manner...For **they all were trying to make us afraid,** saying, "Their hands will be weakened in the work, and it will not be done." Now therefore, O God, strengthen my hands. Afterward I came to the house of Shemaiah the son of Delaiah, the son of Mehetabel, who was a secret informer; and he said, **"Let us meet together in the house of God,** within the temple, and let us close the doors of the temple, for they are coming to kill you; indeed, at night they will come to kill you." And I said, "Should such a man as I flee? And who is there such as I who would go into the temple to save his life? I will not go in!" Then I perceived that God had not sent him at all, but that he pronounced this prophecy against me because Tobiah and Sanballat had hired him. For this reason he was hired, that I should be afraid and act that way and sin, so that they might have cause for an evil report,

> that they might reproach me...So the wall was finished on the twenty-fifth day of Elul, in fifty-two days. And it happened, when all our enemies heard of it, and all the nations around us saw these things, that they were very disheartened in their own eyes; for they perceived that this work was done by our God.
>
> –Nehemiah 6:1–4, 9–13, 15–16, emphasis added

During this intense time of warfare, there were times when those around me tried to get me to stop what I was *building* in the Lord. Do not be deceived, for even those who call themselves *prophets* or who are *ministers* in the Lord will try to tell you that you are out of God's will. Believe me, when you begin to build the wall that God is telling you to build, you will come into *much* opposition. Nehemiah's life is a perfect example of this. The enemy will mock you, call you a fool, and try every *trick* in his book to bring you down and to cause you to stop building. He will tell you that you are *nothing* and that you are too weak to walk in the High Place that Jesus has called you to walk in. The enemy will "hire" those that you love and that you respect to try to intimidate you even as he tried to discourage Nehemiah. Nehemiah would not come down off the *wall*, and neither must you, no matter what comes against you. God will give you the courage and the strength that you need to finish building the *wall of protection* that He has called you to *build*. We must work until there are no *breaks* in the *wall*, for this *wall of protection* must be completed in order for the Church to walk in the fullness and the glory that He has called Her, the Church, to walk in.

When this work is completed in the Church and God reveals His glory in a fullness that He has never done before, all will see and know that God alone is the One who built His *wall of protection* around His people through His servants and His true ministers. God will receive all the glory, honor, and praise, not man. The Holy Spirit will be a "Wall of Fire" around His people, and the Church will come into the glorious destiny that Jesus has prepared for His *Ekklesia*.

> And I will be to her a wall of fire all around, declares the LORD, and I will be the glory in her midst.
> –Zechariah 2:5 – ESV

> So we labored in the work, and half of the men held the spears from daybreak until the stars appeared. At the same time I also said to the people, "Let each man and his servant stay at night in Jerusalem, that they may be our guard by night and a working party by day." So neither I, my brethren, my servants, nor the men of the guard who followed me took off our clothes, except that everyone took them off for washing.
> –Nehemiah 4:21–23 – NKJV

Every true intercessor knows that standing in the "gap" for another soul or for a nation is hard work; it is a *labor of love*. A powerful example of this would be the prophet Elijah as he prayed and interceded for rain and stood in the "gap" for Israel. He *travailed* before the Lord until he saw the answer manifesting in the natural. This is perseverance in prayer, a *never give up* stand. He saw the abundance of rain coming in the Spirit before it manifested in the natural. This is true faith, and this shows the importance of listening to the voice of the Spirit in prayer and then bringing forth the will of God into the earth. Elijah *heard* the sound of Heaven and then released this *sound* through his *travail!* This is true intercession, and all of God's people can participate in bringing God's will into the earth realm through prayer and obedience.

> Then Elijah said to Ahab, "Go up, eat and drink; for there is **the sound of abundance of rain."** So Ahab

> went up to eat and drink. And Elijah went up to the top of Carmel; then he **bowed down on the ground, and put his face between his knees,** and said to his servant, "Go up now, look toward the sea." So he went up and looked, and said, "There is nothing." And **seven times** he said, "Go again." Then it came to pass the seventh time, that he said, "There is a cloud, as small as a man's hand, rising out of the sea!" So he said, "Go up, say to Ahab, 'Prepare your chariot, and go down before the rain stops you.'" Now it happened in the meantime that the sky became black with clouds and wind, and there was a heavy rain.
>
> –1 Kings 18:41–45a, emphasis added

Nehemiah was not the only watchman who was building this *wall of protection*. When you read through this Book, you will see that *many* were involved in this rebuilding of Jerusalem's wall. God has called the Church to unite in love and in unity and to work together, for many workers are needed in this very hour. In John chapter 17 God is calling us to be *one with Him* and *with each other*. There is power in unity, and it is in unity that God will "command the blessing" and show His might and power. There is a *pattern* that God is using to build His Church, and those who have "ears to hear" are building according to His design and His purpose for this generation. This is God's Gideon army, and they will not take off their "clothes," their "armor," but will complete the work that God has given them to do. Day and night God's watchmen, both men and women, are watching on the wall, and they will not be moved, come hell or high water, until the work is completed!

> And they shall rebuild the old ruins, they shall raise up the former desolations, and they shall repair the ruined cities, the desolations of many generations.
>
> –Isaiah 61:4

There have been many *watchmen on the wall* in the past, and there are some in this very generation. David Wilkerson was a true watchman. This man of God was transformed internally by the Spirit through obedience to the Father's will and through the many, many trials and hardships that he went through. He warned the Church of coming destruction and cried out to God's people to repent and to surrender their lives to Christ. He warned of coming calamities and prophesied concerning the "filth" that our nation would embrace, and we have already seen much of this come to pass. David did not care if men accepted him but was true to his calling in the Spirit. What an example he has been to me and to the Body of Christ.

We must be fearless, passionate warriors in this generation and follow David Wilkerson's example of faithfulness and courage. Jesus is looking for those who will lay aside the comforts of this world and press deep into His heart of love, His heart of passion, for the lost and the dying. Yes, the corruption in our nation is great, but I believe the coming revival and awakening will release many souls from the *trap* of the enemy as we cry out for them in deep travail before the Lord's throne of grace. God is not finished with our nation or the nations of this world, and His travail in us will birth millions upon millions of souls in this new era. The best is yet to come through an outpouring of the Spirit this world has never seen!

> Then I said to them, "The gates of Jerusalem are not to be opened until the sun is hot, and while they are standing guard, the gatekeepers are to keep the doors shut and bolted. Also appoint guards from the inhabitants of Jerusalem, each at his post, and each in front of his own house."
>
> –Nehemiah 7:3 – NASB

God's watchmen, His guardians, are His *"gatekeepers."* They guard the *doors* of the Church, and the only time they will open them is when the "sun is hot," meaning when the fire of God invades the Church with His Holy Presence! They open to God's presence alone. The gatekeepers are called to bolt the doors of the Church against darkness and evil. These "guardians of the ark" make "straight the paths of the Lord" in all that they say and do. (See Isaiah 10:3.) I believe that in each local church God has appointed *guardians* to *watch* and to *protect* His people.

> A single day in Your courts is better than a thousand anywhere else! I would rather be a **gatekeeper in the house of my God** than live the good life in the homes of the wicked.
>
> —Psalm 84:10 – NLT, emphasis added

> And there was a prophetess, Anna, the daughter of Phanuel, of the tribe of Asher. She was advanced in years and had lived with her husband for seven years after her marriage, and then as a widow to the age of eighty-four. She did not leave the temple grounds, serving night and day with fasts and prayers.
>
> —Luke 2:36–37 – NASB

> On your walls, O Jerusalem, I have appointed and stationed watchmen (prophets), who will never keep silent day or night; you who profess the Lord, take no rest for yourselves.
>
> —Isaiah 62:6 – AMP

We are called to pray and to intercede day and night, to pray without ceasing. We are called to warn and to encourage others in their walk with Christ and to be a burning candle, even a blazing fire, and never allow our *light* to be diminished. We must not be silent, for we are His witnesses in this generation to our families, to our neighbors, and to this world.

> And He went a little beyond them, and fell on His face and prayed, saying, "My Father, if it is possible, let this cup pass from Me; yet not as I will, but as You will." And He came to the disciples and found them sleeping, and He said to Peter, **"So, you men could not keep watch with Me for one hour? Keep watching and praying, so that you do not come into temptation; the spirit is willing, but the flesh is weak."**
>
> –Matthew 26:39–41 – NASB, emphasis added

God is calling each one of His children to *stand watch* with Him in this desperate hour, but many have *fallen asleep* and have neglected their prayer life and their *quiet time* with Jesus. May we not be found *sleeping* as the disciples were in their weariness, but may we ask the Holy Spirit to empower us in prayer and in intercession. The Lord desires to share the passion of His heart with us, especially in the hour that we live in. So many of God's children want the "joy of the Lord," but few are willing to drink of His "cup of suffering."

> I will stand at my guard post and station myself on the watchtower; and I will **keep watch to see what He will say to me,** and how I may reply when I am reprimanded.
>
> –Habakkuk 2:1, emphasis added

We are not only called to pray and to intercede but to listen to the voice of the Spirit and to obey Him. Many are good at praying a list of prayers and then running off without listening to what the Spirit would say to them. We need to "be still and know" that He is God, to listen for His guidance, and to receive what He has for us that day. (See Psalm 46:10.) It is a two-sided conversation. We know what it feels like to have a person talk to us but never listen to what we have to say. This kind of relationship never develops into a true friendship.

> His watchmen are blind, all of them know nothing. All of them are mute dogs unable to bark, dreamers lying down, who love to slumber.
>
> –Isaiah 56:10

> For this is a rebellious people, lying sons, sons who refuse to listen to the law and instruction of the Lord; who say to the seers, "You must not see visions from God"; and to the prophets, "You must not prophesy to us what is right! Speak to us pleasant things and smooth words, prophesy [deceitful] illusions [that we will enjoy]. Get out of the [true] way, turn aside from the path [of God], stop bothering us with the Holy One of Israel."
>
> –Isaiah 30:9–11 – AMP

> I set watchmen over you who warned you: "Listen for the sound of the trumpet! It will let you know when trouble comes." But you said, "No! We won't pay any attention!"
>
> –Jeremiah 6:17 – The Living Bible

There are many "blind watchmen" in our nation and in this world, and many of God's children love it so! Many of God's children do not want to hear about the cross that Jesus requires us to pick up daily. They want a smooth and easy path to Heaven, but *internal transformation* will never happen in their lives without the working of His cross in their souls. They come against God's true prophets when told that they are called to live a holy life of full surrender to the will of the Father. They go to *compromising churches* where they are told that they only need to pray a *sinner's prayer* and that nothing else is required of them. These are the "lying sons" who refuse to listen to the instruction of the Lord and the ways of the Lord. They throw out the true prophets of the Lord and *stone them to death* with their slanderous words and lies. They love the smooth words of the minister that tells them: *"You're okay, and I'm okay! Jesus paid it all, and there is nothing more to do on your part except come to church and get involved in some kind of ministry."*

In this new era God is putting an end to this, and true prophets, pastors, and leaders will now come forth and tell the whole Truth of God's Word. God is exposing corruption in the Church, and every false prophet and leader will be *uncovered* for all to see. This is God's time, and He will not be hindered; neither will He be stopped from accomplishing His whole will in this generation!

> This is God's message to Edom: Someone from among you keeps calling, calling to me: "Watchman, what of the night? Watchman, what of the night? How much time is left?" The watchman replies, "Your judgment day is dawning now. Turn again to God, so that I can give you better news. Seek for Him, then come and ask again!"
>
> –Isaiah 21:11–12

> For the Lord GOD does nothing without revealing His secret to His servants the prophets.
>
> –Amos 3:7 – ESV

True prophets will speak only what they hear the Spirit of God saying, no matter if it is received or not. Their one desire is to please the Lord their God. They do not look for the approval of man but only a smile from their Heavenly Father. They live "behind the veil" and will not speak only comforting words to God's children but the truth about the full nature of God and His righteous judgments.

Jesus would say to you:

> *"Get up into the High Place, that Place in Me that is safe and secure! Get up and out of the 'lowlands' of fear and unbelief. This is the time when you must make an all-out effort to get to the top of My Holy Hill. This is not a time to be fearful or timid, for I have called you to follow Me into the greatest adventure of your life! Do not turn back! Do not look back, for your future is before you, and in Me I will now release the 'new things' that I have for your life! I have called you to come and to join My 'rescue team,' to rescue the lost and bound souls in this generation.*
>
> *"Abandon all, and do not hold onto anyone or anything that will hinder you from joining My team of rescuers. Let go, children, and give Me your all. Why would you hold onto the 'dead' things of your past when I have a glorious future prepared for you? Come to Me with everything that confuses you, binds you, and every sin and iniquity that is trying to cling to you. Close your ears to the devil, for some of you are listening to his lies. Remember: the devil is the 'father of lies.' I will give you discernment in this hour, discernment to know My voice and to rebuke the voice of the evil one. He wants you to think that what you are hearing is My voice, or even your own voice, telling you the Truth! Rebuke him in My name, and I will reveal to you My plans and My purposes for your life.*
>
> *"Come now and take a deep breath...a deep spiritual breath and move on into the next level. New things! New and more powerful revelations in My*

Spirit is what awaits you! You are loved! You are valuable! No one can take your place in My heart. You belong to Me, and I belong to you.

"Get out of the 'shadowlands' and into My High Mountain where you will find relief and total victory over the evil one. In this Light you will see Truth and know that I am the Lord your God who never fails you. Nothing will hinder you; nothing will remove you from My presence or take you off of the path that I have you on. Believe this; receive this, and you will experience My perfect peace deep within your soul.

"Now is the time to move forward. Let nothing, let no one, take your crown, your overcoming crown, from you. I have already gone before you and have overcome every obstacle for you, only keep moving up and onward in your walk with Me. Be discouraged no longer, for I have overcome this world, and I have overcome every sin, every 'block' from the enemy. I will delay no longer! Only believe—says your God!"

I have said these things to you, that in Me you may have peace. In the world you will have tribulation. But take heart; I have overcome the world.

–John 16:33

Noah as God's Watchman

Noah is a perfect example of someone who was God's "guardian of the ark." He built an *ark* to protect his family from the coming flood even as Nehemiah built a *wall* to protect God's people from their enemies. A true *guardian* will protect others through their obedience in building the *ark*, their lives, according to God's design. Noah was set apart in his generation and was a "preacher of righteousness" (2 Peter 2:5). Noah listened and obeyed the Lord in his generation; may we be faithful in ours to do all that the Lord commands us to do! Only Noah, his wife, three sons, and his son's wives were saved: eight total. Eight is the number of new beginnings, and we have now entered into a time of transition and change!

> And God said to Noah, "The end of all flesh has come before Me, for the earth is filled with violence through them; and behold, I will destroy them with the earth. Make yourself an ark of gopherwood; make rooms in the ark, and cover it inside and outside with pitch...And behold, I Myself am bringing floodwaters on the earth, to destroy from under heaven all flesh in which is the breath of life; everything that is on the earth shall die. But I will establish My covenant with you; and you shall go into the ark—you, your sons, your wife, and your sons' wives with you. And of every living thing of all flesh you shall bring two of every sort into the ark, to keep them alive with you; they shall be male and female."
>
> –Genesis 6:13–14, 17–19 – NKJV

Noah followed the design and the pattern of the Lord when he built the ark even as Moses did in the building of the tabernacle. He closed his ears to the taunting of naysayers. They mocked him just as people mocked Nehemiah in the repairing of the wall. Noah stood firm in faith and completed what God told him to do, and God established an eternal covenant with Noah. (See Genesis 9:8–17.) Our Heavenly Father has established a covenant with us through the blood of His Son, and only in Jesus will we be safe in the coming floods of judgments. God will no longer flood the earth with natural flood waters, but there is coming a tidal wave, a tsunami flood, of judgment along with a flood of His glory that will cover the whole earth.

I have had quite a few prophetic dreams concerning flood waters. Several years ago I dreamed of many people drowning in deep waters. I was in a High Place, and I was hanging on a "Door" (Jesus is the Door – see John 10:7–9). People were reaching up to me and crying out as I reached down and lifted them up and out of the "angry waves." In another dream I saw a storm come suddenly with great flood waters. I was in the *attic* of my house which represents the "High Place." I saw these waters coming up the stairs and into the attic. I immediately rebuked the waters in Jesus' name, and they stopped; they never reached me. God was showing me His protection in my personal trials and in the floods of judgment that are coming.

In another dream I was in my old neighborhood standing on **Washington Street.** All of a sudden I saw a flood of water coming, and it flooded the whole area. When I tried to cross the street, I had to swim across because the waters were so deep. I believe I was on **Washington Street** for 2 reasons. God showed me that in the flood that was coming many would be "washed" and would come to know His great salvation. The other revelation that came to me was that our government in **Washington, D.C.** would come under the judgment of God, and that God was going to do some deep cleaning and removal of evil in our nation.

In another dream I was standing on the sidewalk, and all of a sudden as I looked to my left, I saw a huge *tidal wave of water* coming right toward me. I was then lifted up on top of this wave along with several others. I saw only a few people walk in safety on top of this wave which I felt represented the remnant of God. Truly, God is speaking, and He has a *prepared people* who are ready to ride this *wild wave of glory* with Him!

> Then the LORD said to Noah, "Come into the ark, you and all your household, because I have seen that you are righteous before Me in this generation"...And it came to pass after seven days that the waters of the flood were on the earth. In the six hundredth year

> of Noah's life, in the second month, the seventeenth day of the month, on that day all the fountains of the great deep were broken up, and the windows of heaven were opened. And the rain was on the earth forty days and forty nights. On the very same day Noah and Noah's sons, Shem, Ham, and Japheth, and Noah's wife and the three wives of his sons with them, entered the ark—they and every beast after its kind...All in whose nostrils was the breath of the spirit of life, all that was on the dry land, died. So He destroyed all living things which were on the face of the ground: both man and cattle, creeping thing and bird of the air. They were destroyed from the earth. Only Noah and those who were with him in the ark remained alive.
>
> –Genesis 7:1, 10–14a, 22–23

God has a righteous remnant in this generation that He has been preparing, positioning, and transforming in order to stand with Him in the tumultuous days ahead. They have been building an *ark of safety* for themselves, their families, and the Church little by little and plank by plank through prayer and obedience. What we have gone through in the past has conditioned us to stand firm in the days ahead. We are about to live out Psalm 91 as we walk in the High Place with Him.

> Watch therefore, for you do not know what hour your Lord is coming.
>
> –Matthew 24:42

I hear the Lord say:

> *"Come up to higher ground, for the flood waters are about to be released. Make sure you are prepared for the coming judgments and the glory of your God. Come*

to the place where the 'waters of destruction' cannot harm you or cause you to go down. My Ark of Safety is the only safe Hiding Place, and as you abide in Me and I in you, you will know the safety and the protection of My loving arms. But woe unto those who will not listen to My voice...who have hardened their hearts and will not turn to Me and repent. I have been speaking, but few are listening; few are taking My words seriously. Open your heart and open your spiritual ears and hear what the Spirit of God is saying in this hour.

"I am about to release 2 floods, says your God. One will be a flood of glory, and the other will be a flood of judgment. Make a choice this very day, step over the line, and give Me your full surrender and consecration to do My will. Only in full surrender to Me will you experience My keeping power and My mercy. Do not listen to those who tell you that you are safe, that you have prayed a prayer and are now on your way to Heaven. This false Gospel is now being exposed and will come down quickly, for many souls have been given this 'placebo' and feel safe when in reality they are in grave danger. I will hold ministers and leaders accountable for giving this false message of hope and telling others that their hearts are right with Me. I will shake up individual souls now and expose their true hearts before Me. This is My mercy in the judgments that are coming.

"Those who have given Me their all and are walking on the High Road of obedience with Me, these very souls will walk in the High Place of glory and will know and experience My miracle-working power. They will now enter fully into My rest and will experience joy unspeakable and full of glory! Their joy will be without measure, and they will know the

love of the Father in a measure they have never known. Their reward will come now, and they will be overwhelmed in My presence. They will know that their lives of self-sacrifice have not been in vain.

"There is a 'harvest' coming forth in the lives and hearts of many. Those who have sown to the flesh will experience great sorrow, but those who have sown to the Spirit will know a harvest of righteousness that will not be taken from them. Yes, this is the time of the unveiling of hearts, and those who call themselves after My name but do not truly know Me will now be exposed for all to see. My judgments are starting to come forth in this very hour. Get ready My children, for the hour is later than you think—says your God!"

The Children's Teeth are Set on Edge

Then the LORD came down in a cloud and stood there with him; and He called out His own name, Yahweh. The LORD passed in front of Moses, calling out, "Yahweh! The LORD! The God of compassion and mercy! I am slow to anger and filled with unfailing love and faithfulness. I lavish unfailing love to a thousand generations. I forgive iniquity, rebellion, and sin. But I do not excuse the guilty. I lay the sins of the parents upon their children and grandchildren; the entire family is affected—even children in the third and fourth generations."

–Exodus 34:5–7 – NLT

I feel it is necessary, at this point, to set forth some truths about how iniquities can hinder our walk with Jesus and keep us from the full power of His transforming glory. Notice I used the word iniquities instead of sins. A simple way to explain the difference between sin and iniquity is that **iniquity** is like the **root of a tree** while **sin** would represent **the leaves.** The reason why so many are still caught in the "iniquitous traps" of the enemy is because they (iniquities) have never been truly confessed and repented of. People try to deal with the leaves (sin) instead of dealing with the root of the problem (iniquities).

Many prayers that are prayed concerning sin and iniquities are generalized, and God's people say: *"Lord, forgive all my sins."* This prayer may be well-meaning, but what God requires is repentance for specific sins and iniquities that His people are trapped in. For example: *"Father, I come to You and confess the iniquity of addiction to pornography. I confess my selfishness and my greed. I confess to you my gluttony and my pride. I have been jealous of my sister Mary. Please cleanse and release me from this. Father, I have been rebellious and disobedient and have not obeyed you because of the fear of man."* These are humbling prayers, and I believe that these kinds of prayers and repentance is what our Father wants to hear. Many times God's children do not even see their deep iniquities and sins until the Light of the Spirit shines into their soul, but I believe this is the day and the hour when the Lord is taking His "ax" and going to the root of the problems within our souls. He will no longer allow us to hide under our "good works," our "fig leaves," for the time of uncovering has arrived.

> People who conceal their sins will not prosper, but if they confess and turn from them, they will receive mercy.
>
> –Proverbs 28:13

> If I had not confessed the sin in my heart, the Lord would not have listened. But God did listen! He paid attention to my prayer.
>
> –Psalm 66:18–19

Through all the shaking that is happening in our nation and this world, I believe the *cover* has come off of many souls, including those within the Church. This uncovering is nothing to fear, for our God is a merciful God; I have found this to be true. As *guardians* of our own souls, the Lord wants us to confess our sins and our iniquities and allow the Spirit to free us completely from our iniquitous past.

> The word of the Lord came to me again, saying, "What do you mean when you use this proverb concerning the land of Israel, saying: 'The fathers have eaten sour grapes, and the children's teeth are set on edge'? As I live," says the Lord God, "you shall no longer use this proverb in Israel. Behold, all souls are Mine; the soul of the father as well as the soul of the son is Mine; the soul who sins shall die."
>
> –Ezekiel 18:1–4 – NKJV

Many "fathers have eaten sour grapes," and millions of children's "teeth are set on edge." If these iniquities are not dealt with, they will *bind souls* even into adulthood and will cause many spiritual and emotional problems. These "sour grapes" are offenses, sins, and iniquities committed by previous generations.

According to Dictionary.com, *teeth set on edge* means: **"irritate, annoy, make one cringe, as in: That raucous laugh sets my teeth on edge. This expression alludes to the shuddering feeling evoked by a grating noise or similar irritation."**[xv]

Multitudes have been infected with iniquitous sins that have been passed down from generation to generation. These sins have been as "sour grapes" in the hearts and lives of so many. Bitterness, hate, and revenge have been passed down from one generation to another, and millions do not know how to be free from these strongholds.

You've heard people say: *"I don't know why I do what I do! I try so hard to do right, but I keep falling into the same pit of sin!"*

Even some of God's people fall into the "sour grape syndrome" of perversion, bitterness, jealousy, pride, and many other sins of the flesh. It is taught that when we come to Christ, we are new creatures, but few teach the *process of the cross* and how to stand against iniquities in the bloodline. Millions do not know how to overcome these *strangleholds* of the enemy in the power of the Spirit. Millions of Christians just ignore these strongholds and do not believe they can ever be free from them until they die. Their Christian lives lack joy and the power of the Spirit, and they believe this is "normal" for a Christian, but this is far from the Truth. They believe because their parents had these issues that it is normal for them to suffer as they do, regardless if they are Christians or not. Their "teeth are on edge." They are filled with fear and unbelief, and they wonder why they are not experiencing the "abundant life" that Jesus promised them. God has seen this lack of knowledge, understanding, and bondage in so many of His children's lives. When we come to Jesus and surrender our all, we no longer need to use the proverb so many use: *Like father like son* or *like mother like daughter*, for whom the Son sets free is free indeed! (See John 8:36.)

The Word tells us that the soul that sins will die. Just because your parents or mine suffered from iniquitous sins and didn't know how to be freed from them does not mean that you must live in the same turmoil or sin. Jesus died to free us from **all** sin and **all** iniquity, and we do not have to wait to die a physical death to be freed from them.

Jesus not only forgives our sin and iniquities when we truly repent of them but His desire is to *wash them away fully*, to *cleanse us completely*, but few truly believe this. Many just ignore these nagging feelings of guilt, hoping they will just go away. They believe that when they confessed their sin when they came to Jesus that every *hidden sin and iniquity* was *automatically* removed. I believe because of deep shame and guilt, many of these "hidden iniquities" are never confessed and forsaken.

> For day and night Your hand was heavy upon me; my vitality was turned into the drought of summer. I acknowledged my sin to You, and my iniquity I have not hidden. I said, "I will confess my transgressions to the Lord," and You forgave the iniquity of my sin.
>
> –Psalm 32:4–5

You see, it is in the **confession of our sin and our iniquity** that the Spirit cleanses us. We can be *forgiven* of our sin, but if we are not cleansed, we will struggle with what is "hidden" in our souls. Many people wonder why they are depressed and downcast and why their vitality has diminished. They are spiritually dry and wonder why the Lord seems so far from them. I can tell you from experience that it is the work of the Holy Spirit deep inside of our souls that frees and cleanses us as we open our hearts fully to Him. As we allow the Light of the Spirit to shine on and expose what is "hidden" in our hearts, we can then be freed by His power.

> Who forgives all your iniquities, Who heals all your diseases.
>
> –Psalm 103:3

> But if we confess our sins to Him, He is faithful and just to forgive us our sins and to cleanse us from all wickedness.
>
> –1 John 1:9 – NLT

> Judah, you are he whom your brothers shall praise; your hand shall be on the neck of your enemies; your father's children shall bow down before you. Judah is a lion's whelp; from the prey, my son, you have

gone up. He bows down, he lies down as a lion; and as a lion, who shall rouse him?

–Genesis 49:8–9 – NKJV

He washed his garments in wine, and his clothes in the blood of grapes.

–Genesis 49:11b

Jesus is the "Lion from the tribe of Judah," and He has paid the price for us to be freed from all evil. He defeated the enemy through the blood of His cross and the power of His resurrection. Jesus is the One we praise and bow before, for He alone sets us free and lifts us up to the High Place!

Jesus was washed in the "blood of grapes" so that we no longer have to eat "sour grapes." Our "teeth" no longer need to be "set on edge." He has tread down all of our enemies in the "blood of grapes," and now all that is "sour" in our lives can be turned into the *sweet wine of His love.* Through His bloody sacrifice we can be completely freed from all that the enemy has bound us with in our past. Come, be washed in His blood and be freed completely from your past iniquities and every stronghold.

When we receive the infilling of the Spirit of God through the *baptism of the Spirit,* He then begins to possess our souls more fully. As we are transformed by the "renewing of our minds," we begin to think His thoughts and to hear the voice of the Spirit more clearly. (See Romans 12:2.) We have the responsibility to *watch* what goes into our souls through the media: what we watch and read, the activities we engage in, and how we live our daily lives altogether. We are the "guardians of the ark," of God's presence inside of us, and the Word admonishes us not to grieve the Holy Spirit. (See Ephesians 4:30.)

I believe there is another reason why I was standing in front of the garbage can in my parent's kitchen besides *standing in the gap.* This dream also represented the *garbage of our iniquitous past.* A dark cloud of depression lies over the hearts of many, and they can't understand the reason for this. We must ask the Holy Spirit to reveal to us what is binding our hearts and then allow Him to *cut away* all that is dark in our iniquitous bloodline. Because millions of God's children have not allowed the Spirit to do this work in their souls, they are still drawn to what is impure and unclean. They go where they want to go, watch what they want to watch on the TV, and enjoy the entertainment that they want, regardless of its evil content. Many believe they can watch any movie as long as it is not rated R, but any *worldly program* has the power to influence us in one way or another. In the sight of God, this is *garbage.* We see pastors and leaders falling into iniquitous sins of perversion and filth because of unrepented sin and iniquity. This is why God's Holy Fire is coming in greater intensity to this generation.

God desires to narrow down our interests and give us a greater hunger and thirst for His holiness and presence. Many want to be used by God and have a preaching or healing ministry, but they refuse to pay the cost. I see many youths that desire to be apostles and prophets, but they do not want to pay the cost to be purified and prepared for these offices. I remember reading about Smith Wigglesworth, who had a powerful healing ministry, and how he would not even take a newspaper into his house. He did not want any *worldly influence* in his life. People may see this as a little "overboard," but he was making a strong statement about his total commitment to the Lord. He carried his Bible with him everywhere and honored God's Word above all.

Those who have given their all to Jesus in this *new era* will be blessed abundantly. God's children who have sacrificed their lives in full surrender and who worship their King extravagantly will now know the full reward of Jesus, and everything they touch will be blessed by Heaven. Being a *guardian of the ark* will require a full sacrifice of our lives before the Lord, not a half-hearted commitment to His Lordship. This next move of the Spirit will be led by those who walk in purity and who know how to be true *guardians of the ark.*

Let's open our hearts fully to the work of the Spirit inside of us, and we will find that repentance, surrender, and obedience is the pathway to the Lord's "abundant life" within us.

Listen to the Spirit's voice saying:

> *"A tidal wave of glory and of judgment is on the way, and soon you will see it; soon you will experience it! Those who have abandoned all for Me and for the sake of My Kingdom will ride this glorious wave of power and of strength, but for those who have refused to surrender their lives to me, they will know what it is to fall into 'sinking sand.' Only those who have built their 'houses,' their lives, in Me, on My foundation of Truth, only these will walk in the High Place with Me. They have climbed the 'Mountain of Faith' and have walked with Me through the 'valley of the shadow of death.' (See Psalm 23:4.) They have 'died' to the things of this world and have chosen the High Road of holiness and of obedience to My will. These are the ones who will now 'ride this glory wave' with Me.*
>
> *"Those who have prepared their hearts and their lives for this day and this hour will not fear the intensity of this 'wave,' for they will know that this is of Me, and they will not back down in the face of this 'violent wave.' They have learned how to trust Me and to stand in Truth, and they will not be shaken neither will this wave overwhelm them. The enemy has tried to take the life of My remnant. He has tried not only to discourage them but to destroy them, but I have kept them safe for this season of glory.*
>
> *"I will now show My strong arm of power and might to those who have cried out to Me. They have stood in faith against 'impossible odds,' and now I*

*will show them My favor and My delivering power. They have not looked to man but to Me for healing and for deliverance and have not backed down in fear and unbelief. This does not mean that they have not **felt** the fury of the adversary, but they have refused to believe his lies and have walked on the High Road of victorious faith in Me and My power to deliver and to heal them. These are My 'qualified' ones; these are the ones who have paid the price and have abandoned all for My sake, and these are the ones I will use, that I will flow through to awaken My people and to show them the path of Truth and the ways of My Spirit.*

"*Some will be offended when they see these 'weak' ones raised up to great heights of glory, and they will wonder why they still live in the lowlands of fear and of unbelief. I have chosen who I have chosen, and no man, no devil, will stop this unstoppable company. These are My Jehu's; these are my Elijah's and Elisha's, and now is the time for this Great Awakening in your nation and in the nations of this world. It is here! It is NOW—says your God!*"

Chapter 4

My Personal Testimony

I struggled with and prayed about this chapter before writing it because I knew the Lord wanted me to share more of my life's story. I have come to such a place of healing and forgiveness that, to be honest with you, I think little of my past but am enthralled with the future that God has for me. I guess this must be why I am ready to share with you my painful past without shame or guilt.

In this book, unlike the others, I felt compelled by the Lord to share more of my background and my struggles with the *iniquities* that were passed down in my family's bloodline and how the Lord brought total victory into my life. Jesus showed me that in my openness and honesty others will be touched and will be more willing to open their hearts and their painful past to Him in order to be healed and set free.

I believe what the Word says about *"love covering a multitude of sin"* and that we need to love, forgive, and *cover* others as the Word teaches. (See 1 Peter 4:8.) As I prayed about this the Lord gave me many examples of sin being uncovered and repented of in His Word, and one of them was Noah. In the Scriptures below concerning Noah, he was **first** uncovered and then his "nakedness" was covered. What the Lord showed me was that our sin and shame must first be uncovered before He can cleanse us: **"If** we confess our sins..." (1 John 1:9a). The Holy Spirit also showed me that King David was confronted by the prophet Nathan concerning his sin. His sin had to be uncovered **first** before he could be forgiven. (See 2 Samuel 12:1–14.) When Adam and Eve sinned in the garden, God confronted them, and in His mercy and grace He will confront us also.

> Then Noah began farming and planted a vineyard. He drank some of the wine and became drunk, and uncovered himself inside his tent. Ham, the father of Canaan, saw the nakedness of his father, and told his two brothers outside. But Shem and Japheth took a garment and laid it on both their shoulders and walked backward and covered the nakedness of their father; and their faces were turned away, so that they did not see their father's nakedness.
>
> –Genesis 9:20–23 – NASB

> Then the Lord God called to Adam and said to him, "Where are you?" So he said, "I heard Your voice in the garden, and I was afraid because I was naked; and I hid myself." And He said, "Who told you that you were naked? **Have you eaten from the tree of which I commanded you that you should not eat?** Then the man said, "The woman whom You gave to be with me, she gave me of the tree, and I ate." And the Lord God said to the woman, **"What is this you have done?"** The woman said, "The serpent deceived me, and I ate."
>
> –Genesis 3:9–13 – NKJV, emphasis added

Before I start to share my story, I want you to know that both my parents are with the Lord in Heaven. My mother went home to Jesus at 58 years old, and my father went home 4 months later. A friend of mine was at a conference, and the Lord had her buy a cross for me with 2 roses in the center of it. He spoke to her and told her to tell me that those 2 roses represented my parents and that they were safe in His arms. What a comfort that was to my heart.

My Childhood Memories

I am the second born in a family of 6; I have 4 sisters and 1 brother. They are precious and dear to my heart. I grew up in a middle-class neighborhood and attended a Catholic school and church. I was quite shy, but I would always make at least one friend that I would be close to. I was very thin, and some of the children would make fun of me and call me "Olive Oyl." I was withdrawn and took every tease deep into my heart. I felt alone and isolated in my heart and truly believed that this was normal. I experienced many bouts of depression and never understood why. Outwardly, I probably looked like a *normal* child but inside there was a devastating fear that no one else could see. I thought: *"Who can I talk to? Who would really understand what I am feeling and going through?"* I felt like an outsider and that my life would never change for the better.

I remember cleaning St Patrick's church and having a sense of God's presence while I was cleaning, but that *comfort* was always short-lived. Years later, I realized that this was a prophetic sign from the Lord that I would be His prophet and that He would flow through my life to bring forth Truth to His people, to bring forth the whole counsel of God. I always felt dirty inside and would go to confession and tell the priest some "dark" secrets of uncleanliness. He would tell me to say some prayers, and that would help for awhile. I would step out of the church and feel clean, but that was always a short-lived feeling for my *"teeth were set on edge."* (See Ezekiel 1:2.) I remember one priest, Father McGary, who showed me a little attention. This attention made me feel loved and special, but when I saw him in a casket a short time later, I knew my *comfort* was gone. I was always looking for someone to love me. I was loved by my mother, but my heart had a hard time believing that I was loved unconditionally. It was hard for me to receive the love that I longed for so deeply. There was a hard covering over my heart, and it was something only the love of God could break open and cut away.

My mother was a great mom. I remember her *always* doing the wash, and every line in our basement was always filled with clothing. She seemed to be forever buying socks and underwear for us kids. But even though she was busy raising 6 children, she would make time for us and take us for walks in the park. Many times she would take us to a Tastee Freeze for an ice cream cone and some chips or cram all 7 of us into a taxi and take us swimming. These are good memories that I will never forget. I remember looking up at the stars on a clear night, and I would feel a sense of peace and rest, but then the feelings of grief and shame would return with a vengeance.

My mom was very religious, and I know that she loved the Lord. When I was older we went to an all-night vigil at Holy Hill in Wisconsin and even to some Catholic charismatic church meetings. I remember my mom having all of us children kneel in the dark in our dining room with candles lit while we prayed the rosary. She was a woman of prayer and would kneel by her bedside and pray. God heard the prayers of my mother, and even though none of us children truly *knew* the Lord at that time, God had His hand on us. My mom did the best she could with the knowledge that she had, and the Lord blessed her for that. When I was older and had a born-again experience, my mom and I would talk about Jesus and Mary and would have great conversations. I didn't judge My mom, for I knew her heart was right with Jesus; she loved Him.

Before my mother passed on to glory, she spent some time with me and stayed overnight at my house. We had several heart to heart talks, and I began to open up a deep place in my heart with her that I never had before. We both wept and hugged each other as I shared how I longed to be loved and cherished. It was such a healing time between us. As I shared my grief with her, God did some deep healing in my heart. I never felt as close to my mom as I did during this time. We sang "Great is Thy Faithfulness" together and worshipped our King. Even to this day this is one of my all-time favorite hymns.

When my mom was spending her last days in a hospital, she slipped into a coma. One day as I entered her room the Holy Spirit told me to do my Bible study with her. I knew she was in a comatose state, but I obeyed anyway. As I read the Scriptures from Revelation, I looked over at my mom, and she was weeping. I was touched deeply, for I knew that her spirit-man was being ministered to by the Holy Spirit.

> Then I saw a new heaven and a new earth, for the old heaven and the old earth had disappeared. And the sea was also gone. And I saw the holy city, the new Jerusalem, coming down from God out of heaven like a bride beautifully dressed for her husband. I heard a loud shout from the throne, saying, "Look, God's home is now among His people! He will live with them, and they will be His people. **God Himself will be with them. He will wipe every tear from their eyes, and there will be no more death or sorrow or crying or pain. All these things are gone forever.**" And the One sitting on the throne said, "Look, I am making everything new!" And then He said to me, "Write this down, for what I tell you is trustworthy and true." And He also said, "It is finished! I am the Alpha and the Omega—the Beginning and the End. To all who are thirsty I will give freely from the springs of the water of life. All who are victorious will inherit all these blessings, and I will be their God, and they will be My children."
>
> –Revelation 21:1–7 – NLT, emphasis added

During this time I attended West Layton Assembly of God, and as Mother's Day approached someone asked me if I would sing at a gathering that they were putting together in honor of *mothers*. I immediately said: "Yes," and in a flash the Holy Spirit spoke to me and told me to sing "Great is Thy Faithfulness" in honor of my mother. I esteem my mother and all that she was to us, her family, and to many others. I believe that it was her prayers and faithfulness to God that kept our family together. I see the hand of God on each one of my siblings, and I know, even though we went through much trauma, that all of us will come forth as "pure gold." Our God is faithful!

My father went through much in his lifetime, and some of the most traumatic times were during World War 2. My dad would point to his leg and show us kids where a bullet went through. He also shared about a time when he was supposed to *watch* for the enemy at his bunker, but his friend stood watch for him instead. That night his friend was killed, and my dad carried that guilt, I believe, throughout his lifetime. My dad did not know how to process all his pain. I remember seeing him in agony as he looked at a picture that was sent to him from Yugoslavia showing his mother in a casket. He didn't know the Lord personally even though he went to church. He went to Mass and then straight to the tavern where he *drowned* his sorrows with alcohol. Alcohol could not remove the grief and the pain that he was feeling, and it took its toll on our whole family.

My dad worked 2nd shift, but he did have the weekends off. The only time that I remember going somewhere with my dad was to a baseball game. I believe it was a Brave's game. I tried to avoid my father as much as I could. When my dad would be sitting at the kitchen table, there was only a small space to get past him if I wanted to get something from the refrigerator. When I would see him sitting there, I would turn back and go into another room. I lived in almost constant fear of him except when I saw him in a good mood. Then he would show off his muscles, and we would swing on his arms. There were times when my dad would have some of his brothers over at the house, and he would take his *squeeze box* and play his heart out. Sometimes we would all join in and sing with him. These are pleasant memories. My father had a very deep and tender heart, and when others would reach out to him, whether it was for money or for help, my dad was there to help. Many alcoholics have deep, sensitive hearts and many good qualities, but when the enemy of their soul takes over, it can be frightening and even dangerous.

I remember frightening times when all would seem calm, and then there would be an outburst of anger, and all of us would have to run out of the house for safety. My mom would go back after awhile and calm him down, and then we would go back into the house for the night. There were times when I was older when we had to stay at my boyfriend's (now husband's) parents' house to be kept safe. We never knew when there would be an *outbreak of violence,* and so I lived walking on *eggshells* when my dad was home. I remember having dreams as a young girl and feeling a dog biting me while I was sleeping. I would wake up and still feel pain in my leg. I was under demonic attack even as a young child.

Some of you may be thinking at this point: *Why didn't her mom divorce him to keep her children safe?* My mom was a devout Catholic, and she was taught that when you marry, you marry for life. My mom felt that this was her "cross" to carry, not realizing what it truly meant to carry the cross according to Scripture. Many times while growing up I wondered the same thing, and I truly believed that I would have been so much more emotionally stable if I would have grown up without a father, but now I know that God works ALL things together for good to those who love Him.

I remember what happened one night when I was sleeping with my older sister. My father walked into the room, singled me out, and started to hit me. I cried out in pain and fear and asked him why he was hitting me. He said: *"This is for when you do something wrong in the future."* There were times I was singled out and hid from him, and I would hear him yell: *"Where's that skinny girl?"* as he searched for me. You must understand that my dad was not angry with me but with himself. He was filled with guilt and shame, and he didn't know how to handle the pain. I look a lot like my dad. Maybe he saw himself in me and that is the reason why I was singled out at times. But I wasn't the only one who suffered; our whole family did. There were times when my dad, in a drunken rage, would go after my older sister, and my mom would stand between them. At times when my sister would be on the phone, he would tell her to get off, and when she wouldn't he would rip the phone out of the wall.

When these rampages would happen, one of my favorite places to hide was in a metal clothes closet. This was my *"secret place,"* but I have to say: *"I now have a secret place in Jesus where I feel safe and secure from all evil!"* I want to emphasize that in no way am I making excuses for my dad. My dad suffered great grief and torment because of his refusal to repent and to yield his life to Jesus. I have forgiven him, but it took many years of excruciating grief and pain to reach that point.

I remember seeing my dad sitting on a couch in the living room smoking cigarette after cigarette in torment. He suffered physically, mentally, spiritually, and emotionally in ways that only God knows. All of us can thank God for His mercy or we would be spending an eternity in Hell. Many people judge others as so much more wicked than them. This is because the Light of the Spirit has not entered into their souls and revealed their deep hidden sins. I have learned that all of us have sinned in a depth and severity that only God recognizes. If the Lord would show us the depth of our depravity, we would shudder in utter horror. Thank God for His mercy and grace! Many refuse to look inside and to allow the Spirit to come into their hearts with His searching Light, and so they, like the Pharisees, sit in judgment of others and call them *incurables.*

Troublesome Years of Grief

In High School I remember sitting and drawing unclean pictures, not even realizing why I was doing this. There was a deep darkness in me that I believed I could never be free from. I was tormented and lonely and was heading in the same direction as my father. I started drinking, partying, sneaking out at night, and meeting with others who were hurting and rebellious. I would go to church dances, but before I arrived I would get drunk with the person I was going with. I thank God, for during this rebellious time in my life, God was watching over me and never allowed the enemy to really hurt or to destroy me. The Spirit was teaching me invaluable lessons through all these hard years though I didn't realize it at the time.

I met my husband, Ron, in High School through his sister, Denise, and at 19-years-old I got married. When I told my mom I was getting married, she told me that she thought I was marrying Ron to escape my home life, but that was not true. This was all in God's plan for my life. One day while I was still living at home and dating Ron, I heard a voice telling me that this was the man I was going to marry. I knew I was going to marry Ron, for God had given me a deep peace in the direction I was going.

In our early years of marriage, I was drawn to pornographic movies, and I felt this was the most natural thing in the world. I never stopped to reason out why I was drawn to such filth until the Lord showed me why. I believe many are caught in this web and do not even realize that they were victims of incest or some form of perversion in their lives. Many pastors and leaders have fallen as King David did so long ago, not realizing that these iniquitous sins and strongholds are in their bloodline. King David did not realize that the temptation that brought him down when he committed adultery was there because of an *iniquitous stronghold* of "harlotry" that was passed down from his great, great, grandmother Rahab. Jesus is more than willing to free every captive soul, but these sins must be uncovered, confessed, and forsaken.

When I was pregnant with my first daughter, April, my sister, Jeanie, was witnessed to by her aunt about salvation in Jesus. She accepted the Lord and was gloriously saved. She called me and shared the wonderful news of salvation through Christ, and I was thrilled. We went to a church called Brookfield Assembly of God, and when they gave the *altar call,* my 2 sisters and I, with tears streaming down our faces, went to the front and gave our hearts to Jesus. That was the best day of my life!

Years of Warfare, Grace, and God's Purifying Fire

At the beginning of my journey in Jesus, I was already learning the ways of Jesus in a *hard* way. As I was giving birth to my firstborn, April, doctors and nurses were suddenly all around, and I heard: *"Let's get this baby born quick!"* My husband and I knew that something was drastically wrong. As soon as she was born, I saw that she was blue, and they took her away quickly. It turned out that as I was birthing her, the cord was wrapped around her neck, and she was swallowing meconium which is the earliest stool of an infant. The doctor came in hours later and explained to me the seriousness of her condition. As a very young Christian, I prayed to the Lord and surrendered my baby to Him. I told Jesus that I sure would like to keep her, but I left the results in His loving hands. When the doctor came back the next day, he told me that she was going to be fine. He also told me that a baby was born in the same condition as my daughter and had died a day after I gave birth. I knew that Jesus had healed my daughter, and I was so grateful. As I look back on this, I realize the great grace that the Lord gave me at that time. Our God is so good; His faithfulness knows no end!

God gave me some powerful dreams early in my walk with Him. In one of them I was back at my parent's house, and I was sweeping the floors and the walls of the basement. Dreaming of a basement always stands for the deep heart or the subconscious. Suddenly, the *trap door* opened, and a mighty wind like a *whirlwind* came through the basement and removed all the debris. In another dream I was out on a boat in the middle of a large body of water. Out of the sea came a huge "leviathan" creature. I fell out of the boat and into the water, and as I did this "sea serpent" wrapped around me from the top of my head to the soles of my feet. In the next scene I was lying by a tree *dead*. Then a man with a white robe walked up to me, and He (Jesus) began to remove all the venom from my body, and I started to come to life. Our God is faithful to not only save us but to make us whole in every area of our lives!

Early in my marriage God gave me many dreams concerning my past and revealed to me the sexual abuse that I had suffered. He desired to *uncover* me so I could be free from my past and the guilt that I was living in. I had a dream of going into my father's bedroom and taking a brown suitcase out of his closet. Inside of it there was an object that symbolized something sexual. In the next part of the dream, I was sitting next to my dad, and he had this object in his possession. When I looked at the suitcase, I realized that it was now completely empty except for this one object. I believe God showed me that sexual abuse can be one of the deepest roots in the soul of a person; though everything else may be emptied out of the heart, there can still be a *lingering root* that needs to be uprooted. I do not believe that I was ever raped, but what I suffered emotionally was akin to this. I believe in this hour the Spirit of God is exposing the things that are hidden, the things that are hiding in closets, and the time to be free is now.

When a child suffers great trauma, they escape the trauma in one way or another, emotionally, and this is what happened to me. I remember a time as a teenager when my father went to hug me and grabbed my breast. This was not only done to me. There were times when we would bring friends over, and if the girl was *well-endowed*, he would touch her breast by acting as if he was brushing a crumb off of her top. My father suffered from unclean spirits because he never repented of these iniquities nor did he surrender his heart to Jesus until he was on his deathbed. The enemy had access to his soul because of disobedience and rebellion. During my healing process God showed me that I had a *spirit of murder* and great hatred against my father, and this was why I was in a *dungeon* of hate, fear, and guilt. I struggled many times during this process, and even in my early years at church, the enemy would bring unclean thoughts, and this would bring feelings of guilt and condemnation.

During this season of *deep internal cleansing and warfare,* God was dealing with me to surrender *fully* to His will, no matter what the cost. I remember having suicidal thoughts, and the enemy would even tell me how to accomplish my demise. I remember getting on the floor and crying out to Jesus because the demonic attack was so fierce, but God gave me the victory.

At a conference around this time, a Messianic Jewish brother preached on the Jezebel spirit. He said that most people believe that this spirit *binds* with *lust* and *perversion* alone. He explained that the Jezebel spirit does bring many souls into bondage through adultery and lust, but what many do not see is that this spirit is keeping millions of God's children in a place of *compromise* and *idolatry.* At that moment the Holy Spirit spoke to me and said: *"This is what is binding you!"* He told me that I had to decide that very moment either to stay where I was at, spiritually, and not enter into the fullness that He had for me or to step over the line into full surrender to His will. This had nothing to do with my salvation but with my *destiny* and *calling* in Jesus. I was weeping and trembling from head to foot as I got down on the floor and travailed before the Lord. That day I made a solid decision to go *all the way* with Jesus, and I have never regretted it. There were times when I wanted God to lessen the pain, but I knew that my heavenly Father knew what was best for my life.

As a young Christian God was preparing me for my future in Him, and it required much spiritual growth and learning the ways of the Spirit. I remember God speaking to me during a service at West Layton Assembly of God and telling me that He *chose me* out of the multitudes, but little did I realize the training and the preparation that God would take me through to fulfill this calling. I'm glad that God doesn't show us all that will be required of us to fulfill our destiny. One thing I found is true; the Lord is faithful, and He will never give us more than we can bear. God's grace is always sufficient for us, no matter what we go through, even if it is through the *"valley of the shadow of death."*

At a conference one day I was alone in my room, and I opened my Bible and these words from Luke 1:76–80 (AMP) jumped off the page as the Spirit spoke personally to me about my calling: *"'And you, child, will be called a prophet of the Most High; for you will go on* BEFORE THE LORD *(the Messiah)* TO PREPARE HIS WAYS; *to give His people the knowledge of salvation by the forgiveness of their sins, because of the tender mercy of our God, with which the Sunrise (the Messiah) from on high will dawn and visit us,* TO SHINE UPON THOSE WHO SIT IN DARKNESS AND IN THE SHADOW OF DEATH, *to guide our feet [in a straight line] into the way of peace and serenity.' The child continued to grow and to become strong in spirit, and he lived in the deserts until the day of his public appearance to Israel [as John the Baptist, the forerunner of the Messiah]."* I would now come to know, by experience, what it means to be "battered into the shape of the vision."

God takes us from "glory to glory," and to get to the *next level* we will encounter a *new devil* as Joyce Meyer has said.[xvi] As the years continued the trials intensified, not because I was disobedient but because I was fully yielded to the work of the Spirit inside of my soul. Trial after trial came upon me, personally, in my family, and in the church; it seemed as if my trials would never end. Just when I would feel that I was catching my breath, spiritually, another hard-hitting trial would try to overtake me and even destroy my life. During these years of intense warfare, God was building me up spiritually, and He would not let me go. The Spirit of God was out to possess me fully and free me completely from every chain that was trying to strangle my life. God had a purpose for my life, a destiny and a calling, and the Spirit held me firm in His grip.

I remember a time when I fell on my knees and cried out to the Lord because of great pain and pressure; Jesus spoke to my heart and told me that the enemy had demanded to *"sift me like wheat."* (See Luke 22:31.) These were the words that Jesus spoke to Peter, and now God was showing me that I was being "sifted like wheat." Everything that I held on to so tightly was being removed from my heart and my life. All the *props* that I was leaning on were being taken from me. Every idol was being crushed and burned up in my life. I felt as if I was being turned upside-down, inside-out, and even *destroyed!* I was in the Spirit's *whirlwind,* and it seemed as if this shaking would never end!

During this time God told me to memorize a Psalm a week and then confirmed this by sending me an article entitled: *"My experience with memorizing a Psalm a week."* This helped me tremendously, for my mind was being renewed and cleansed through the *"washing of the water of the Word."* (See Ephesians 5:26.) I spent countless hours in the presence of God gazing into His face and receiving His love. This was where I developed my "secret place" and encountered Jesus in glorious ways. Through the deep waters I was going through and copious tears, Jesus was drawing me deeper and deeper into His heart. I was "fellowshipping" with Him in His sufferings. His *presence* was bringing *deep transformation* into my soul, and His perfect love was casting out all fear. Every time I laid down my own will for the Lord's will, the *transforming work of the cross* was realized in my life.

One of the hardest seasons of my life was in a church I attended for about 12 years. Never had I felt such pain and rejection as from the pastor and the leadership at this church. Blow after blow, I endured the greatest feelings of pain and rejection in my life. This was my season of suffering the *"loss of all things."* Many of my loved ones did not understand what was truly happening in my life as God took me through a *spiritual ringer!* Very few stood with me at this time, but Jesus was my Help and Stay! This was the season in my life when Jesus wanted me to find Him as my All in All!

Every time I went to church during this purifying season, I would experience the greatest fear and demonic attacks, but God, in His mercy and grace, kept me faithful to continue to praise Him and to serve Him where He had placed me. Later, when God released me from this church and ordained me through a beautiful ministry called SON RISE MINISTRIES, the pastor of that ministry could not understand why God would have kept me in a church where I suffered so much abuse, but I knew why. God was purifying me under a Saul ministry and preparing me *"to rule and to reign with Him."* Jesus was emptying me of pride, rebellion, fear, and unbelief through it all. I was learning to respect and to honor God's anointed ones even if *their* hearts needed deep purification and they were hurting others because of their pain. God was having me look past their ungodly actions and showing me their deep wounds.

Many leaders have not dealt with generational curses or the pain of their past. There is still a little boy or a little girl inside of them crying out for *daddy's* love and acceptance. God was teaching me so much during this time of suffering, and He was accomplishing a deep inner healing in my soul. I spent so much time alone in my car crying out to God and going through deep deliverance. God was also bringing reconciliation between my father and I, even though he was not with me physically. I had much deliverance in my parked car, for in that *quiet place* I poured out my heart to Jesus with loud cries.

Through the many years of healing, Jesus was preparing me for the ministry that He has me in now, one that He has told me is only the beginning of what He desires to do through my life. I know God has so much more for me, and for *you*. He only desires our full surrender and an abandonment to His will above all. God does not take all of His children down the same path of suffering that He took me on. Our God is sovereign, and He looks at each one of His children as a unique individual. The prophetic word below confirms this. He will conform our lives to His image in His way and in His timing.

The Spirit is saying:

> *"Trust Me when all is dark and you do not know the direction that I am taking you. I am looking for your trust and your surrender at all times, no matter what you feel or see. I have you on a path of intense and extreme faith. This is the path of the fully surrendered; this is the path that I have called you to walk on. Not all of My children are on this path, this extremely narrow path that you are treading. This is the path that I have chosen for you, so do not look at anyone else's path. I have called you to extreme obedience to My will, and you will not walk off of the path that I have placed you on. I will keep you steady, and I will keep you strong.*
>
> *"Never look around and wonder why others are not going through the 'ordeals' that you are going through. Every path is different; every path is designed specifically for each one of My children. There are no two paths that are exactly alike. This is where many get confused; they look at others through their own experience in Me, and they wonder why this person or that person is struggling. They give flippant answers to very complicated situations...about a very special and unique individual. Only I know the human heart and what I need to take them through in order to fulfill My plan and My purposes, not only for their lives but for what I would have them accomplish in My name. This is where I need My children to let go of the lives around them when they see them on a*

path that is confusing and even disturbing to them. I control the direction that I am leading My people on, the path that I alone have designed for their lives. All of My children must learn this lesson and trust Me with every life that looks 'confusing' to them.

"Pastors and ministers, along with all of My children, must learn this. You cannot look through the lens of your own eye and experience and believe that each one of My children will be led as you are. Trust Me in this, and let Me remove the 'cataracts' from your eyes, and you will see more clearly than you ever have before. Let go and let Me be God to each one of My children, for I am more than capable to lead them all the way Home—says your God!"

Many souls have generational curses broken off of their lives in a much shorter time. I believe that in this very generation millions of souls will be freed from iniquitous strongholds quickly as sin and iniquity is confessed and forsaken. True repentance and surrender to the Father's will is always a requirement in order to be set free and to enjoy the abundant life that Jesus promised us.

We can go as deep as we desire into the heart of Jesus. The Apostle Paul's passion was to *know* Jesus in the *"power of His resurrection"* and in the *"fellowship of His sufferings."* (See Philippians 3:10.) He counted the cost and considered everything else *"rubbish"* in order to truly know the deep love of Jesus. (See Philippians 3:8.) My heart has the same passion, and I will press on to *know* Him, no matter the cost. We can have a 30, 60, or a 100-fold harvest. (See Mathew 13:8.) The choice is ours. We can choose life or death. (See Deuteronomy 30:19.) *The choice is ours.* God will never force us into His fullness, but He will draw us with deepest love into His cross and into the power of His resurrection.

The Healing Power of God's Word

In 2019 I was diagnosed with cancer of the bladder. Before this I knew that my body was going through some *changes,* and I was standing on God's Word to bring me full healing. When I would get a symptom, I would speak the Word of God and claim His healing promises for my body. This went on for some time, and I was truly believing for a total healing, miraculously. As my symptoms worsened I prayed more earnestly and claimed God's covenant promises. When I suffered a severe headache that wouldn't go away, I prayed, and I told God that if the headache continued this would be His sign to go to the ER. I go into detail concerning this in my **God of War** book.

I couldn't understand why God didn't immediately heal my body because I was standing on His Word diligently. Later I learned that God had more lessons in faith that He wanted to teach me as I battled through months of suffering and continued to *"fight the good fight of faith"* (1 Timothy 6:12 – NKJV). God deepened my faith and His humility in my soul during these battles, and I have greater empathy for those who struggle with fear and grief when suffering in their bodies.

I know what it feels like to go down into the *"valley of the shadow of death"* (Psalm 23:4) when I lost 9 pints of blood, and they had to rush me back into surgery to try and stop the bleeding. I felt panic and fear when I woke up in ICU intubated and tied down, unable to move, feeling as if I was choking and unable to breathe. I kept pushing the intubation tube away from the center of my throat with my tongue, for I felt as if I was being strangled. I remember staring at a cross on the hospital wall all night in this state and asking Jesus how He could have ever gone through His cross of suffering. I remember the trauma, and for weeks afterwards I could barely talk about it without weeping and reliving the experience.

I had to have a 3rd surgery, and the enemy tormented me that I would again have to go through the painful ordeal of being intubated, but we prayed that there would be *minimal bleeding*. In Day Surgery as I waited for them to take me into the surgical room for my 3rd surgery, I felt angels around me, and the joy of the Lord flooded my soul. In the recovery room, the first words that I heard were: "minimal bleeding." Our God is so faithful, and what I learned during this year of physical suffering, I would not trade for the world. Do I want to go through this again? Do I ask for suffering? Heavens, no!

Jesus said that in this world we will have many trials and sorrows but that we are to be of good cheer, for He has overcome the world. (See John 16:33.) During this time of suffering Jesus told me that I lived out Psalm 18: the warfare, the victory, the strengthening, and the deliverance of God. I give God all the glory for bringing me through these hard times. I will forever and eternally be grateful for all the lessons I have learned and for the transformation that the Spirit of God accomplished, and is accomplishing, in my life.

As I climbed the *spiritual mountain* that God put before me, I felt and experienced a sense of *weakness* that I had never felt before. I experienced in my life what Paul stated in 2 Corinthians 12:10 (TPT): *"So I'm not defeated by my weakness, but delighted! For when I feel my weakness and endure mistreatment—when I'm surrounded with troubles on every side and face persecution because of my love for Christ—I am made yet stronger. For my weakness becomes a portal to God's power."* I found that in my weakest moments Jesus was my Strength and that He was transforming me more and more into His image.

> Stop imitating the ideals and opinions of the culture around you, but be inwardly transformed by the Holy Spirit through a total reformation of how you think. This will empower you to discern God's will as you live a beautiful life, satisfying and perfect in His eyes.
>
> –Romans 12:2

I can't finish my testimony without expressing the importance of God's Word in the transformation process. If I hadn't had the Word of God for my foundation of Truth, I never would have made it through the myriad of trials and temptations that I endured. His Word in our lives is what brings deep internal change in the way we think and in the way we live. The Word empowers us to walk through the darkest valleys and to climb the highest mountains.

Jesus never promised us an easy road, but He promised that He would be with us and always see us *through* every difficulty. His Word tells us that we when we *"walk **through** the valley of the shadow of death"* He would be with us. (See Psalm 23:4.) Jesus was with the three Hebrew men in the fiery furnace. He did not keep them from it but brought them *through* it. God was with them and freed them from their "bonds" in the fire. (See Daniel 3:16–27.) Jesus didn't keep Daniel *from* the lion's den but delivered him *in* it and then *from* it. God took him *through* the ordeal and then promoted him.

> When you pass **through** the waters, I will be with you; and **through** the rivers, they shall not overwhelm you; when you walk **through** fire you shall not be burned, and the flame shall not consume you.
>
> –Isaiah 43:2 – ESV, emphasis added

God's purpose and desire in all that we go *through* is to make us whole: spirit, soul, and body, and He is passionately desiring to complete this work in each of our lives. Our God is faithful, and He will never waste anything that we go through as we walk on His path of surrender and obedience. I look back on my life, and all that I see is the love and faithfulness of my Heavenly Father. He is a good, good, Father.

My thesis in Bible College was: *"The Power of the Cross in the Life of the Believer,"* and this was what I have been experiencing throughout my life, through all the ups and downs. My pain and sorrows were not wasted, for God used each *stroke of adversity* for His glory and for my good. God used these adversities to refine me and to draw me deep into His heart. Truly, He is closer than my breath, and I wouldn't trade my relationship with the Father, Jesus, or the Holy Spirit with anyone else on the face of this earth. I am living the Song of Songs; Jesus is my life, my song, and My greatest joy and delight! I can say from the bottom of my heart that it was, and is, worth going through the cross so that I can experience the *"power of His resurrection"* which is ever increasing in my life.

I had a dream recently, and I titled it: **The Tiger and the Mouse.** I feel it is so significant in showing how the Holy Spirit's power inside of us transforms us from a *mouse* to a *tiger*. In a dream a tiger can represent power, raw emotion, and fearsomeness[xvii] while a mouse can represent timidity, fear, shyness, and insecurities.[xviii] In this dream I put a mouse and a tiger in a cage together. As I looked at them I noticed that the mouse was actually overcoming and destroying the tiger. When I looked again the tiger had the mouse on the ground and had killed it. I then saw the tiger coming out of the cage, and I tried to stop it. I had his neck in the door of the cage and was trying to close him in, but he got out. When I turned around, the tiger was lying peacefully on the floor, but I wanted to get him back into the cage.

Jesus showed me that in my past I was in a cage of timidity and insecurity. He showed me that the *tiger* represented His presence in me and that His presence and power *in* me has *swallowed up* the timidity and insecurity in my life (the mouse). At times in the past, I was fighting against this transformation, and that's why I saw the mouse winning. Like Jacob I had *wrestled* with Jesus in the process He was taking me through. Jesus showed me that now the *tables have turned,* and the *tiger* in me has won.

I believe the reason I tried to keep the tiger caged is because sometimes we fear to feel our *raw emotions,* all the *strong emotions* that we try to *keep at bay* deep within us. But we do not need to fear. We can handle our emotions when they are controlled by the Spirit, and He will help us not to *lose it!*

Many souls fear change, and sometimes we are comfortable with the way things are, fearing we may open a Pandora's box deep inside of our souls! We try to hide our deep emotions from the Lord, but in so doing we squelch the power of the Spirit in us. I have been open and honest with Jesus, but it has not always been easy. Jesus told me that I will never again be able to *cage* His presence in my life. The tiger was in a *resting position,* and this is the place that Jesus has brought me to: His deep rest.

Most of my life I have been fearful and timid, but not anymore. Jesus has transformed me from being a timid, *fearful mouse* into a *tiger.* This is the transforming power of the Spirit that He desires to work out in each one of His children's lives, but we must be open and honest with our raw emotions. Many have been fearful of taking off their *masks of piety,* for they think they will be loved less. We want love and acceptance from others and from the Lord so we put a smile on our face when our hearts are bleeding and cover up our true feelings. God wants us to be real with Him so that we can be made into *tigers in the faith.* His desire is to release His glory in and through us, but the *covering* over our hearts must be removed. It is painful, but it is worth going through His fire in order to be completely freed from every bondage.

> The Lord God is my strength, and He has made my feet like deer's feet, and has me walk on my high places.
>
> –Habakkuk 3:19a – NASB

In His Glory – Transformed!

Only in God's Glory can we know His transforming power. It was in the very glory of God that I was delivered from my past and am being transformed internally. What is God's Glory? How do we receive His transforming power into our lives, practically?

Mark Ballenger's definition of glory is the best one I found online: **The glory of God is the invisible qualities, character, or attributes of God displayed in a visible (or knowable) way.**[xix]

God's glory is the display of His magnificence. This is God's Shekinah glory, His *manifest presence,* that comes to us when we seek Him with our whole heart. These are His invisible qualities, His beautiful character and attributes, made known to us in a *tangible* way, in a way that will overwhelm us and cause us to cry out in ecstasy! When souls and bodies are touched by His tangible presence, some will weep profusely while others will fall to the floor as *dead*. Others will cry out or moan in deepest repentance. Depending on what God is doing in a soul, there will be many different responses when God's Holy Presence touches a life.

> Then Moses asked to see God's glory. The Lord replied, "I will make My goodness pass before you, and I will announce to you the meaning of My name Jehovah, the Lord. I show kindness and mercy to anyone I want to."
>
> –Exodus 33:18–19 – TLB

Moses passionately desired to see God's glory, and so do I! God's "goodness" in our lives reveals His glory. Jesus is *always* speaking to us and blessing us in hundreds, if not thousands, of ways as we walk with Him. When our eyes are opened to His love and presence, we see Him in everything that transpires in our lives. We realize that every *good thing* that comes to us comes from our Father in Heaven. Millions do not know the glory of God in His goodness, kindness, and mercy. They see God as a vengeful and mean deity that is only out to destroy them. I was blind to the love and mercy of God for years because of my painful relationship with my father, and this is where millions of souls are in this very hour. They do not realize how much God loves them and desires to free them. They see Him only as a *faraway* God who cares nothing for them. They believe, as I did, that God is just like their earthly father or someone who hurt and abused them. They may fear God, but they would never draw close to Him and believe that He loves them passionately.

> All who claim me as their God will come, for I have made them for My glory; I created them.
>
> –Isaiah 43:7

We were created by God for His glory, and He desires to transform us into His image. God is LOVE; it's who His is. I've learned that there is nothing greater or more powerful than the glory of His love, for this is what transforms us in the depths of our being. Nothing is more all-consuming than the fire of His love; it is what draws us into the depths of His heart. The passionate love of Jesus is what changed my heart and life more than anything else; He drew me close to Him with strong "cords of love!" All who come to Jesus and surrender to His design for their lives will experience His love, glory, and power and will be changed internally.

> And the Word became flesh and dwelt among us, and we have seen His glory, glory as of the only Son from the Father, full of grace and truth.
>
> –John 1:14 – ESV

The glory of God is **Jesus.** Jesus is the manifestation of Shekinah glory! He is the Living Word of God. When we behold Jesus, how He lived and what He taught, we behold His glory and the glory of our Father. The Holy Spirit reveals who Jesus is deep in our souls and spirits as we open our hearts in worship. As we follow in the footsteps of Jesus and learn His ways, we experience who He is in His manifest glory! We experience the fullness of His grace and Truth in our lives. We behold the glory of God in the face of Jesus as we gaze on His beauty. As we embrace our cross daily, His glory will be made known to us, and we will walk in resurrection power. ***The cross of Jesus is the portal into His glory!***

> Jesus replied, "Have I been with you all this time, Philip, and yet you still don't know who I am? Anyone who has seen Me has seen the Father! So why are you asking Me to show Him to you?"
>
> –John 14:9 – NLT

So how do we experience God's transforming power in His glory when our hearts are heavy with grief and sorrow and when we are going through a deep valley of loss? Let me tell you a deep and powerful secret though I believe it is not a secret to everyone. At the beginning of my trials, God taught me the power of praise and worship even when I didn't *feel* like praising. Jesus told me that I would *dance* my way into freedom and victory, and I have found this to be true. God *"inhabits our praises,"* and when the Spirit comes in the midst of our worship, the enemy flees; our hearts are ignited with His fire, and we are transformed. (See Psalm 22:3.)

When my heart feels the *coldest* and *farthest* from the Lord, I worship Him in song and in worshipful dance; I lay prostrate before Him and cry out to Him from the depths of my heart. During the many years of transformation as I followed His command to praise Him no matter what I felt or what I was going through, I would experience His Shekinah, manifest glory covering and filling me. When we worship and praise Jesus even when He feels farthest from us, we show our God that we trust Him and believe His Word, no matter what we feel or see.

I didn't always *feel* God's transforming glory covering and filling me, but as I continued to praise Him and to walk in obedience to what He was telling me to do, the transformation process continued as tears flowed and, at times, great cries of pain came forth from my heart. It was not an easy path but a glorious one, and to this day when my heart is heavy, I run to the Lord and praise and thank Him for His goodness and mercy in my life as He continues to take me from *"glory to glory!"*

I know I am a walking, living *miracle of transformation,* for though my relationship with my earthly father was fearful and painful beyond words, my walk with my heavenly Father is glorious! His transforming power in my life took me from fearing God and seeing Him as a God who didn't love or care about me to a living, vital relationship with Him whereby I can call Him "Abba," daddy God. I know that my Heavenly Father loves me with an everlasting love and that He will never leave me nor forsake me; truly, there is no fear in His love. It was worth all the years of pain and sorrow, for through the *"fellowship of suffering"* with Jesus and His *"resurrection power,"* God has transformed me, and is transforming me daily, into the image of Jesus. Glory to God!

The Transforming Power of Forgiveness

I cannot end this chapter without writing about the *power of forgiveness* and how it frees us internally. I have found, through all of my struggles and years of bondage, that true freedom comes as we release those who have hurt and wounded us. This process of letting go frees us from chains of destruction and from deep, debilitating fears. Without forgiveness, without releasing those who have wounded us, we will stay in a *prison* of bitterness and of unbelief. The Word of God talks much about forgiveness, and we will look at a few of these powerful Scriptures.

> For if you forgive others their trespasses [their reckless and willful sins], your heavenly Father

will also forgive you. But if you do not forgive others [nurturing your hurt and anger with the result that it interferes with your relationship with God], then your Father will not forgive your trespasses.

–Matthew 6:14–15 – AMP

Many times in my past pain and rejections, I have struggled with forgiving others. I've learned that it is not a matter of your *feelings* but of obedience to God's Word. I remember having clenched fists when I would see someone that I was holding a grudge against, and my whole body would react in fear and anger. I know what it is like to struggle with forgiving those who you believe have betrayed and hurt you. The enemy is right there feeding your heart and mind with lies so that you continue to hold a deep grudge against those you believe have rejected you. Unforgiveness kept me in a prison of fear and unbelief until I was willing to let the Spirit of God release me from my anger through His purifying fire. I had to confess my bitterness and allow the Spirit to come with His sharp knife of truth and cut out of my heart deep roots of hatred. This did not happen overnight but through years of God's hand resting upon me heavily and dealing with me in mercy and grace.

I struggled deeply with my relationship with my Heavenly Father because of the bitterness I held in my heart against my biological father. If our relationship with our earthly father was painful and filled with deep fear and grief, we can be sure that we will need to go through some deep healing in our souls in order to know the love of our Heavenly Father. If I had continued to hold onto bitterness and anger against my earthly father, I would never have come to know my Heavenly Father's love. If we hold onto unforgiveness we will never know the freedom of the Father's forgiveness in our lives. We can try to *skirt* this issue in our lives, but God will continue to confront us with this issue of unforgiveness.

> Bearing graciously with one another, and willingly forgiving each other if one has a cause for complaint against another; just as the Lord has forgiven you, so should you forgive.
>
> –Colossians 3:13

In order to live a life of joy and freedom, we must be willing to confront those who have hurt or rejected us. While doing this, we must be led by the Spirit of God, and this confrontation must be done in His *way* and in His *timing*. Even though we may be willing to reconcile with someone, they may not be ready, and it may do more damage than good. First, we must make sure that our hearts are filled with love for the one who we believe has wounded us. It may take weeks, months, or even sometimes years before we see God move and bring reconciliation in a painful relationship, but we can be sure that in God's perfect timing restoration will come.

> Then Peter came to Him and asked, "Lord, how many times will my brother sin against me and I forgive him and let it go? Up to seven times?" Jesus answered him, "I say to you, not up to seven times, but seventy times seven."
>
> –Matthew 18:21–22

There may be times when the same person who has wounded you in the past will continue to wound you. In your pain you may think that because they continue to hurt you God no longer requires that you forgive them. Forgiveness is always necessary if we are to know true freedom in the Spirit. Forgiving those who have hurt you and continue to hurt you does not mean that you will have a relationship with them, but on your part you will experience an intimate relationship with God and freedom in your soul to love them in spite of what they have done against you. The Lord may have you sever the friendship, and if it is a family member, you may have to place boundaries in your life in order to protect yourself from constant harassment. God will give you wisdom in doing this as you seek Him with your whole heart. Only the Spirit can bring true healing and reconciliation between two parties that have been separated because of pain and misunderstanding. Jesus has not called us to live in constant abuse from someone but to live in peace and joy.

> Whenever you stand praying, if you have anything against anyone, forgive him [drop the issue, let it go], so that your Father who is in heaven will also forgive you your transgressions and wrongdoings [against Him and others].
>
> —Mark 11:25

We must allow the Spirit to remove from our hearts every *blockage* that is keeping us from loving Him and others. If we hold onto unforgiveness, we will never experience the deep love and intimacy that we desire to have with our Father and Jesus. If we refuse this deep work in our hearts, we will forever struggle, and the bitterness that lies within will continue to *eat* away at our love and joy until our hearts cry out in emptiness and grief!

> When I kept silent, my bones grew old through my groaning all the day long. For day and night Your hand was heavy upon me; my vitality was turned into the drought of summer. Selah. I acknowledged my sin to You, and my iniquity I have not hidden. I said, "I will confess my transgressions to the Lord," and You forgave the iniquity of my sin. Selah.
>
> —Psalm 32:3–5 – NKJV

Have you ever experienced God dealing with you as He did with David? I know that I have, and believe me, it is NOT a pleasant experience! I felt the heavy hand of God on me day and night. I was angry, and I tried to ignore what I was feeling; I tried to cover it up by keeping busy and doing good works. But this never works, for the Lord will continue to deal with us until we confess our sin and iniquities before Him. I was weak, depressed, and angry; I felt spiritually dry and fearful until I allowed the Spirit to bring to the surface my bitterness and anger against not only others but even the Lord. It frightened me to see the deep darkness that was in my soul, right below the surface, for I felt that God would forsake me if these deep iniquities and sins surfaced. Isn't that foolish? Do we truly believe that God can't see all that is in our hearts? As I allowed God to bring up these deep sins, He then flooded me with His love, grace, and mercy. Only as I was honest with the Lord did I begin to experience the love and freedom that I so longed for. As I released and forgave others, I experienced the love and forgiveness of my Heavenly Father.

> Hatred stirs up strife, but love covers and overwhelms all transgressions [forgiving and overlooking another's faults].
>
> —Proverbs 10:12 – AMP

> Whoever hates his brother is a murderer, and you know that no murderer has eternal life abiding in him.
>
> —1 John 3:15 – NKJV

> You have heard that it was said to those of old, "You shall not murder, and whoever murders will be in danger of the judgment." But I say to you that whoever is angry with his brother without a cause shall be in danger of the judgment. And whoever says to his brother, "Raca!" shall be in danger of the council.

> But whoever says, "You fool!" shall be in danger of hell fire.
>
> –Matthew 5:21–22

Multitudes in the Church do not realize the strictness of the New Covenant or the high standard that we are called to live in Christ. Jesus spoke the above Scripture and told us that being *angry* with a brother without cause puts us in danger of hell fire. The words we speak in anger can destroy our souls and bring the judgment of God into our lives. So many of God's children speak against others and think nothing of it, but God's standard for our lives is holiness and obedience to His will. Jesus looks at hate and unforgiveness as murder, but many just overlook these abominable sins and believe that committing them is just the *normal* way of life. The Word tells us that no *murderer* has eternal life abiding in him. We must take this seriously! Hatred will always stir up strife, but if God's love is in us, we will learn to *cover* others, even when they hurt and wound us. If we must confront someone, let's always do it in love.

Only in Jesus can we walk on this path of righteousness, and it is paramount that we live a life of repentance before our God. I know what it is like to be filled with hate and unforgiveness against my own father, and God had to deal powerfully with me in order to free me from this damnable sin. The Lord does not wink at anger and unforgiveness in our lives, but in mercy He will forgive us as we repent and turn from our wicked ways. Our God is holy, and the Word tells us that we must be holy as He is holy.

> But be holy now in everything you do, just as the Lord is holy, who invited you to be His child. He Himself has said, "You must be holy, for I am holy." And remember that your heavenly Father to whom you pray has no favorites when He judges. He will judge you with perfect justice for everything you

do; so act in reverent fear of Him from now on until you get to heaven.

–1 Peter 1:15–17 – TLB

Jesus said, "Forsake the habit of criticizing and judging others, and you will not be criticized and judged in return. Don't condemn others and you will not be condemned. Forgive over and over, and you will be forgiven over and over."

–Luke 6:37 – TPT

The *"tongue is a fire," "a world of evil"* that *"corrupts the whole body."* How can we praise the Lord and then turn around and curse a brother or sister made in the image of God? (See James 3:6–12.) Daily we must pray and ask the Holy Spirit to control our tongues so that what comes forth from our lips will be pleasing to the Lord. God is asking us to live a life of forgiveness and to stop condemning others, for He alone is the righteous Judge.

Let's press on into the fullness that Jesus has for our lives and release all hate and unforgiveness into His fire of holiness so that we can experience the full mending of our hearts and the deep and intimate relationship that God wants us to have with Him. We will experience this freedom as we release forgiveness to those who have deeply wounded us. Father, our prayer is: *"Forgive us the wrongs we have done as we ourselves release forgiveness to those who have wronged us"* (Matthew 6:12).

I end my testimony with this powerful Scripture:

Not that I have already obtained it [this goal of being Christlike] or have already been made perfect, but I actively press on so that I may take hold of that [perfection] for which Christ Jesus took hold of me and made me His own. Brothers and sisters, I do not consider that I have made it my own yet; but one thing I do: forgetting what lies behind and reaching forward to what lies ahead, I press on toward the goal to win the [heavenly] prize of the upward call of God in Christ Jesus.

–Philippians 3:12–14 – AMP

Listen to what the Spirit would say:

"Come near to Me this day, and I will whisper My secrets into your ear.

"Nothing is out of My control, and I have made a way for every seeking soul. Can you feel your spirit-man ascending to Me? Do you know that you are 'seated in heavenly places' with Me? (See Ephesians 2:6.) Your trials and troubles have brought you near to My heart, and now I have you on My spiritual 'spring-board,' and I am ready to 'launch' you into the full plan that I have for your life!

"Step by step you have been building a strong foundation in your life, and now you will see that when this storm hits, you will be as steady as a mountain. You will not be moved neither will you be intimidated by the adversary any longer. This has been My plan and purpose for your life all along, not to destroy you but to make you strong and sure-footed.

"I want you to look now with your spiritual eyes and see what I am doing in your midst, for I have removed your blinders, and I will now show you a 'panoramic view' of what I have in store for your life. You have had only a glimpse of what I have designed and planned for you, but now you will see the full picture, even a world-wide view, of what I have planned for you. You think to yourself at times: 'All of those wasted years,' but now you will understand why you

have had to wait so long to come into the full plan of your life in Me.

"The foundation and preparation for your life is more important than any ministry. You have given up 'lesser' ministries in order to have My very best. You have let go of so many opportunities that you could have taken in the natural realm in order to soar with Me in the High Place of perfect love and My perfect will for your life. What you may see as 'wasted years' will now be turned into a future of fullness, power, and delight such as you have never seen or experienced. These next years will be the most fruitful and glorious years that you have ever known!

"I want you to look at My own life and see how the Father worked out His glorious plan for Me. I spent most of my years on this earth in preparation for My glorious ministry, and for you, My beloved, it has been the same. What seems wasted has been for your good and for My glory! You will now have some years of power and glory such as you have never known.

"Your foundation in Me is now sure and strong, and you will never be shaken. These past many years have been necessary in order for you to build a strong foundation of trust and obedience, and now you are ready to move forward into the full plan, the full destiny, for your life! So, rejoice! I have saved the best for these last years in your life. This is the finale; this is the final chapter of your life, and it will be the most glorious— I promise you—says your God!"

Chapter 5

Divine Reversal

Hear what the Lord would say:

"This is the time of the changing of the guards, and the time has come for a 'Divine Reversal' of all things. What has looked right-side up will now be turned upside-down, and all will see and know that I am 'reversing the tables' and revealing My Divine purposes in this generation. Many that have been in the forefront in the past will now step down from their positions as I raise up My end-time leaders and miracle-workers.

*"Those who have been used in the past in releasing miracles and healings will now step down and make room for My remnant, for those who have been prepared for this time and this season. Some will resist, for their desire will be to keep their name and fame going, but I have decreed that a **new generation** of prophets and ministers will now come forth into the 'limelight.' These are My 'unknowns,' My forgotten ones, and they will now come forth out of their 'caves of seclusion' and make themselves known. They care not for fame or for a name in this earth, for their one desire will be to lift Me up and make Me famous throughout the world. They care not for the applause of man nor*

do they look for man's approval in what they do. They are out to accomplish the will of My Father, and nothing, no one, will stop this mighty 'force of power' from moving with Me. These are My chosen ones, My strong 'mouthpieces,' who will come forth now and show this world the wonder of My name and My glorious power.

"You have not yet seen them nor would you have chosen them, but know this: I have chosen them to move across the face of this earth and to make changes in My Church and in the hearts and lives of My people. They will bring in this final harvest and will raise up a mighty end-time army that will finish My work on the earth.

"Some will be shocked at who I have chosen, and others will be offended and even turn from Me, for they thought that they were the 'high ones,' the ones that I would choose to make a mark on this earth. Get ready to be shocked and to wonder how I could ever choose those whom I have chosen.

*"Those who have been applauded by man will now step down as I lift up this end-time remnant and use them in miraculous and even unusual ways. You will see them now, for the time has come for the 'changing of the guards.' These 'guardians' will move with Me; they will follow the 'Cloud of My Glory,' My 'Shekinah' presence, into the fullness that I have for them. The old pattern and ways of man are coming down, and I am raising up a 'new breed' of people who will do My **whole** will, and no one will make them afraid or shut them down! I have spoken, and I will perform My Word in this very generation—says your God!"*

What glorious days we have entered into! These are days when we will see evil empires topple and the glory of God released in a measure that we have never experienced before. Now we will see millions of souls set free and the enemy fall into the pit that he has dug for individuals, our nation, and the nations of this world.

Thousands upon thousands of souls have experienced this *divine reversal* in their lives as Jesus took them out of the darkness of sin and into His marvelous Light. (See 1 Peter 2:9.) Many of God's people have been healed in their bodies by the power of the Living Christ. We have experienced *divine reversals* in our circumstances and miraculous *turn-arounds* that we know only God could perform. All of this is glorious beyond words, but what God has in store for our generation, the new things and feats of glory that He is about to perform, defies human comprehension. What the Spirit is about to release in our midst, the work that He is going to perform, will "shock" multitudes, not only in the Church but in this world!

> Then the Lord said to Samuel, "I am going to do a shocking thing in Israel."
>
> −1 Samuel 3:11 − TLB

We have seen a demonic invasion in our nation in a measure that we never believed possible. We will stand in awe when we see and hear of the wonders and marvels that the Lord our God will do in exposing and releasing His judgments against the evil rulers in our nation and this world. Only God can expose and remove the deep roots of evil that satan has planted for many decades in our nation and this world. It will take the Almighty hand of God to pull up and to remove these demonic roots and to release His righteous judgment in our midst.

I believe with all of My heart that we are on the verge of the greatest outpouring of the Spirit and of a release of glory so great that no tongue will be able to express the magnitude of it. We will now see the "sleeping giant," the Church, waking up and taking *Her* rightful place before the Lord.

As I pondered the words: divine reversal, the Spirit spoke to my heart and said: *"Dress Rehearsal!"* I looked it up, and according to Merriam-Webster a dress rehearsal is: **1: a full rehearsal (as of a play) in costume and with stage properties shortly before the first performance 2: a practice exercise for something to come: DRY RUN.**[xx]

The Lord showed me that these have been days of *rehearsal* before the *first performance* or, as my pastor says, before 'the real deal' breaks forth! The curtain is about to be lifted, and we will walk in the glory and destiny that Jesus has prepared for our lives. This has been a *dry run,* a time of *testing* and *preparation,* in order for God to bring forth His *divine reversal* and His glorious outpouring of the Spirit.

Through these recent delays in judgment, God has been preparing His people and drawing them close to His heart. Jesus has been revealing and establishing His identity in His people in a depth they have not known in the past. God is *awakening* their hearts to realize the authority that they have in Him, and His Church is taking the "keys" that Jesus has given them and are "loosing" and "binding" according to His will and His purpose for their lives, this nation, and the world. (See Matthew 16:19.) The Ekklesia is taking her authority in Christ and beginning to rule and to reign with Jesus in a new and powerful way. She is feeling the passion of the Lord in her heart and is bringing down evil fortresses in the mighty name of Jesus. The Church is releasing spiritual decrees from the heart of Jesus, and we will see the glorious changes that we have long waited for!

> Encourage those who are afraid. Tell them, "Be strong, fear not, for your God is coming to destroy your enemies. He is coming to save you." And when He comes, He will open the eyes of the blind and unstop the ears of the deaf. The lame man will leap up like a deer, and those who could not speak will shout and sing! Springs will burst forth in the wilderness,

and streams in the desert. The parched ground will become a pool, with springs of water in the thirsty land. Where desert jackals lived, there will be reeds and rushes! And a main road will go through that once-deserted land; it will be named "The Holy Highway." No evil-hearted men may walk upon it. God will walk there with you; even the most stupid cannot miss the way. No lion will lurk along its course, nor will there be any other dangers; only the redeemed will travel there. These, the ransomed of the Lord, will go home along that road to Zion, singing the songs of everlasting joy. For them all sorrow and all sighing will be gone forever; only joy and gladness will be there.

–Isaiah 35:4–10

This is not the time to be weak-kneed or fearful but a time to rise up with "wings as an eagle" and soar with Jesus. (See Isaiah 40:31.) God is coming to save us in a way that will overwhelm us. No matter where you are spiritually in this hour know that your God has heard your cries and that He is coming to rescue you in a way you cannot fathom.

The eyes of the blind, both physically and spiritually, are going to be opened. Deafened ears will be unstopped as people truly hear the Gospel for the first time, for their ears will be opened in the power of the Spirit. We have heard of, and may have seen, some miracles in our lifetime, but what is coming is beyond our wildest dreams...so great, so powerful will be this next move of the Spirit.

I remember driving home from a ministry meeting in northern Wisconsin, and suddenly, it began to rain so hard that I had to pull over to the side of the freeway. It continued to rain for some time, and as I sat in my parked car, the Holy Spirit spoke some powerful words to me. He began to reveal to me the intensity of this Great Awakening and end-time revival that is coming. I remember the Lord telling me that this last outpouring will not be stopped by any devil or any man. Nothing and no one will stop this last glorious outpouring that is going to be released. The Spirit also revealed to me that this revival and Great Awakening will last until His second coming. This does not negate God's judgments from coming forth, but in the midst of all the darkness, millions will run into His Kingdom.

Thirsty souls will be filled to overflowing as the Spirit floods cities and nations with His presence and glory. Where *demonic entities* have controlled nations, God is now going to break these "bands of evil" and release millions. God will deal with the "Pharaohs" that have bound and imprisoned multitudes of souls. No longer will His people be kept in captivity and made to do "hard labor."

God is bringing His people out of bondage, and they will walk on His "Highway of Holiness." The Lord is raising up a *purified people* for His glory and honor. No *lion,* no enemy will be on this path to harass or to harm us. We will live in the "Land of Goshen," and no plague will come near our dwelling. We are entering into a time of peace, peace in our hearts, even though there will be *hurricane force winds* all around us. God's people will be kept in the "eye of the storm," in the very center of God's will, deep in His heart. All of our sorrow and sighing will flee away, and our hearts will be filled with His continual joy. Love and laughter will be our daily portion, for God will prepare a table, a feast, before us in the presence of our enemies. (See Psalm 23:5.)

Are you ready for this *reversal* in your life? Are you ready for the fullness of it? You may have tasted of His goodness in the past, but the glory that God's *prepared ones* will now know will be beyond words! God has saved the best "wine" for this generation. Do we have any idea what it will be like in the coming months and years? I believe we will be so flooded with God's glorious presence that in the midst of horrendous judgments on this earth we will walk in perfect peace above all the darkness and catastrophic events. We will realize that all of our past suffering and trials have brought us up to this High Place in Jesus where no evil will be able to touch us. The transformation in our lives will be so great that we will know that the evil one has "nothing in us." (See John 14:30.)

Joseph – From the Pit to the Palace

> Look how the wicked conceive their evil schemes. They go into labor with their lies and give birth to trouble. They dig a pit for others to fall into, not knowing that they will be the very ones who will fall into it. Every pit-digger who works to trap and harm others will be trapped by his own treachery.
>
> —Psalm 7:14–16 – TPT

God has taken many of His children through a *period of testing* in a variety of ways. Many have fallen into the traps of the enemy. Sometimes it has been through other people or even so-called *ministers*. These *snares* may have come through our circumstances or even family members. Satan has many, many ways to trap souls in a pit of depression, fear, unbelief, sickness, lies, lethargy, bitterness, hate, and a myriad of other strongholds to keep them bound and ineffective for the Kingdom of God. Little by little he *digs a pit* for millions of souls, believing that he has captured them for good, not knowing that he is digging his own pit. Our very nation has been ensnared by the evil one, but we have yet to see what our mighty God will do. He is not done with our nation or the nations of this world!

God uses the schemes of the devil and turns them around for His own purposes, and one of them is to **PRUNE** us in the pit so that we can bear more *spiritual fruit* in our lives. A perfect example of this was the life of Joseph. (See Genesis 49:22; Psalm

105:17–22.) His brothers mocked him, betrayed him, and threw him in a pit. In order to get rid of Joseph, they sold him as a slave, and he spent many years in Egypt. At the beginning he was a slave in Potiphar's house taking care of his master's goods. Joseph **PROSPERED** in Potiphar's house because of His faithfulness to God in the midst of his trials and his diligence in all that was required of him in his master's house.

During his time of slavery the Jezebel spirit, through Potiphar's wife, tried to seduce Joseph, but he ran from this temptation and passed his fiery test. His character was being developed in every trial and test, and he was being **PURIFIED** deeply. But instead of being promoted after this severe test, God prepared a time of *transformation* for him in prison. The enemy may have desired to destroy Joseph in his pit, but God had a higher plan for His servant's good. Even in prison Joseph knew that the Lord was with him, and because of this Joseph found favor with the prison guard.

When Joseph interpreted dreams for two of Pharaohs officials, they came to pass just as he interpreted them. He may have thought that because of the accuracy of these interpretations his time of release had come, but this didn't happen. God was out to purify His son in His way and in His timing, not Joseph's. The Lord needed to work in the depths of his heart the strength, wisdom, and stability that he needed in order to stand in the high position that God had ordained for him. Joseph spent many years in his pit, and because he trusted the Lord, God transformed his heart and elevated him to a High Place in Egypt. Joseph experienced **PROMOTION** and *divine reversal* after years of suffering. All of the dreams that God had given Joseph so long ago came to pass, but they sure didn't materialize in the way or timing that he thought they would.

God deals with us in much the same way. He whispers into our ears and reveals our destiny and calling in Him, and we are thrilled. We try to figure out, in our own understanding, how He will bring it to pass, and when it looks like Jesus is taking us in the opposite direction, we get offended and angry. For some reason we think that God should deal with us differently than others. Many times we think: Why would God have to take us through a valley of suffering? Aren't we special? We are people of faith, and our sins aren't that bad, are they? We believe because sister "Mary" isn't suffering, or so we think based on what we see, then why should we? We ignore hundreds of Scriptures that talk about suffering and the way that Jesus led many of His children through a wilderness of pain and loss. We close our hearts to the deeper truths and ways of the Father and think that we can escape the "cross" that Jesus tells us to pick up and to carry daily. We believe there is some easier way to enter into His glory, and we fashion a "god" after our own *imagination* instead of the God of the Bible. If we desire to walk in the High Place with Jesus, we will experience some *pits* along our journey with Jesus. Like Joseph we will find that we are being transformed in our pit as we are *pruned, purified, prospered, and promoted* in the very things that we thought would bring *death*. Instead we find His abundant life as we walk into the glory that our Father has planned for us!

> God has sent me ahead of you to keep you and your families alive and to preserve many survivors. So it was God who sent me here, not you! And He is the one who made me an adviser to Pharaoh—the manager of his entire palace and the governor of all Egypt...Pharaoh said to Joseph, "Tell your brothers, 'This is what you must do: Load your pack animals, and hurry back to the land of Canaan. Then get your father and all of your families, and return here to me. I will give you the very best land in Egypt, and you will eat from the best that the land produces.'" Then Pharaoh said to Joseph, "Tell your brothers, 'Take wagons from the land of Egypt to carry your little children and your wives,

and bring your father here. Don't worry about your personal belongings, for the best of all the land of Egypt is yours.'"

–Genesis 45:7–8, 17–20 – NLT

Now this is **divine reversal!** And will not our God do the same for me and for you? Let's believe God for the best of all the "land," all His provision and promises for our lives. We serve a good God; a God who will never fail us!

The Number 40 – A Time of Testing

When the number 40 was accentuated in a recent dream that I had, I knew that God was speaking to me and that this number was important. According to **Rabbi Aish** the number 40 is significant throughout the Torah and the Talmud. It means **transition or change; the concept of renewal; a new beginning. It has the power to lift a spiritual state.**[xxi]

The number 40 can stand for a period of *probation, trial, and chastisement*. It will *end* with **revival or a new beginning if** we are faithful and submit to the discipline of the Father. (See Hebrews 12:4–11.) 40 is also the number of **perfection or completion.**[v]

During these past years many of God's people have gone through a time of testing. Through Covid, upheavals in our government and nation, unemployment, and many personal issues, many have been confused, disheartened, and even angry at the turn of events. Those who have understood God's purposes during these times of trouble have found themselves *changing* and *transitioning* more fully into the image of Christ. If we have learned to trust and to praise Him during this time of probation, we will find ourselves entering into a time of renewal, refreshing, and new beginnings. I believe that during this time of testing God is "weeding out" those who are not truly serious about being in His end-time Gideon army. Just as God *whittled down*

Gideon's army to 300 men so is God drawing a line of division and seeing who will surrender fully to His will and ways in this season of glory.

God's whole purpose during our times of testing is to transform and to transition us so that He can catapult us into the next glory that He has prepared for us. So many just want to skip the discipline of the Father and move on into glory. It just doesn't work that way, for if we are not disciplined, we will not have the inner strength and character that is needed to stand strong in the *greater floods* that are coming. God will waste nothing in our lives, but if we fight against what God wants to accomplish in us, we will not come to that place of maturity that He desires us to walk in.

> For after seven more days I will cause it to rain on the earth **forty** days and **forty** nights, and I will destroy from the face of the earth all living things that I have made...Now the flood was on the earth forty days. The waters increased and lifted up the ark, and it rose high above the earth. The waters prevailed and greatly increased on the earth, and the ark moved about on the surface of the waters... Then the ark rested in the seventh month, the seventeenth day of the month, on the mountains of Ararat.
>
> –Genesis 7:4, 17–18; 8:4 – NKJV, emphasis added

When God takes us through *flood waters*, fiery trials, and suffering, God is cleansing us and removing from our lives all that is not of Him. We will not drown in these waters; they will only flow *through us* and remove all the debris of sin and shame. As these waters increase in our lives, God will lift us higher and higher, and we will learn to *float* on these *troubled waters*. We are God's "ark," and His desire is to lift us higher and higher until we reach the pinnacle of His "Holy Mountain." As the ark came to rest on the mountains of Ararat so does the Lord desire that we enter fully into His rest in this hour. (See Hebrews 4:9–11.)

> Afterward, the Holy Spirit led Jesus into the wilderness to experience the ordeal of testing by the accuser. And after fasting for **forty** days, Jesus was extremely hungry.
> –Matthew 4:1–2 – TPT, emphasis added

Before Jesus began His public ministry, the Holy Spirit led Him into the wilderness to experience the ordeal of testing. Before God can release us fully into His divine plan for our lives, we, too, must go through a time of testing. If an earthly machine or vehicle has to be tested before it can be sold or used how much more do we need to experience trials and temptations in order to *weather* us, spiritually, and to form us into that "vessel of honor" that is useful in His Kingdom? As the Spirit brings us through our wilderness experience, we will experience great hunger in our souls for the "Bread of Life," Jesus, and He will satisfy our souls fully. We must follow in the *footsteps of Jesus* all the way if we are to come into the fullness of our calling. This time of preparation is more important than anything else in our lives, for it is building a strong foundation under us that will not be shaken.

> After **forty** years had passed, an angel appeared to Moses in the flames of a burning bush in the desert near Mount Sinai.
> –Acts 7:30 – NIV, emphasis added

During Moses' **40** years in the wilderness, he experienced the *transformation* that God was after in his life. Some may wonder why it took Moses so long to be transformed. Remember: His *high calling* required many, many years to prepare and to spiritually *condition* him. God was with Moses in the desert place and was working diligently in his heart and life so that when the time came Moses would be able to withstand the pressure and temptations that would assail him. Moses was *emptied* in the desert, and when the call came Moses knew that his total dependence would have to be on God, for in himself he knew he could do nothing. This is God's purpose in our transformation process also. We are emptied of the things of this world in order to be filled with the Spirit. Moses realized that nothing would be accomplished apart from God's power, and we must learn this same lesson, no matter how long it takes.

After his 40 years of discipline, Moses then experienced his *Great Awakening*. I'm sure Moses didn't expect this powerful "burning bush" encounter with God. You may not be expecting an encounter with Jesus either, and you may even have given up on ever coming out of your fiery ordeal, but God has not forgotten you! God has a "burning bush" experience for you as you wait on Him and "turn aside," as Moses did, in order to see the "sight." (See Exodus 3:3.) We *turn aside* by waiting on the Lord in our *secret place*, for this is where we will encounter our King in marvelous ways! When Moses *least expected* this encounter with the Living God, God showed up as a mighty *Flame of Fire*. Moses was overwhelmed in the presence of God and was afraid to look into the face of God. Moses felt inadequate as God commissioned him to set His people free. God was not looking for someone who felt strong and adequate in themselves, but someone who knew that their strength had to be found in God alone. The Lord is calling the weak and the foolish in this hour, not the strong and self-assured. (See 1 Corinthians 1:27.)

In this dream I had concerning the number 40, I remember being with Jesus and my *destiny child*, and we were heading for breakfast. I remember saying: *"I am thirsty."* God told me that now is the time when He will "break the fast" in my life and, I believe, your life as well. God is going to satisfy us with His glorious presence in this hour, and we will hunger no more!

For those of you who are hungry and thirsty for God, your time has arrived to have the greatest encounter with the Living God that you have ever had.

> How He satisfies the souls of thirsty ones and fills the hungry with goodness!
>
> —Psalm 107:9 – TPT

> For **forty** days, every morning and evening, the Philistine champion strutted in front of the Israelite army.
>
> —1 Samuel 17:16 – NLT, emphasis added

The enemy's time of taunting, harassing, and binding God's people is over! We have endured **40** days, months, or even years of his relentless persecution. It has worked for our good in transforming us and making us into the warriors God has called us to be. It has refined our character so that now we walk more fully in the likeness of Jesus. God has filled us with His righteousness and with the fruit of the Spirit, and we are ready to not only knock our giants down but to take off their heads! The adversary has strutted before us in pride and arrogance, but now our Champion, through us, is bringing him down! We have waited; we have worshipped; we have obeyed, and now our season of *full* victory over the enemy has arrived. I believe that from the time we surrendered our lives to Jesus, satan was under our feet, but now we have reached a place of maturity where we will see him *crushed under our feet.*

> And the God of peace will swiftly pound Satan to a pulp under your feet! And the wonderful favor of our Lord Jesus will surround you.
>
> —Romans 16:20 – TPT

The Changing of the Guards

There has been so much change in our nation, and much of it has looked disastrous. In the midst of all the turmoil, God is telling us *not* to be discouraged, for His dynamic changes are on the horizon and, in truth, are already happening. There is a great *spiritual shift* coming that is beyond anything we are expecting or dreaming of. It is so much greater than we realize. If the Holy Spirit would reveal to us what is coming in its fullness, we would not be able to take it in! Words cannot express the *full glory* that we are about to see manifested in our nation and in this world. This is so much bigger than a *turn-around* in our nation and government; this involves the whole earth. We are in a time when the whole "earth will be filled with the knowledge of the glory of the Lord" (Habakkuk 2:14– NKJV).

Through this time of intense testing, God has chosen His end-time "guards" who will now take their place and position before Him. This is a new season, and God has a *hidden* people who will now come out of their *caves* to release God's plans and purposes for this nation and the nations of this world. (See 1 Kings 18:4.) When Elijah's ministry on earth was nearing its end, the Lord spoke to Him and revealed to him what he was to do next.

> Then the Lord said to him: "Go, return on your way to the Wilderness of Damascus; and when you arrive, anoint Hazael as king over Syria. Also you shall anoint Jehu the son of Nimshi as king over Israel. And **Elisha the son of Shaphat of Abel Meholah you shall anoint as prophet in your place.** It shall be that whoever escapes the sword of Hazael, Jehu will kill; and whoever escapes the sword of Jehu, Elisha will kill. Yet I have reserved seven thousand in Israel, all whose knees have not bowed to Baal, and every mouth that has not kissed him."
>
> –1 Kings 19:15–18, emphasis added

This was a time in Elijah's life when he would experience a *changing of the guard*. Elijah was nearing the end of a season, and when Elisha was anointed in his place, the *new season* would begin. As Elisha experienced a "double portion" of the Spirit for his generation so is the Lord releasing in this new season, this new era, a double portion, a measure of His Spirit that His people and this world have never seen before. Elijah's ministry was coming to an end, and he completed the work that God had given him to do. It was time to pass the mantle on to his successor. In the same way many faithful servants of the Lord have gone home to their eternal reward, and some on earth have completed what God has called them to do. Many ministers and leaders will now step down and make room for this *new breed of warriors*, those who God has selected to bring in this final worldwide revival. A *greater anointing* is needed in this generation because of the *greater evil* that has invaded our nation and this world. We will get into a greater understanding concerning this in the next chapter.

According to Wiktionary, *changing of the guard* means: **(1) A ceremony during which the soldiers or other officials guarding a major government building or state residence, especially Buckingham Place in England, are replaced by a new shift. (2) Any situation in which an individual or group charged with a task or responsibilities in an organization is replaced by another individual or group.**[xxii]

There is a new *shift change* coming; a new and fresh prophetic army will now rise up and take this *land* and this *world* in the name of Jesus. We will see unusual anointings on men and women that will shatter the powers of hell that have ruled over our nation and this world for so long. As these "gates of hell" are crushed, we will see millions upon millions of souls released from demonic chains. These *new* "wine-skins" will replace the *old order*, the old way of doing things in the traditions and ways of men. Church services will not continue as they always have. The Spirit is about to invade church services and take full control.

Many will not recognize Jesus, for He is coming in *warlike* ferocity and zeal to "overturn tables" in the Church and to tear down the works of the enemy. (See Matthew 21:12.) For too long the enemy has had his way in the Church, but now he is coming down! Controlling spirits that have ruled over the Church, cities, and nations will now be demolished, and this will come about as God raises up His end-time *special forces unit;* they will complete this task. They are a fearless company that will not back down, no matter what they face, no matter what demonic forces come against them. They are walking in the Elisha anointing, a double portion of power and strength from the Spirit, and devils will tremble in their presence, for they will see Jesus in them and working *through* them in this generation.

What are some of the *qualities* and *qualifications* for God's end-time *guards?* Many believe that God will choose them, no matter how they live, no matter if they are faithful and obedient to the Lord or not. Thousands who call themselves Christians are living a "sloppy agape" lifestyle, and they believe that God will overlook their sinful way of life. Thousands, if not millions, believe the lie that because they have "accepted Christ" His grace now covers *all* and that this gives them a license to live as they please. But now we will see that God looks for faithful, disciplined, and obedient children to "guard" their own lives and His people. This *changing of the guard* has arrived.

> Lift up a signal flag against the walls of Babylon; post a strong guard, station sentries, set up an ambush! For the LORD has both planned and performed what He spoke concerning the inhabitants of Babylon.
>
> –Jeremiah 51:12 – NASB

God is looking for spiritually strong leaders, not necessarily those who have been Christians for a long time. There are some Christians that have served the Lord for many years, yet they are spiritually weak and immature. They have not allowed the

Spirit to transform them on the inside, and they are what is called "carnal" Christians, babes in the Lord. (See 1 Corinthians 3:1.) They still walk in the flesh; they walk by what they see and feel. They do not qualify to stand as the Lord's end-time guard.

> He was honored among the thirty, but he did not attain to the [greatness of the] three. David appointed him over his guard.
>
> −2 Samuel 23:23 – AMP

It doesn't matter if you do not attain to the "greatness of the three," those around you who seem to have greater strength than you do or a greater ministry in Christ. God is looking for *faithful* warriors who are willing to come out of their comfort zone and to walk with Him in the High Place. Do not look at others but keep your eyes and your focus on Jesus alone and know that He has chosen you, not man.

> Therefore, [let me warn you] beloved, knowing these things beforehand, be on your guard so that you are not carried away by the error of unprincipled men [who distort doctrine] and fall from your own steadfastness [of mind, knowledge, truth, and faith].
>
> −2 Peter 3:17

The Spirit is looking for men and women of the Word, those who not only talk the talk but walk the walk. These are disciplined warriors who close their ears to the lies of the enemy and to the false doctrines of men. They meditate on God's Word day and night and walk on the "High Road of Holiness." (See Joshua 1:8.) Studying God's Word daily will keep us from the danger of deception and being steered off of God's path of Truth.

> Set a guard, LORD, over my mouth; keep watch over the door of my lips.
>
> −Psalm 141:3 – NASB

God's end-time guard is one who has tamed his tongue through the power of the Spirit. This does not mean that we never fail in what we say, but we should be growing daily in this area of our lives as the Spirit takes possession of our lives and our tongues. The Book of James speaks much about this. God's Word admonishes us to speak only about things that are lovely, good, pure, of good report, and praiseworthy. (See Philippians 4:8.) In the natural this is near impossible, but with God all things are possible. We need the Holy Spirit to set a *guard* over our mouths. As we yield to the Spirit, He will accomplish this work in our lives, and we will marvel as we see the transformation take place.

> The one who guards his mouth [thinking before he speaks] protects his life; the one who opens his lips wide [and chatters without thinking] comes to ruin.
>
> –Proverbs 13:3 – AMP

> Allow the healing words you've heard from me to live in you and make them a model for life as your faith and love for the Anointed One grows even more. Guard well this incomparable treasure by the Spirit of Holiness living within you.
>
> –2 Timothy 1:13–14 – TPT

The Spirit is looking for men and women of faith. He is looking for faithful ones who will do His whole will in this hour. Jesus is looking for those who are rooted and grounded in His love, for faith works through love. (See Galatians 5:6.) We are called to *guard* the precious gifts that the Lord has given us, especially His glorious presence within us. His Life in us is our greatest treasure.

> Timothy, guard what God has entrusted to you. Avoid godless, foolish discussions with those who oppose you with their so-called knowledge.
>
> −1 Timothy 6:20 – NLT

Those who engage in foolish discussions and are argumentative will not be one of God's called and chosen ones. They may be in the Kingdom, but God will not entrust them with His higher gifts or put them in high places of authority in the Church. We are to stand in Truth and not back down, but we are called to do this in love and gentleness not with a loud and brassy spirit. God is looking for humble servants who are spiritually strong and who know how to keep peace and unity in the Body of Christ.

> So guard yourselves and God's people. Feed and shepherd God's flock—His church, purchased with His own blood—over which the Holy Spirit has appointed you as leaders. I know that false teachers, like vicious wolves, will come in among you after I leave, not sparing the flock. Even some men from your own group will rise up and distort the truth in order to draw a following. Watch out! Remember the three years I was with you—my constant watch and care over you night and day, and my many tears for you.
>
> −Acts 20:28–31

These end-time warriors and guards are called to keep watch over their own souls and also over God's children as we have seen in prior chapters. We are called to feed others with the Living Bread from Heaven, Jesus, the Word of God. God is calling His *seasoned warriors* to rise up in His strength and to stand firm in Truth. The Spirit is calling intercessors to *travail* with Him and to know the passion of His heart for the lost and for His people. Paul knew the heart of Jesus because of his "fellowship of suffering" with Jesus, and God's chosen "guards" will know the deep passion that is in the heart of Jesus. This powerful dream that the Lord gave me reveals this truth.

In the first part of the dream, I was talking to Jesus and telling Him how concerned I was that so many of His people are not loving Him in the way that He deserves. Jesus looked at me and said: *"But they will!"* I believe Jesus was showing me that in this glorious awakening, in His *divine reversal* and outpouring, the Spirit is going to awaken His people to His deep, passionate love. Where God's children have been cold and distant from Jesus, they will now be awakened through God's end-time *guards* who will be the vessels that God uses to pour His glory through. God's people will be ignited through the *fire* that is in His *guards*, fire that comes through the power of the Holy Spirit.

In the next part of the dream, I heard deep moaning, but I wasn't sure where it was coming from. I went down into the basement and walked into a room, but I couldn't find anyone. I then went into another room, and there I found Jesus in great pain. I ran over to Him and took Him in my arms and comforted Him. As we search for Jesus with our whole heart, we will find Him, and when we do we'll *fellowship with His suffering*. (See Philippians 3:10.) Those who are one with Jesus share His passion and pain, but He also shares ours.

After this scene I looked at Jesus, and He was standing with a man. They both had "warrior paint" all over their chests and faces. Jesus looked so different, and I remember thinking that few of His children would recognize Him because of all the "war paint" that was on Him! I laid my hands on Jesus and prayed. The prayer was not for Him, but I believe for myself, that this *Warrior Spirit* would enter fully into me. Jesus showed me through this dream that those who are *fellowshipping with Him in His sufferings* are the very ones who are called to be His end-time warriors. Through this "fellowship" they are being transformed more fully into His image, and they will come forth as mighty warriors. Jesus is the "Lion of Judah," and He showed me that many of His people have not known Him as a "Lion" but only as a meek and gentle Savior.

In the dream, Jesus walked outside and dropped 5 small items around a chair; they looked like jeweled stones. I, along with a few others, picked them up. I believe the *chair* represented a *seat of authority and power.* Jesus told me that the 5 stones represented two things. First, His remnant who pick up their calling and mantle in this hour, the ones who will be His mighty end-time warriors. Secondly, they were also *stones of truth.* The Lord showed me that many are frightened of who He really is: The "Lion of Judah" and the "Warrior of Heaven." So many *reject* His call to *pick up their cross daily and follow Him* and to *fellowship with His sufferings.* The Lord then gave me these Scriptures to confirm this.

> But Peter **followed Him at a distance** to the high priest's courtyard. And he went in and sat with the servants to see the end.
>
> –Matthew 26:58 – NKJV, emphasis added

> Now they were on the road, going up to Jerusalem, and Jesus was going before them; and they were amazed. And **as they followed they were afraid.** Then He took the twelve aside again and began to tell them the things that would happen to Him: "Behold, we are going up to Jerusalem, and the Son of Man will be betrayed to the chief priests and to the scribes; and they will condemn Him to death and deliver Him to the Gentiles; and they will mock Him, and scourge Him, and spit on Him, and kill Him. And the third day He will rise again." Then James and John, the sons of Zebedee, came to Him, saying, "Teacher, we want You to do for us whatever we ask." And He said to them, "What do you want

Me to do for you?" They said to Him, "Grant us that we may sit, one on Your right hand and the other on Your left, in Your glory."

—Mark 10:32–37, emphasis added

Peter followed Jesus *at a distance* and even denied Him 3 times because of fear. Let's not be hard on Peter, for apart from the power of the Holy Spirit, we would have done the same. Fear of suffering is strong in every soul, and a desire to live permeates through everyone's soul, whether they admit it or not. When the disciples followed the Lord, there was a time when Jesus was *going before them.* At that time they could not handle the *full truth* that they, too, would someday lay down their lives for Jesus. (See John 16:12.) Right after Jesus told them what He was about to suffer, all they could think about was who would sit next to Jesus in His glory. Many of God's children are in this *mode* right now, and few are willing to go through *His passion* and *fellowship* with Jesus in His sufferings.

In the last scene in this dream, I was singing a beautiful song about Jesus, and I remember singing: *"It's all about Jesus!"* Another woman, who represented compromise and the mixing of natural reasoning with God's Word, tried to sing, but her song was *worldly,* not godly at all. The Lord showed me that we will sing a *new song* in this *new season,* but those who live in compromise will not sing for Jesus because their hearts are far from Him. I pray that all who read this will be able to sing a *new song* in this generation and be used mightily as the Lord's end-time "vessel of honor."

> Then Moses and the people of Israel sang this song to the Lord: I will sing to the Lord, for He has triumphed gloriously; He has thrown both horse and rider into the sea. The Lord is my strength, my song, and my salvation. He is my God, and I will praise Him. He is my father's God—I will exalt Him. The Lord is a warrior—Yes, Jehovah is His name. He has over-

thrown Pharaoh's chariots and armies, drowning them in the sea. The famous Egyptian captains are dead beneath the waves.

–Exodus 15:1–4 – TLB

Listen as Jesus speaks words of life to you:

"When you come to the end of yourself and you wonder where you are going, know that at that moment I am standing at the crossroads and beckoning you to follow Me. Follow Me into the fullness that I have for you, for this is the path that I have ordained for you. When you give up all of your striving, all of your trying to figure things out in your own understanding, this is the very time that you will have your 'burning bush' experience in Me.

"I am the God of Revelation, and I will come to you and say: 'This is the way, now walk in it.' (See Isaiah 30:21.) I have waited for this season and for this time in your life, and now it has arrived. I have seen your years of struggle and pain, your years of doubt and fear, but you have now entered into a time of transition, a time of the turning of the tables, and you will stand in awe as My Spirit moves in great power in and through your life. You thought that your life was over and that all you had to look forward to was the same old routine, the same 'going around that mountain of difficulty.'

"I say to you now: 'Step forward into the fullness of your calling!' Your destiny has arrived, and you are standing right before a door, a double door of opportunity that you never dreamed you would see! Step into My 'Whirlwind of Glory' and let Me take you where I want you to go. Let Me accomplish My purposes through your life. I told you many times

that this was not the end, but you could scarcely believe it because of your painful circumstances. But now it will be different; now you will see what I have been after, and you will step into 'Waters of Glory' that will take you into the fullness that I have for you. These 'Waters of My Spirit' will refresh you as you encounter Me in ways that will overwhelm you and that will position you as I take you into this new realm, this 'portal of glory' that you have longed to experience.

"These have not only been days of transition and transformation but a time of 'birthing' through My Spirit all that I have desired for your life, all that I have placed within your spirit and soul. This birthing will come forth quickly, for now is the time of transference; now is the time of release. This avenue of glory that you will now walk on will be unlike anything you have known in the past, for I am now making all things new for you. This newness will take your breath away, for you have not traveled on this path before. It is a new path filled with My glory and My power in a measure that will astound you. You will feel and know that you are walking in the High Place with Me and that nothing, no one, will ever move you again.

"I have promised you greatness and power, and now you know that this greatness and glory is found in Me alone. There will be no pride, no self-exaltation, for your life is consumed in Me alone, and you will lift Me up for all the world to see. I will honor you in this late hour, and you will lift all of this honor back to Me, for your heart is one with Me. I am your Life; I am your Love, and I am your Passion, now and forevermore—says your God!"

Mordecai and Esther – A New Breed and Anointing

In this new era God is raising up a company of men and women who will walk side by side with each other and release an anointing so strong that millions of captives will be freed. They are a radical, transformed, and uncompromising group of Believers that will tear down evil forces of darkness and remove evil empires that have ruled over this earth for centuries. They do not fit in the *norm* but are *spiritual revolutionists,* world-changers, like Paul and Silas. (See Acts 17:6.) This company of warriors will *turn the tables* in our nation and in this world, for they have been called for such a time as this. Where it was once said: *"The curse on this city or nation can never be reversed"* God's people will now say: *"God has released His power and glory, and millions of souls are running into the Kingdom of God! The Great Awakening has begun, and this whole world is being shaken!"*

God is forming and sovereignly putting together *teams* in this hour that will release His Light and Glory into the nations. This is not something that man will do, but God will bring together, through divine appointments, those that He wants to work together in this hour. They will have the same heart and mind, for they will be one with the Lord and with each other. Great power will be released through them because of the unity and love they will share in Christ. They will *turn the tables* on the enemy, even as Queen Esther (Hadassah) and Mordecai did so long ago.

Because Hadassah was orphaned at a young age, she was raised by her cousin Mordecai. Hadassah must have felt great pain and grief in losing her parents, but God took this pain, *reversed* it, and brought good out of it. She was obedient and submitted to the authority of Mordecai, and in the same way this new company of Believer's will obey the Lord at all costs. They have learned that in *loss* there is *gain* in Christ. God was preparing Hadassah for the throne even at a young age; little did she realize that some day she would sit on the royal throne.

Never would she have believed the *divine reversal* that was going to take place in her life, in God's perfect timing. (See Esther 2:5–18.) This *changing of the guards* began when Queen Vashti lost her position and Queen Esther took her place. Queen Vashti was removed because she refused the kings invitation to come to him, for he wanted his people to see the queen's beauty. (See Esther 1:10–12; 2:17.)

Many messages have been released about Queen Esther, but I believe that without Mordecai she would never have been able to *reverse the tables* on evil Haman and save her people. Mordecai stood at the king's gate; he was a *prophetic guard* who *stood in the gap* and interceded for the protection of his people, the Jews. He *influenced* Esther to go before the king and petition him for the Jewish nation. (Esther 4:1–3, 12–14; 5:13.)

Mordecai would never bow down to evil Haman, who represented the enemy, and that drove Haman crazy! (See Esther 3:2–6.) No one and nothing could make Mordecai bow to this evil man, even though Haman held a high position in the land. Mordecai was a *type* and a *shadow* of the *new breed* that God would raise up in the last days. This company of Believers in this new era will not bow down to the devil, no matter what he throws against them, and as we shall see in this story when the tables were turned on evil Haman, Mordecai was given the king's signet ring and he was appointed over Haman's estate. As God was working out His *divine reversal,* the enemy, Haman, was commanded by the king to exalt Mordecai to Haman's shame and dishonor. (See Esther 6:6–12; 8:1–2.) In the same way God is going to restore what the enemy has stolen from His people. God has given us His "signet ring," His power and authority over the evil one. God will release the shame that has covered our face in the past season and will restore to us double honor and blessing for our shame. (See Isaiah 61:7.) God is *turning the tables* on our enemy, and *his* face will now be covered with shame!

> Each young woman's turn came to go in to King Ahasuerus after she had completed twelve months' preparation, according to the regulations for the women, for thus were the days of their preparation apportioned: six months with oil of myrrh, and six months with perfumes and preparations for beautifying women. Thus prepared, each young woman went to the king, and she was given whatever she desired to take with her from the women's quarters to the king's palace.
>
> –Esther 2:12–13 – NKJV

We see in these Scriptures that Esther had to be *prepared* before she had her night with the king. She had to bathe in *oil of myrrh* and also *perfumes*. Myrrh represents suffering,[xxiii] and those who God chooses must not run from the fiery trials that God allows for their purification. She also soaked in perfumes which represents our need to soak in the presence of our King through prayer and worship.[xxiv] This is where our transformation takes place and where this *new breed* is being fully prepared for this next move of the Spirit.

> For we are a sweet perfume of Christ to God in those being saved and in those perishing.
>
> –2 Corinthians 2:15 – BLB

> Now it happened on the third day that Esther put on her royal robes and stood in the inner court of the king's palace, across from the king's house, while the king sat on his royal throne in the royal house, facing the entrance of the house. So it was, when the king saw Queen Esther standing in the court, that she found favor in his sight, and the king held out to Esther the golden scepter that was in his

hand. Then Esther went near and touched the top of the scepter. And the king said to her, "What do you wish, Queen Esther? What is your request? It shall be given to you—up to half the kingdom!"

–Esther 5:1–3 – NKJV

Jesus is calling His bride to remove her old *clothes of mourning* and to adorn herself with *royal robes*. God's remnant has found favor in His sight, and our King is holding out to us His golden scepter, His rod of authority. Hear Him say to you this day: *"What do you wish, My bride? What is the desire of your heart? Only ask, and it will be given to you!"* Jesus has given us His Kingdom authority, and those who are *one with His heart* know His heartbeat and His desire is their desire. Jesus is asking us to decree and to command His will into the earth in this dark hour, and in the Spirit we will bring forth His divine purposes.

> For if you remain completely silent at this time, relief and deliverance will arise for the Jews from another place, but you and your father's house will perish. Yet who knows whether you have come to the kingdom for such a time as this?
>
> –Esther 4:14

The Church must not remain silent in this hour but speak His words of Truth to all who will listen. This is not the time to be timid or to allow the intimidation of the devil to keep us silent. Just as Esther had to *do* something in order to free her people from destruction so is God calling us to *do His will*, to *speak His words of life*, and to *accomplish all that He desires* in this generation. It will cost us, but we must not love our lives even to death. We must say, even as Esther said so long ago: "If I perish, I perish!" (Esther 4:16).

Now Harbonah, one of the eunuchs, said to the king, "Look! The gallows, fifty cubits high, which Haman made for Mordecai, who spoke good on the king's behalf, is standing at the house of Haman." Then the king said, "Hang him on it!" So they hanged Haman on the gallows that he had prepared for Mordecai. Then the king's wrath subsided.

–Esther 7:9–10

I believe the wrath of our King Jesus has been ignited in this hour, and His judgments are on the way. Our God will not hold His peace until all of our enemies are "hung on the gallows" that they have built for our lives, our nation, the Church, and this world. We will yet see this great *divine reversal* in a measure that will astound us! We have waited for this day, and it has now arrived! Blessed be His Holy Name!

For the Lord would say:

> *"You have only seen in part what I am about to do! What I have planned and what I will bring forth in this new hour no tongue can tell! I am ripping off the 'veil,' and you will see Me now face to face. No more will I hide behind the veil, for I am releasing a full measure of glory and power to this very generation. Now you will see it! Now you will know that all that I have spoken to you in the past has been My Truth. Now you will see all of these Promises come to pass in a short period of time. Like a train that has no end these blessings and Promises will come forth now in full force, and you will not be able to catch your breath.*
>
> *"What you have so long waited for is now coming to you in a way and in a power that you are not expecting. In this 'divine reversal' nothing will be withheld from you, My bride, for I will adorn you with My beauty and splendor, and all will know that*

you belong to Me. You are My queen, My Esther; I have called you to be My royal queen. Never again will you wear the worn-out clothes of depression and fear. Never again will you wear the 'rags' of spiritual poverty. You are called to My abundance, and I will show you and this world that I am the 'God of Restoration.' What the 'canker worm' has eaten I will now restore back to you, not seven-fold but 100-fold! (See Joel 2:25.)

"*Come near to Me now, and do not walk at arm's length from Me any longer. Don't look back, but give Me everything, your whole life, every part of it, and no longer allow your past iniquities to have a hold on you. I died to free you! I died in order to release your soul and body from every stronghold.*

"*Be bold and come to Me with every request. There is a 'portal' over you, an open Heaven, that you can enter into right now, in this very season, and receive all that I have for you. Don't delay any longer, but move into the fullness that I have for you. There is a ladder before you, 'Jacob's ladder,' that leads into Heaven and to all of My blessings. (See Genesis 28:12.) Praise Me, and continue your climb heavenward, and you will, at last, leave behind every dark cloud that has discouraged you in this past season.*

"*See, even now, I make all things new in your life, but you must grab hold of it, and don't let go! I am here just for you. Receive My Life, receive My Love, and you will know, even now, Life Eternal—says your God!*"

Jesus Reversed the Curse

I cannot complete this chapter without giving all the glory to Jesus for what He accomplished for us on the Cross and in His glorious Resurrection. The greatest *divine reversal* that this world has ever known is the *Cross of Jesus,* His blood, suffering, and death, which *reversed the curse* and released us into the *power of His Resurrection and Eternal Life.* Words cannot express my gratitude for the greatest love ever expressed to mankind through the Cross. What our Beloved King suffered for us is beyond human comprehension or words to express. To Jesus be all the glory, honor, and praise, now and forevermore.

> Don't yield to fear. I am the Beginning and I am the End, the Living One! I was dead, but now look—I am alive forever and ever. And I hold the keys that unlock death and the unseen world.
>
> —Revelation 1:17b–18 – TPT

Jesus *reversed the curse,* and now He holds the *"keys of death and hell."* All who *abide in Christ* now have Eternal Life pulsating through them. Death cannot hold us, and we now have a living relationship with Jesus that daily grows more and more glorious. He is our love, our Life, and our All in All!

> He will swallow up death [and abolish it] for all time. And the Lord God will wipe away tears from all faces, and He will take away the disgrace of His people from all the earth; for the Lord has spoken.
>
> —Isaiah 25:8 – AMP

The Lord is wiping the tears from our eyes even now, and as we behold His glory we will run with Him to the nations. God is taking away our disgrace, all of those humiliations that we have suffered in the past. We will walk with Him in "white" and will know, deep in our hearts, our true identity in Jesus. This is the *divine reversal* He is accomplishing in the hearts of His people in this new era.

> Therefore, since [these His] children share in flesh and blood [the physical nature of mankind], He Himself in a similar manner also shared in the same [physical nature, but without sin], so that through [experiencing] death He might make powerless (ineffective, impotent) him who had the power of death—that is, the devil.
>
> –Hebrews 2:14

We realize now, more than ever, that the enemy of our soul has no power over us. For too long we have allowed the adversary to rob us through sickness, poverty, grief, shame, loss, and so many other *issues* that put us in a pit of depression and fear. No more will we tolerate the enemies lies and deception, for we have come to know our identity in Christ and the authority that He has given us in His name. The Church, the Ekklesia, God's governing Body, is now rising up and taking her rightful place before His throne. These past delays and sufferings have purified and conditioned us to see and to know that we can do all things through Christ who strengthens us! (See Philippians 4:13.)

> When the perishable puts on the imperishable, and the mortal puts on immortality, then shall come to pass the saying that is written: "Death is swallowed up in victory."
>
> –1 Corinthians 15:54 – ESV

No more fear of death! No more fear of suffering! We have come to know His transforming glory, and we will never be the same! We will never truly *know death,* for it is swallowed up in His victory, in His very Life. Death no longer holds us captive. It has lost its "sting!" (See 1 Corinthians 15:55.)

For our sake He made Him to be sin who knew no sin, so that in Him we might become the righteousness of God.

–2 Corinthians 5:21

Through the transforming work of the cross, we can know resurrection life, even now, on this earth. We can rise above all the darkness and all the pain of our past and enter into the fullness that the Lord has for our lives. Jesus became sin for us so that we can walk in *His* righteousness even now. We don't have to wait until we die physically for His power and love to free us from sin and iniquity. Let's honor the Lord by believing His Word that tells us that in Him we are free indeed!

Hear the word of the Lord:

"Get ready, children, get ready for the greatest 'reversal' that this world has ever seen! It is here! It has come, and I will show Myself strong to a generation that has fallen asleep, spiritually, and to a Church that does not believe that I will bring this Great Awakening! I am coming in a way that will shock most of My people, in a way that is powerful, radical, and even frightening to many. I am coming with a 'warlike' move of My Spirit that will awaken this generation as I move throughout this world in phenomenal ways, in ways that will confound 'conservative' church people, in ways that will shock and awaken the secular world!

"Watch and see now what I am doing, for I am pushing over the first 'domino,' and it will awaken millions. Get ready, saints of God, for what you are about to see has not even entered your heart or mind. Let Me show you now the power that I have reserved for this generation, a power and a love, a fury and a zeal, that no man has yet seen or known. This end-time move is now being released in a measure that will

shake the 'gates of hell' as I move through My people and shatter these gates in the power of My Spirit.

"Look to Me! Look to Me alone, for the glory will be greater than you realize. This outpouring, this flood of My Spirit, is going to sweep you off of your feet, and you will know, without a shadow of a doubt, that this is from Me, for I will confirm this move of My Spirit with signs and wonders that you have never seen or heard of in the past. What has been done in past revivals is NOTHING compared to what I am about to release! Get ready, get ready, for I say again: 'Ready or not, here I come!' I am here, and I am releasing My passion in My end-time warriors in a measure that is measureless, in an anointing that is stronger than they have ever known. Even My 'prepared ones' will stand in awe and wonder when they see what I will do through their lives.

"Never has there been a time or a season like the one you have now entered into, an unprecedented 'new era of glory' that this world will now see. This is not just for My Church but for the whole earth! This last outpouring will bring renewed hope to My people as I refresh them in this 'River of Life' that is being released. Now is the time and the season for this to break forth.

"It is BREAKTHROUGH time...a time when I will breathe on My people and this world 'New Life.' As I have shown you this is My time, a NOW time, an end-time move that I have promised you so long ago. You have waited; you have been patient, and it has NOW arrived. Reversal, reversal, reversal of all things now! My 'divine reversal' is here, and I release it right NOW into your life, your ministry, the Church, and this world. Divine reversal is here! Believe it; receive it, for the time has come—says your God!"

CHAPTER 6

Walking in the High Place of Sacrifice and Victory

So many of God's children have given up on the promises and visions that God gave them many years ago, but God is about to "resurrect" them in this new era. Like Peter from long ago they have gone back to their *secular* jobs and have given up hope of ever seeing them come to pass. Peter needed a powerful visitation from Jesus in order to restore him and to bring him back into the center of God's will for his life. Peter failed miserably when he denied the Lord and said that he didn't know Him. His heart was crushed, and he felt that the Lord would never forgive him. Maybe he couldn't forgive himself and was punishing himself for his failures, but God did not forsake His servant neither did the Lord change His mind concerning Peter's destiny and calling.

> Peter told them, "I'm going fishing." And they all replied, "We'll go with you." So they went out and fished through the night, but caught nothing...After they had breakfast, Jesus said to Peter, "Simon, son of Jonah, do you burn with love for Me more than these?" Peter answered, "Yes, Lord! You know that I have great affection for You!" "Then take care of

My lambs," Jesus said. Jesus repeated His question the second time, "Simon, son of Jonah, do you burn with love for Me?" Peter answered, "Yes, my Lord! You know that I have great affection for You!" "Then take care of My sheep," Jesus said. Then Jesus asked him again, "Peter, son of Jonah, do you have great affection for Me?" Peter was saddened by being asked the third time and said, "My Lord, You know everything. You know that I burn with love for You!" Jesus replied, "Then feed My lambs! Peter, listen, when you were younger you made your own choices and you went where you pleased. But one day when you are old, others will tie you up and escort you where you would not choose to go—and you will spread out your arms." (Jesus said this to Peter as a prophecy of what kind of death he would die, for the glory of God.) And then He said, "Peter, follow Me!"

–John 21:3, 15–19 – TPT

God is about to rekindle His fiery love in millions of hearts that have given up on Him, on themselves, and on ever fulfilling their destiny and calling in Jesus. Their zeal for the Lord has grown cold, and their hearts are embittered. Like Peter they need to be reinstated into the dream that Jesus has for their lives. They will hear Jesus say to them: *"Come, follow Me!"* Jesus will touch their hearts, and they will know that God has healed their deep wounds.

Only Jesus can touch this deep place in our hearts. No matter what others say or do they cannot restore a person back to the heart of God. This is something that only the Holy Spirit can do in our hearts. Every wound in our soul that has denied and rejected Him will now be touched in a miraculous way. Even as Peter was eventually crucified upside-down because of his love for Jesus so will we, in the power of the Spirit, fulfill our destiny in Jesus and be willing even to die for Him if this is God's will for our lives.

For thus says the High and Lofty One who inhabits eternity, whose name is Holy: "I dwell in the high and holy place, with him who has a contrite and humble spirit, to revive the spirit of the humble, and to revive the heart of the contrite ones.

–Isaiah 57:15 – NKJV

God is calling His broken and contrite ones to draw near to Him and to press into His heart of love. God's passion and longing is to revive His weary ones and those who have grown depressed because of delayed answers and constant demonic attacks from the enemy of their souls. I pray this prophetic word below will encourage and lift you up as you realize that God has not forsaken you.

The Spirit is saying:

"If you only knew the things that I have planned for your life, your heart would be overwhelmed. You have a God who dreams big, bigger than you realize, My children. My plans for your life exceed everything that is in your heart this day. Come, dream with Me; take My hand, and let's move into the fullness of My dream, My vision, for your life, for My Church, and for this world. I am widening your heart in this hour so that I can 'download' My passion and desires into you. For so long you have been 'squashed,' spiritually, and have not known the full life that I have planned for you. So many times you have been rejected and ignored, and you are near giving up of ever seeing these past dreams and visions come to fruition.

"Children, hear My heart's cry in this hour. I need every one of My children to come to Me...to come deep into My heart of passion and to know My deep desires for their lives. My heart is bursting with love and a deep longing for this earth, to bring in this final harvest.

Know that I have called you; I have called each one of My children, but so many have closed their ears and cannot hear My cry. Oh, children, if you only knew how much I love you and this dying world you would run to Me and fall before Me!

"Break open your heart and allow My Spirit to refill you with My glorious Life. Come closer and lay your hand on My broken heart, and you will be changed forever. You will never go back to your old way of life, your old way of doing things. Peter was so discouraged because of his failures that he decided to go back to fishing in the natural realm. He needed a deep encounter with Me to bring him back to his destiny; this is what turned his heart back to Me, and he was never the same. I called him to be a 'fisher of men,' and as you know, I turned his life around, and he became a glorious soul-winner for Me. Don't give up! Don't look at your past failures but know that I have new and glorious things planned for your life.

"This is turn-around time; this is the time and season to cut all 'ties' that are binding you to this earth, this world-system. It's time to let go and let Me be God in your life. There's nothing in your past or present circumstances that can hold you down. Come to Me, and I will restore you quickly, and your 'dead dreams' of the past will come alive once more, never to die again—says your God!"

God is visiting and restoring His people in this hour, and He has, even now, a prepared people, a remnant, who have come to know the power of sacrificing all on God's "fiery altar." They are walking the "High Road of Holiness" of full surrender to God's will. They have overcome the evil one through submission to God and have resisted all of the lies and the deceptions of the devil. They are called and chosen and are now dwelling on heights of glory. When the greater fires come many will question how anyone could survive the catastrophic events that are being released, but they will see a people who will not only survive but thrive when these judgments are released.

> They ask themselves, "Who could possibly survive this all-consuming conflagration? Who can live through the unrelenting heat, the flames, the smoke?" I will tell you who: the one who goes through life with integrity and speaks truth with conviction, refusing to take part in fraud and abuse, whose hands are free of bribes, whose ears are covered to violent schemes, and whose eyes are shut to the temptations of evil. That one **will survive and prosper on the heights of Zion** and take comfort in **the shelter of rock fortresses, and never be hungry, never thirsty.** Ah, you will see for yourself the beauty of the One who rules over all. Your eyes will take in a land that stretches far beyond the horizon.
>
> –Isaiah 33:14b–17 – The Voice, emphasis added

In this chapter we will discuss the importance of self-sacrifice, Mount Moriah, warring from the High Place, the power of praise and worship, and the keys of the Kingdom. I pray you will be blessed and encouraged as you understand more fully what God is after in your life and what He desires to accomplish in this generation.

The High Place of Sacrifice

There is a High Place of sacrifice that the Lord is calling His people to enter into more fully in this hour. This is the place where everything in our lives is laid before Him on His *burning altar*. God is looking for *"living sacrifices,"* those who will go *all the way* with Him and do His *whole* will. This is a call to an all-out surrender to the Holy Spirit so that His will can be accomplished and His glory be known throughout the whole earth. God is calling us to be *"poured out drink offerings"* before Him, but what does this mean? (See Philippians 2:17.) Our Father is asking us if we are willing to pour out our lives before Him in total abandonment and to empty our hearts fully of the things of this world. There is a personal price to pay, a great cost, but it is worth it; Jesus is worth it.

> Beloved friends, what should be our proper response to God's marvelous mercies? To surrender yourselves to God to be His sacred, living sacrifices. And live in holiness, experiencing all that delights His heart. For this becomes your genuine expression of worship. Stop imitating the ideals and opinions of the culture around you, but be inwardly transformed by the Holy Spirit through a total reformation of how you think. This will empower you to discern God's will as you live a beautiful life, satisfying and perfect in His eyes.
>
> –Romans 12:1–2 – TPT

Jesus is calling us to abandon everything that binds us to this earth in order to fulfill His holy will in the earth. God will make a way for you when it looks like every avenue has been blocked by the enemy, when it looks impossible to climb or tunnel through the mountain that looms before you. The Lord is challenging us to step out of our comfort zone and to take the step of faith that He is asking us to take. Jesus desires to put spiritual blinders on us so that we will focus on Him alone and not on the winds and waves that we may see before us. As we take these steps of faith, we will find that our hearts are becoming more and more conformed into the image of Jesus. We will find ourselves walking in the footsteps of Jesus, doing the Father's will.

> And do not present your members as instruments of unrighteousness to sin, but present yourselves to God as being alive from the dead, and your members as instruments of righteousness to God.
>
> –Romans 6:13 – NKJV

Giving our lives as *"living sacrifices"* before the Lord will require us to present our lives: spirit, soul, and body, to the Lord in holiness. We are called to turn our backs to all unrighteousness and present ourselves to the Lord daily as *"instruments of righteousness"* in all that we do and speak. Living before the Lord in holiness will require us to experience a *"baptism of fire"* that will daily cleanse and purify us in the depths of our being. (See Matthew 3:11.) We cannot, in ourselves, clean up our act. Only in the power of the Holy Spirit as we yield our lives fully to Him can we become a "sacrifice" that is acceptable to Him. It is *"Christ in us, the hope of glory"* that will release a pleasing odor before our God. (See Colossians 1:27.) His Life alone in us is the pleasing sacrifice that will release a pleasing fragrance to our Father.

God is asking us to give Him all the emotional grief and pain from our past, all of our bloodline iniquities, and all that is holding us back from the fullness of His love and power. If we *stuff* our emotional grief and pain down and keep it *buried* in our hearts, it will eventually come to the surface and release great havoc in our lives. It will come forth in anger, bitterness, and sickness and will block many of the blessings and the goodness that the Lord desires to release into our lives. This is *not* God's will or destiny for us. If we embrace the pain of our past and do not ignore or deny it, it will bring genuine transformation in our lives and will enhance and deepen our love relationship with Jesus. The truth of our painful past, as we allow the Spirit to reveal it and then release us from it, will set us free!

Are we willing to lay down our lives for the One who gave His all for us? Are we willing to give up the comforts of our home, where we live, and go where the Gospel is so desperately needed?

If we truly knew the depths of His love for us and for the lost, we would not hesitate to say as Isaiah did so long ago: *"Here am I, send me!"* (Isaiah 6:8b).

> We know what real love is because Jesus gave up His life for us. So we also ought to give up our lives for our brothers and sisters. If someone has enough money to live well and sees a brother or sister in need but shows no compassion—how can God's love be in that person? Dear children, let's not merely say that we love each other; let us show the truth by our actions.
>
> —1 John 3:16–18 – NLT

So many Christians miss the full plan God has for their lives on this earth. They never realize the *higher purpose* they are called to. There is so much more for us than getting *saved,* going to church, and enjoying our loved ones and this beautiful earth, as great as all of this is. This is why it is so important to experience an inner transformation by the Spirit, for when we do we come to realize that God has so much more for our lives.

Even as young Christian I asked the Lord: *"Is this all there is for my life? Is this all that it means to be a Christian?"* Deep in my heart I knew that there was so much more for me, and God heard the cry of my heart and answered me through the years. We are called to lay down our lives before Him and to follow the Spirit wherever He would lead us. Can you hear the Lord's voice calling you in this hour and saying: *"Come, follow Me!"*

I recently had a dream about someone singing so beautifully before Jesus, but He was <u>not</u> *moved* by her singing. I then went with several others through a door, and I knew we were headed for the *washroom.* The Holy Spirit showed me from this dream that *obedience* is the sacrifice that Jesus is looking for from His people, *not* beautiful singing. He does not want our outward works but obedience to do His will above all. To obey Jesus is better than any other "sacrifice" that we could give Him. Many people say that they love Jesus, but they live to please their flesh. They live to accomplish their own will and desires, not God's. If we truly loved Jesus, we would obey Him. The Spirit is calling us to come and to *wash our souls* and *bodies* in His "Life-giving Stream." God desires to cleanse us in the deepest recesses of our hearts so that we can obey Him without fear or dread. Jesus gave me these Scriptures after this dream.

> And Samuel said, "Has the LORD as great delight in burnt offerings and sacrifices, as in obeying the voice of the LORD? Behold, to obey is better than sacrifice, and to listen than the fat of rams.
>
> –1 Samuel 15:22 – ESV

> If you love Me, you will obey My commandments.
> –John 14:15 – GOD'S WORD Translation

A life of sacrifice is a life of obedience in doing God's will. Obeying the Lord is not always easy, but He brings us to the place where we can say: *"I delight to do Your will!"* (Psalm 40:8a – NKJV). Every step that we take in abandonment to His will brings us into greater freedom and power to accomplish all that He desires. It will cost us, but it will be worth it, for the end result will be "joy unspeakable" and the fullness of His love and presence in our lives.

In this High Place that Jesus is bringing us to, we will find that our path is getting narrower by the day until our whole heart is consumed with His love and presence. Daily we will ask the Lord: *"What would You have me do this day? How can I please you?"* Jesus wants us to know Him, to know who He is in the depths of our heart. Bobby Connor often stated: *"The Church is far too familiar with a God we hardly know!"*[xxv] This statement, sad to say, is true for many who profess to be Christians. Millions say that they know Jesus and walk with Him, but in reality, they know very little concerning His ways and His deep heart.

As we continue to walk with Jesus on His Holy Mountain, we will come to know Jesus and to enjoy true and deep intimacy with Him. Jesus will truly become our *"first love."* We will sacrifice our time, money, earthly pleasures, and anything else that He might ask of us. It will not be a burden or depressing, but we will experience His *"joy unspeakable and full of glory"* (1 Peter 1:8 – KJV) as we walk on His path of surrender.

Day by day, as we walk with the Spirit of God, we will find that He is taking more and more possession of our lives and that He is controlling our thoughts and actions more fully. We gladly give up our own will to do His will. We will say with Job: *"Though He slay me, yet will I trust in Him"* (Job 13:15a). We will find that as time goes by there is no greater joy than to love and to serve Jesus and to walk daily with the Holy Spirit.

There will be times of great persecution, but as we lay our lives before Jesus in total abandonment, we will experience His passionate love for us and for the lost and the dying. We will have encounters with our King and revelations that will overwhelm us. Many believe that if they surrender all to Jesus others will love and bless them, but many times they will find greater persecution, not only from the enemy but even from ministers and other Christians who live *compromised* lives. The pain of persecution is not meant to destroy us but to conform us more fully into the image of Jesus and to prepare us for our calling and destiny. The Holy Spirit will allow these trials for our greater good, but His heart will grieve deeply when others come against us.

> Instead, rejoice as you share in the sufferings of Christ, so that you may also rejoice with great joy when His glory is revealed. If you are ridiculed for the name of Christ, you are blessed, because the Spirit of glory and of God rests on you.
>
> –1 Peter 4:13–14 – Christian Standard Bible

I remember an experience I had at a church that I attended years ago. There was great freedom in this church to worship the Lord, and during one evening service, I laid prostrate before the Lord and cried out to Him as I worshipped Him deeply. After the service the pastor came up to me and questioned me concerning my *mode* of worship, even though it was the way I and others had always worshipped. He told me a family questioned the way I worshipped, and he was concerned that this family would leave the church because of this. When I left the church I didn't *feel* much of anything, but when I got into my car, I began to wail loudly as the Holy Spirit *travailed* through me. I realized later that the Holy Spirit was grieved that the pastor cared more about what this family thought than what the Spirit wanted. The depth of grief was great; little do people realize how easy it is to grieve the Holy Spirit and to care more about what man thinks than what He thinks.

> Through Jesus, therefore, let us continually offer to God a sacrifice of praise—the fruit of lips that openly profess His name.
>
> –Hebrews 13:15 – NIV

> But as for me, I will sacrifice to You with a voice of thanksgiving. I will fulfill what I have vowed. Salvation belongs to the LORD.
>
> –Jonah 2:9 – CSB

Our worship and praise are a beautiful *sacrifice* before the Lord, especially when we are going through deep fires of suffering. This is a *"sacrifice of praise"* that is very pleasing to the Lord. God wants us to give Him the *"fruit of our lips"* by singing continual songs of praise to Him, maybe not for what we are going through but in the *midst* of the suffering. This shows our King that we trust Him no matter what we see or feel, and it hastens His deep work of transformation in our lives. I don't believe that many of God's children realize how much our worship in *"Spirit and Truth"* means to our God. It touches our Father's heart deeply when He sees our pain and tears, and yet we choose to praise Him anyway! I believe tears of love and joy pour down His beautiful face as He beholds the love sacrifices we give to Him. How our God loves us! I believe only in eternity will we know the fullness of His joy over us and how much He loved us during our times of deep turmoil and pain.

My prayer for you and for me is that we will become a *pleasing fragrance* before our God as we lay down our lives fully before Him. I pray that as we come to know Jesus more intimately and walk in the High Place with Him daily we will come to know the joy of being a *"living sacrifice"* before Him. In earnestness, I desire and pray that the Holy Spirit fulfills His work *in* and *through* us for the sake of His Kingdom. We are loved more than words can express, so let's abandon all for His sake and for the sake of His Kingdom. Truly this is our *"reasonable service"* for all that He has done for us.

Hear what Jesus is saying:

> *"If you truly loved Me, children, you would obey Me. (See John 14:15.) I am not moved by your singing or your good works. I am moved by your obedience and your full surrender to My will. You can sacrifice everything for Me in the natural, but if your heart is not truly Mine, if your heart is not obedient and filled with My love, it counts for nothing. (See 1 Corinthians 13:3.) Everything that is done in your own will, in your own strength and power, no matter how good it looks outwardly, means nothing to Me unless it is in My will and 'birthed' in My Spirit.*
>
> *"Are you offended by this, children? Do you truly believe that I will accept your own works? I see this only as rebellion and as 'wood, hay, and stubble,' and*

truly, it will burn when you stand before Me on that Day. (See 1 Corinthians 3:12–13.) I want your heart and your obedience. I want to see brokenness in your heart so that I can fill you with My Life. This is the sacrifice that is pleasing to Me. This is the sacrifice that I will accept. (See Psalm 51:17.)

"Many want to walk with Me in the High Place of Holiness and Power, but few truly surrender their all on My 'altar of sacrifice.' I have not changed My mind concerning this full abandonment to My will, and I never will. The 'road is hard' and the 'gate is narrow' that leads to Life. (See Matthew 7:13–14.) I have not widened the gate neither have I made the road easy. It remains the same. I am God, and I change not. I am 'the same yesterday, today, and forever' (Hebrews 13:8). Many of My children want to change the rules so that the road becomes easier. They feel that if they do a few good works and sing loud enough that I will accept their sacrifice. This will NEVER do. I see this as a 'Cain offering,' an offering of the flesh, an offering of their own making. (See Genesis 4:3–6.)

"Get back to the foundational Truths of My Word. For it is in Truth, My Truth, that you will find My pattern for life and freedom. Let Me redirect your thinking, and then your life will line up with My Truth—says your God!"

Mount Moriah – Our Hearts, God's Altar

Moriah: "The chosen of Jehovah. Some contend that Mount Gerizim is meant, but most probably we are to regard this as one of the hills of Jerusalem. Here Solomon's temple was built, on the spot that had been the threshing-floor of Ornan the Jebusite (2 Samuel 24:24–25; 2 Chronicles 3:1). It is usually included in

Zion, to the north-east of which it lay, and from which it was separated by the Tyropoean valley. This was 'the land of Moriah' to which Abraham went to offer up his son Isaac (Genesis 22:2). It has been supposed that the highest point of the temple hill, which is now covered by the Mohammedan Kubbetes-Sakhrah, or 'Dome of the Rock,' is the actual site of Araunah's threshing-floor. Here also, one thousand years after Abraham, David built an altar and offered sacrifices to God."[xxvi]

Jesus was crucified in that same "region of Moriah" more than 2,000 years later. He alone is the perfect sacrifice for this world, and in Him we are now called to be a *"living sacrifice"* for Him. Jesus has called us to walk in obedience and to trust Him, no matter what He would ask of us. The Word tells us to walk in the footsteps of Jesus and to do only what we see the Father doing. (See 1 Peter 2:21; John 5:19.)

Solomon's temple was built on this same spot, Mount Moriah, and this was also a place of sacrifice. It was here that they burned thousands of animals as a *pleasing aroma* to God in obedience to His commands. (See 2 Chronicles 7:1–22.) Solomon's temple was a place of prayer, and as *true worshippers* we are called to live lives of prayer, seeking the Lord daily with our whole heart in order to know His will for our lives. We are now the "temples" of the Lord, as we have seen in previous chapters, and as we climb "God's Hill of Sacrifice," we will be a *pleasing odor* to the Lord. (See 2 Corinthians 2:15.)

When I think about obedience and sacrifice, I first remember the ultimate sacrifice of Jesus on the cross, and then I think about Abraham and his son Isaac. When God told Abraham to take his son, his only son, the one he loved and to go to the land of Moriah and offer him there as a burnt offering on one of the mountains that the Lord would show him, I stand amazed at his faith and trust in the Lord and at the obedience of Isaac in allowing his father to bind him and to lay him on the altar on top of the wood. Isaac had absolute trust in his loving father even as Abraham raised his hand with the knife in it! (See Genesis 22:6–10.)

The Lord stopped his servant from slaying his son and provided a substitute: a *"ram caught in a thicket,"* which of course represents Jesus dying as the ultimate sacrifice for the sin of the world. (See Genesis 22:13–14.) On the same Mount over 2,000 years later, God would provide the ultimate sacrifice, Jesus, and God *will* provide all that we need as we surrender to His plan for our lives and sacrifice all on His altar.

God will test every true servant of His as we walk with Him although the ways will differ. We may not be tested in the exact same way that Abraham was, but it may be just as painful. The Lord has reasons for testing us and for asking us to surrender our lives before Him in trust and obedience to His will. God loves us as much as He loves Abraham and even His own Son. (See John 17:23.) Our God is a jealous God, and He will not tolerate anyone or anything to take His place in our hearts and lives. This world, and even the Church, does not understand the depth and intensity of God's love. He demands our *all* and is calling us to lay down everything on His "altar" that is separating us from Him, including our very lives.

> By faith Abraham, when he was tested, offered up Isaac, and he who had received the promises offered up his only begotten son, of whom it was said, "In Isaac your seed shall be called," concluding that God was able to raise him up, even from the dead, from which he also received him in a figurative sense.
>
> –Hebrews 11:17–19 – NKJV

Abraham knew what God had promised him years before he was tested; he knew that in Isaac his *seed* would continue until God's people would be as the stars in the sky. So Abraham concluded that even if Isaac was slain God would raise him up again! What a man of trust and faith in the promises of God! He never wavered in his faith; he never stopped believing that God would fulfill what He promised him so long ago. This is why he is in God's "hall of fame" and called the "father of faith!" (See Romans 4:16.)

Can we trust Jesus as fully as Isaac trusted his father? Will we stand in faith when everything in our lives and circumstances look contrary to what God has promised us? Will we allow the Lord to take us where He wants us to go, no matter the cost? As long as we cling to our own lives, our own will, and our own desires we will not enter into the fullness of our destiny. We are of the *"Seed of Abraham,"* children of faith and trust; I pray we will honor the Word of God even as our *spiritual father* did. (See Galatians 3:29.)

> Great crowds were following Him. He turned around and addressed them as follows: "Anyone who wants to be My follower must love Me far more than he does his own father, mother, wife, children, brothers, or sisters—yes, more than his own life—otherwise he cannot be My disciple. And no one can be My disciple who does not carry his own cross and follow Me.
>
> —Luke 14:25–27 – TLB

> Brother shall betray brother to death, and fathers shall betray their own children. And children shall rise against their parents and cause their deaths. Everyone shall hate you because you belong to Me. But all of you who endure to the end shall be saved... Don't imagine that I came to bring peace to the earth! No, rather, a sword. I have come to set a man against his father, and a daughter against her mother, and a daughter-in-law against her mother-in-law—a man's worst enemies will be right in his own home! If you love your father and mother more than you love Me, you are not worthy of being Mine; or if you love your

son or daughter more than Me, you are not worthy of being Mine. If you refuse to take up your cross and follow Me, you are not worthy of being Mine. If you cling to your life, you will lose it; but if you give it up for Me, you will save it.

–Matthew 10:21–22, 34–39

The Lord is asking us, in this very hour, to deepen our love and our commitment to Him and to love Him above all, even our most cherished loved ones. So many in our nation are not willing to pay the cost that so many others have paid in other nations. Many crowds followed Jesus as long as it was a *light* message of comfort but turned their backs on Him when He spoke the harder Truths of the Gospel. We cannot call ourselves disciples of Jesus if we refuse to abandon *all* for His sake. Would you go to another nation where you may experience hardship for Jesus? If this endangered your children's lives, would you still say yes to His calling for your life? Have you counted the cost to follow Jesus and to be His disciple? Are you willing to lay down your life for the One who gave you His all?

God has *not* called us to an easy path or a wide gate but to a path that is hard and many times painful, as we see in the above Scriptures. Many teach and preach that God wants to give us a life of ease and prosperity. Jesus *does* gives us *spiritual* prosperity and an *"abundant life,"* but it is not in the way that many teach and preach. They say: *"Just give your life to Jesus, and you will have all that you desire and want."* They do not teach God's children about the *cross* that they are called to carry daily while following Jesus or about the persecution that will come against them as a true follower of Jesus. Just ask thousands upon thousands of souls in other nations such as China, Somalia, parts of Africa, India, and North Korea what it cost them to give their lives to Jesus. Many have lost families, their livelihood, their reputation, and even their lives. They have been imprisoned, tortured, and beheaded for their faith. Talk to them about being *raptured* out of their pain, and they will look into your shame-filled face and talk to you about what it is to live a *life of sacrifice* for Jesus.

These are God's transformed ones, for they have allowed the cross to purify them, and in the Spirit many of them are now walking in resurrection power. They are experiencing the abundant life of Jesus, but it came through the power of the cross. If we have an *escapism theology,* we are dead wrong! God has called us to be His end-time witnesses and to lay down our lives before Him fully...to love Him more than we love our families and friends and even our own lives. Jesus is coming with a "sword" to our nation, and there will be great division in the Church and even in our families. Will we compromise our lives and our witness for Jesus in order to keep *peace* in our families? Or will we allow His "sword" to cut into our hearts as we take a stand for Jesus, no matter what it costs us? The choice is ours to make, but be assured, a greater time of testing is coming to our nation and the Church, and we will have to decide whether to save our lives or to lose them out of love for Jesus.

> And Araunah said, "Why has my lord the king come to his servant?" David said, "To buy the threshing floor from you, in order to build an altar to the LORD, that the plague may be averted from the people." Then Araunah said to David, "Let my lord the king take and offer up what seems good to him. Here are the oxen for the burnt offering and the threshing sledges and the yokes of the oxen for the wood. All this, O king, Araunah gives to the king." And Araunah said to the king, "May the LORD your God accept you." But the king said to Araunah, "No, but I will buy it from you for a price. I will not offer burnt offerings to the LORD my God that cost me nothing." So David bought the threshing floor and the oxen for fifty shekels of silver.
>
> –2 Samuel 24:21–24 – ESV

I find it interesting that Mount Moriah was also the same place that David *sacrificed* before the Lord in order to stop the plague that had broken out as judgment from the Lord. Araunah wanted to *give* the king the threshing floor and even the animals that David would offer up, but the king refused. David would not offer burnt offerings without *paying a price.* He knew that it had to *cost* him something, and yet so many of God's people in this hour believe that following Jesus will cost them nothing. They want the blessing and the power of God without paying the cost. They want God to flow through their lives while they continue to live lives of self-indulgence and self-will. Only those willing to give Jesus their all will be His end-time ambassadors who will go with Him to the ends of the earth. It will cost us *everything* to be empowered fully with His presence and glory. The light-hearted ones and those laying on *couches of ease* will not be part of His end-time army. It will cost us the comforts of this earth and a disciplined life of obedience.

God is calling us to Mount Moriah, to the pinnacle of His Holy Hill, and asking us if we are willing to give Him our all, every part of our hearts and lives, so that we can be a *vital part* in this end-time harvest, this *3rd Great Awakening.* Jesus is calling us to sacrifice all in order to receive His very best in this final hour. It will cost us, but we will then be "vessels" that can carry His glory to the ends of the earth.

> Then Elijah said to all the people, "Come here to me." They came to him, and he repaired the altar of the Lord, which had been torn down. Elijah took twelve stones, one for each of the tribes descended from Jacob, to whom the word of the Lord had come, saying, "Your name shall be Israel." With the stones he built an altar in the name of the Lord, and he dug a trench around it large enough to hold two seahs of seed. He arranged the wood, cut the bull into pieces and laid it on the wood. Then he said to them, "Fill

four large jars with water and pour it on the offering and on the wood." "Do it again," he said, and they did it again. "Do it a third time," he ordered, and they did it the third time. The water ran down around the altar and even filled the trench...Then the fire of the LORD fell and burned up the sacrifice, the wood, the stones and the soil, and also licked up the water in the trench.

–1 Kings 18:30–35, 38 – NIV

Jesus is asking us to give Him our hearts fully in this hour. Our *hearts* are the "altar" that God desires to ignite with His fire, but they must be *repaired,* even as Elijah repaired the natural altar and set it in order before the fire of God could fall on it on Mount Carmel. Elijah dug a trench around it large enough to hold 2 seahs of seed which is equivalent to over 3 gallons of seed. In the same way the Spirit desires to enlarge our hearts by removing the things of this world, distractions, sin, and iniquity, so that we can have room for His holy "seed," His Word, to be planted deep in our hearts.

The bull was *cut into pieces* and *laid on the wood,* and we, as "living sacrifices," must have our hearts circumcised, cut open, as we lay our lives down before the Lord on His altar. Elijah poured water, which represents the Word of God, 3 times over the sacrifice. I believe this shows us that we are to be filled and fully saturated with God's Word in our spirit, soul, and body until we are overflowing with His Word! It was then that the fire of God fell. God has a *pattern* in His Word, and when we meet His requirements, we will know the fire of God in its fullness and be a "vessel" suitable for His glory!

> Why don't you bring Me the sacrifices I desire? Bring Me your true and sincere thanks, and show your gratitude by keeping your promises to Me, the Most High. Honor Me by trusting in Me in your day

of trouble. Cry aloud to Me, and I will be there to rescue you...The life that pleases Me is a life lived in the gratitude of grace, always choosing to walk with Me in what is right. This is the sacrifice I desire from you. If you do this, more of My salvation will unfold for you.

–Psalm 50:14–15, 23 – TPT

A grateful and thankful heart is what God is looking for in His people. Jesus wants to hear a *"sacrifice of praise"* even in the midst of fiery trials and suffering. This brings deepest transformation in our hearts, and it is pleasing to our Heavenly Father. God wants praise and thanksgiving from our *hearts* not just our *lips,* and these true and sincere thanks can only come from a heart that has been broken and transformed in His glory.

We show our gratitude by keeping our promises to God not only when we are in a "pit of despair" but in the good and joyful times. Many times God's children cry out to Him when they are suffering, but they forget all about the promises they made to Him when all is going well. This grieves our God, for He desires our love and faithfulness at *all times.* He wants us to honor Him by trusting Him not only in our days of trial but also in times of joy and jubilation. He wants us to run to Him in our suffering and to cry out to Him in our despair. This honors God when we run to Him first in sickness, pain, and grief and do not go looking for the answers to our dilemma in this present world system.

Every day we should thank the Lord for saving us, for the wonder of His love that was shown through His cross of suffering. We show the Lord how thankful we are when we walk with Him daily and do what is just and right in His eyes. This is the sacrifice that He is looking for, and this is what brings great joy to the heart of our Father. As we walk with Jesus in Truth, greater and deeper revelations will come to us, and we will be filled with His love and joy, even to overflowing.

For the Lord our God has brought us His glory-light. I offer Him my life in joyous sacrifice. Tied tightly to Your altar, I will bring you praise. For You are the God of my life and I lift You high, exalting You to the highest place.

–Psalm 118:27–28

Listen to the heart of Jesus say:

"You are My 'mountain climber'; you are the one that I have called to walk in the High Place with Me. You have not gone backward but forward into all that I have for you. I have called, and you have answered that call. You have not backed down in the face of your enemies but have stood your ground and kept moving forward. I have tested you, and you have passed the test. I have drawn you, and you have not backed away but have come close to Me because of your great love for Me.

"Many waters cannot quench love, child, and I see the fire of My love burning bright within you. 'Troubled waters' could never quench this deep love that I have placed inside of you. The enemy tried to douse this fire, this passion, but it only caused this fire to intensify and to break forth into more glorious flames of love. What the enemy tried to do has failed completely. I have brought you to this place of intense love, and all has been sacrificed on My altar. Now you are wholly Mine, and not one part of you has been left untouched by My holy fire.

"I have called, and you have answered. You have counted the cost and have abandoned all for Me and for the sake of My Kingdom. Like Abraham you have not withheld from Me what is dearest to your heart, and I am well-pleased with you—well-pleased. You

are My child of trust and faith, and no one will remove your crown—the beautiful crown that I have fashioned just for you. You have struggled for years, but your time of 'appearing' has arrived. You are coming out of your 'cave,' your 'cocoon,' and you will soar with Me into the heavenlies. Your 'wings' were clipped, but I have given you new and stronger 'wings' so that you can soar to the pinnacle of glory, the High Place, that I have prepared for you.

"None of these years have been wasted. They have fulfilled My perfect plan for your life and fashioned you after My image. Nothing has been in vain. 'Wasted years,' you thought, but I say: 'No! They have been years of transformation and transition. Now "birth!"' The time has come. Step up and into the full plan for your life. You will not be disappointed but will stand in awe as you spread your 'spiritual wings' and soar with Me near and far, even to lands you have never known—says your God!"

Warring from the High Place

I've always loved this song by Ron Kenoly: "We're going up to the high places. We're going up to the high places. We're going up to the high places to tear the devil's kingdom down."[xxvii]

> For we wrestle not against flesh and blood, but against principalities, against powers, against the rulers of the darkness of this world, against **spiritual wickedness in high places.**
>
> –Ephesians 6:12 – KJV, emphasis added

We are called to pray for ourselves, Israel, the government, our families, the Church, the sick, spiritual leaders, and even our enemies. (See 1 Timothy 2:1–4; Ephesians 6:18–20; James 5:14–15; Matthew 5:44; Psalm 122:6.) We are to be led, always, by the Holy Spirit during our prayer times. We are to live a life of prayer, to pray always as the Word admonishes us to. (See 1 Thessalonians 5:16–18.) Our prayer life gives us the strength and the power to walk the path that the Lord lays out before us. In our "secret place" we meet with our Beloved, lay our requests before Him, and listen to His lovely voice. It is in prayer that we receive guidance and direction for our lives as we follow the Lord into our destiny. Prayer is our daily Bread, Life, and Breath as we receive His very presence and fullness into our spirit, soul, and body.

We come to know our identity in Christ through spiritual growth as we stand in faith on God's Word and refuse to listen to the lies of the enemy. Many, like me, have heard for a large part of their lives that they are nothing, that they are worthless; this is the lie that the devil desires us to believe. As we spend time with the Lord, the Holy Spirit reveals to us how loved and valuable we are. As we read God's Word and have daily encounters with our Father in prayer and worship, we begin to walk in our true identity in Christ. Our beloved King wants us to walk hand in hand with Him and to realize the power and the authority that He has given us over *all* the powers of Hell.

> Submit therefore to God. But resist the devil, and he will flee from you.
>
> –James 4:7 – NASB

As we walk in the place of obedience and submission to God's will for our lives, it is then that we have power to resist the enemy and that he will flee from us. We will no longer hang our heads and feel "unworthy" but realize that Jesus has lifted us up into "heavenly places" in Him. These two keys: *submission to God* and *resisting the devil* are powerful keys that must be utilized if we are to know the full freedom that God has for us.

If one of these keys is missing, we will not experience the full release of divine power in our lives.

I have experienced many demonic attacks in my life and even in my dream-life. In these dreams some of the attacks were violent, and I would feel as if I was being strangled. But as I pleaded the blood of Jesus and rebuked the enemy, I would immediately be released from the enemy's grip. I would come against the enemy with the power of the name of Jesus on my lips. Truly, God has given us authority over all the power of the enemy in the precious name of Jesus.

I remember a time when the enemy was harassing me concerning one of my children and telling me that he was going to kill her. I came against the enemy with Psalm 118:17 (NLT). I made this Scripture personal and changed the wording from: "I will not die" to "**she** will not die; instead, she will live to tell what the LORD has done." The enemy immediately left, for there is power in His Word when we speak His decrees in His authority and anointing.

Satan's fall was great, and his judgment has been sealed. Satan is a defeated foe and doomed to spend an eternity in the *"lake of fire."* (See Revelation 20:10.) Multitudes in the Church are still living under his bondage and lies, for they do not realize the power of the cross and what the blood of Jesus has accomplished for us. It is our responsibility to read the Word, pray, and come to the knowledge of our position in Christ. Satan has been utterly defeated, and he is under our feet.

> There are so many reasons to describe God as wonderful! So many reasons to praise Him with unlimited praise! Zion-City is His home; **He lives on His holy mountain**—high and glorious, joy-filled and favored. Zion-Mountain looms in the farthest reaches of the north, the city of our incomparable King! This is His divine abode, an impenetrable citadel, for **He is known to dwell in the highest**

place. See how the **mighty kings united to come against Zion,** yet when they saw God manifest in front of their eyes, they were stunned. Trembling, they all fled away, gripped with fear. Seized with panic, they doubled up in frightful anguish, like a woman in the labor pains of childbirth. Like a hurricane blowing and breaking the invading ships, **God blows upon them and breaks them to pieces.** We have heard about these wonders, and then we saw them with our own eyes. For this is the city of the **Commander of Angel Armies,** the city of our God, safe and secure forever!

–Psalm 48:1–8 – TPT, emphasis added

I love these Scriptures in the Passion Translation, for they express so beautifully the power and authority of our God. Our God dwells on "Mount Zion," and as we continue our climb, we will have more and more glimpses of His glory and power. His abode is impenetrable, and no devil can touch us. As we walk in this High Place with our God, we will see the enemy flee from us in terror. Our God fights for us with His *hurricane force breath,* and all of our enemies are blown to pieces. No longer will we suffer the devil's torments or be robbed of our glorious inheritance in Jesus.

As we dwell with Jesus on Mount Zion, His glorious city, we find that we have reached a spacious place, a place of rest, and no longer will we succumb to the lies and the attacks of the evil one. As we dwell with Jesus on His "Mountain of Glory," we will be filled with joy unspeakable and will realize more fully that we are favored by our King. Jesus is the *"Commander of Angel Armies,"* and we abide under His shadow, hidden in His strength, forever. He will rescue us from every hidden trap of the enemy. (See Psalm 91:1–3.)

> Yet I have set My King on My holy hill of Zion.
>
> —Psalm 2:6 – NKJV

> Here am I and the children whom the Lord has given me! We are for signs and wonders in Israel from the Lord of hosts, who dwells in Mount Zion.
>
> —Isaiah 8:18

God has created His children for *signs and wonders* as they walk with Him in Mount Zion. His people will be a "sign" of the Lord's power and strength as He releases His miracle power and glory through them in this final hour. We have been given to the Lord, and we are His prized possession. God's people who walk in His power will be a glorious sign to this unbelieving world, and many will repent and come into the Kingdom as they see the wonders that our God will perform through them.

The Power of Praise and Worship

> Around midnight Paul and Silas were praying and singing hymns to God, and the other prisoners were listening. Suddenly, there was a massive earthquake, and the prison was shaken to its foundations. All the doors immediately flew open, and the chains of every prisoner fell off!
>
> —Acts 16:25–26 – NLT

I have learned the *power of praise and worship* in the deepest despair and pain. When we lift our hearts to Jesus in worship, even in a dark valley of suffering, we will see His smile and be released from "chains" of pain and depression; we may even experience one of God's powerful "earthquakes" and see *many* prisoners set free! When we praise God He sends forth "lightning bolts" and sets many captives free. God works powerfully when we praise Him in our "dungeons."

Prayer is powerful, but in a recent dream God showed me that our most powerful weapons in prayer are *praise and worship*. They are like explosive blasts of dynamite that breakthrough demonic barriers and bring healing, deliverance, and the blessings of the Lord into our lives and into the lives of others as well. In this dream I saw a minister that I love deeply standing in my basement in front of the *washing machine*. He had his hands lifted high in worship, and he was wearing a prayer shawl, a tallit. My basement represented the deep place in our hearts, and the washing machine showed the Spirit's cleansing power in our lives as we worship. As I walked over to the room where he was and saw him worshipping, I said to him: *"Praise and worship is the highest form of prayer!"* He looked at me and said: *"I know!"*

When we worship our King Jesus in the High Place of sacrificial love, it releases His love and power into this broken world. Praise is the most powerful weapon of warfare that we can release in the High Place; this is where we will see God's "lightning bolts" of power bring Light into dark areas in this world and free millions of captives. Worship is where true, deep, internal transformation takes place in our lives and where we are washed and released from every chain that would try to bind us.

I have found that when I praise the Lord in the midst of darkness His presence comes, and all darkness and confusion leaves. Praise and worship releases fear and worry and causes faith to rise and to lift us to a place where we can trust the Lord, even in impossible looking situations. When we praise and worship our King even when we don't feel like it, this brings His glorious presence, and all of our enemy's scatter. Our enemies cannot stand in the presence of the Lord! The prophetic word below came from my dream as I sat before the Lord that morning. I pray it will bless you.

Hear what our God would say:

> *"Praise and worship are the highest form of prayer, not 'begging,' not praying individual prayers, but <u>praise,</u> for it lifts you up to Me and sends forth My 'Lightning Bolts' to areas that I know need My help, protection, and mercy. Praise and worship are likened to 'Lightning Bolts of Power' that change hearts and lives, delivers the poor and helpless ones, and releases My presence where it is needed. These 'Bolts of Lightning' are needed across the face of the earth, so move with Me; praise Me; worship Me in your dark place, and I will illuminate areas of darkness across the face of the earth. Yes, these two: <u>praise and worship</u> are needed to change the atmosphere in your home, your church, your nation, and this world. Praise Me more; love Me deeply; worship Me in the depths of your heart, for you are releasing the 'Lightning Bolts' of My Spirit throughout this world.*
>
> *"Prayer is GOOD, but praise and worship are the BEST, the highest form of prayer that you can give to Me. It will release captives and 'wash' you in the deepest place in your heart. Praise and worship will cleanse you as I come to you and remove deepest grief and pain from your heart. The power of praise will lift you up to the High Place, to Mount Zion, and there I will meet with you, and you will know Me as the transcendent God who knows all, who is all-powerful, and who works miracles without number.*
>
> *"Children, now is the time to rise up and to take your rightful place before Me in praise and worship. Join with My angels in this festive joy and know My glory and power in a new and glorious way. Come, take My hand and release My praise, and you will no longer be captive to your emotions or your circumstances.*

Ride with Me up to the High Place of praise and worship. Join the 'festal shout,' and inner walls will come down, not only in your life but in the lives of many.

"It is done! It is finished! Now praise Me with exuberant joy—says our God!"

The Keys of the Kingdom

I am the first and the last, and the living One; and I was dead, and behold, I am alive forevermore, and I have the keys of death and of Hades.

–Revelation 1:17b–18 – NASB

Jesus is the One who holds the *keys of hell and death*. He is the One who was crucified for our salvation and resurrected in eternal power and glory. Jesus alone is the source of all life and all power; all authority in Heaven and on earth has been given to Him. (See Matthew 28:18.) Jesus has given every one of His true children authority over all the powers of darkness. As we embrace the Truth of who we are, our true identity in Christ according to God's Word, it is then that we come to know the power and the authority that Jesus has given us. There are millions of God's children that are walking in the lowlands of doubt and fear. They do not realize the authority and the power that Jesus has given them. They are still in the *prison of law* and don't realize the high position they have in Christ.

> And to the angel of the congregation {Gr. ekklesia – called out ones} in Philadelphia write; these things, saith He that is Holy and True, He who has the key of David, who opens and no one shuts and shuts, and no one opens; I know thy works; behold, I have set before thee an open door, and no one can shut it,

for thou hast a little strength and hast kept my word and hast not denied My name.

–Revelation 3:7–8 – JUB

And the key of the house of David I will lay upon His shoulder; so He shall open, and no one shall shut; and He shall shut, and no one shall open.

–Isaiah 22:22

And I will give unto thee the keys of the kingdom of the heavens, and whatever thou shalt bind on the earth shall be bound in the heavens, and whatever thou shalt loose on the earth shall be loosed in the heaven.

–Matthew 16:19

In 2020, I went to Erie, Pennsylvania, and in one of the messages I ministered from Revelation 3:7–8. Little did I realize when God first gave me these Scriptures as I was preparing for this trip that He was about to "wow" me with a glorious revelation. For years I studied about our authority in Christ, but God was about to put in action and reveal to me just how important these *"Keys of the Kingdom"* and the *"Key of David"* is in our lives.

Before going to Erie, my friend Jane and I went through much warfare in the spirit-realm. I have gone through a lot of spiritual warfare in my life, but this was *over the top*. The discouragement and attacks were so great that it looked like the meetings would be canceled. Because of my walk in Jesus and all of the warfare I had gone through in the past, I knew that God had something very special for us. I knew that the resistance was coming because of what the Lord wanted to accomplish in Erie. Jane was hearing from the Lord, and she was right on target in putting this conference together in Erie.

There was only a remnant that came to these meetings, and I knew that this gathering was not for a large crowd. Those who came were one in Spirit and in purpose, and I knew that God was going to accomplish His will in these meetings. Never look for crowds or for the applause of man but for God's approval in what He asks you to do. Never despise small beginnings, for God may want to accomplish His will with a small remnant of His people. The Spirit of God drew those that He wanted to come, and the outcome was glorious.

During these days of preparation Jane was given a *large key* as a gift from a friend; this key was definitely not like a *regular* house key. After she received the key an inner house lock to her study fell off in her hand. When she went to her basement, the external lock also fell off in her hand. This was a *strange* occurrence. She's lived in her house since 1986, and this had never happened before. She couldn't fix the basement lock at all even though she had all the same pieces for it. She had someone come a month later to fix it with a totally *new lock* because she was unable to put a new one in herself.

Before I left to go to Erie, a small silver key with stones in it suddenly appeared in my bathroom. I wondered where it came from but didn't think much about it at first. But everywhere I went in my house that key was there. I even gave it to my granddaughter to take home, but she forgot to take it. It wasn't until everything came together later that I realized what God was trying to tell me.

When God first led me to Revelation 3, I saw that it was a message to *Philadelphia*, and I knew that this was significant because I was being sent to Erie. As I began to minister these three things: how Jesus has the *"Key of David,"* how Jesus *"opens and no one shuts and shuts, and no one opens,"* and how Jesus has *"set before thee an open door, and no one can shut it,"* a *spiritual light-bulb* suddenly went off inside of me, and I realized that the key that Jane was given represented the power and the authority of Jesus to take the land of Erie and, I believe, *all* of Pennsylvania for Him. In my *lightning-fast* intellect (ha-ha) I realized why God kept putting that *key* in front of me before I left for Erie. God had given us an *open door* to Erie to take the *land* for Him. Jesus gave us the authority to use *His key* to *bind* demonic powers and to *loose* His will in Erie, Pennsylvania.

During one afternoon session we had a glorious time of prayer as we gathered together on the floor in the front of the church and passed the *large key* around to each one that was in the circle. Each person had an opportunity to pray and to turn the key that Jane had received. We turned it 3 times for each of the key cities that would experience God's explosive power in the days ahead, as was revealed through my dear friend, Anita. We prayed repentance prayers for the "First Nations" people, and God had His way in our midst. There was a glorious presence of the Spirit as we prayed and interceded, and I knew that God had accomplished a great work in our midst. I wouldn't have missed that weekend for all the gold in this world!

Getting back to Jane's experiences, I believe that part of the revelation that God was showing us through these broken locks is that no man can shut the doors that God is opening for us. Jesus has set before us an open door, and He is also removing the "old locks" that have kept His people bound to the past and to the lies of the enemy. Jesus is giving *revelation knowledge* concerning the power and the authority that we have in His name. Even as Jane was given a *new key*, a *large key*, so is God revealing, in greater depth, the power and the authority He has given us to open and to shut doors in His name and to loose and to bind in the power of His Spirit. God is *breaking off* old mindsets, all hindrances, and the old "locks" and giving us a greater *anointing of power* to release His will upon this earth! The new locks represent the *new things* that God is now releasing on the earth. We have entered into a new place in Jesus where our old identity is being broken off of our hearts and lives. Jane could not put on this new lock; she needed someone else to *fix it*. Our God is removing what is *old* as we yield to Him and is making *"all things new"* in our lives. This is the work of the Holy Spirit, and *He* will do it. This new key and lock will not be *activated* in our own strength and wisdom but in the Spirit's mighty power. Greater power and authority will be released in this *new era* upon His believing people. Glory to God!

> Assuredly, I say to you, whatever you bind on earth will be bound in heaven, and whatever you loose on earth will be loosed in heaven. Again I say to you that if two of you agree on earth concerning anything that they ask, it will be done for them by My Father in heaven.
>
> –Matthew 18:18–19 – NKJV

God has given us power on this earth to *loose* people from the shackles of sin and to *bind* the works of the enemy in millions of lives. We can open and shut doors, as the Lord leads us, and break through demonic powers over cities and nations. As we grow and mature in the Lord and are Spirit-led, we will be able to move "mountains" in the power of the Spirit. We will walk in the *faith of the Son of God* and realize the Truth of Galatians 2:20a which states: *"I have been crucified with Christ; it is no longer I who live, but Christ lives in me."* Jesus will be the One that is accomplishing the will of the Father *through us*. We will walk in the High Place with Jesus in full maturity as we continue on His path of obedience and walk in His footsteps.

> And have made us kings and priests to our God; and we shall reign on the earth.
>
> –Revelation 5:10

Our identity as kings and priests will become sure and strong in our souls as we continue on this glorious path of transformation, and the enemies lies will no longer torment us or cause us to fall, spiritually. We will walk with our heads held high, not in pride but in the humility of Christ as we realize that it is His Life and His righteousness that we walk in. When we realize fully our identity in Christ and that we *rule and reign* with Jesus even now, nothing on this earth will stop us or hinder us from fulfilling our full destiny in Him.

> When the seventy-two disciples returned, they joyfully reported to Him, "Lord, even the demons obey us when we use Your name!"
>
> –Luke 10:17 – NLT

What a joy it is to know that we have power and authority in Christ to remove demonic strongholds and to rebuke the enemy and see him run, for when the evil one sees Jesus *in* us and we know who we are in Him, demons tremble before us. The devil does not fear us, but he does fear the Holy One who lives within our earthly "temples." The enemy does not want God's people to realize the power and the authority they have in Christ; he wants them to believe his lies: that they are nothing and of little worth in the Kingdom of God. God is about to remove the blinders from the hearts and lives of His people; their *old locks* are breaking off!

> Then He called His twelve disciples together and gave them power and authority over all the demons and to cure diseases.
>
> –Luke 9:1 – JUB

Jesus has given us power and authority to heal the sick and even to raise the dead, for as He was on this earth so are we. We are to walk in the footsteps of Jesus and to do the works that He did, and even greater works! (See John 14:12.) This is the day and hour when our King is releasing many *mantles of power* from Heaven, and I encourage you to seek the Lord and to receive all that He has for you. Jesus has more for you than you realize, and He loves you more than you could ever comprehend.

> Look, I have given you authority over all the power of the enemy, and you can walk among snakes and scorpions and crush them. Nothing will injure you.
>
> –Luke 10:19 – NLT

God has given us authority over *all* the power of the enemy, not just over some of his power. We can go where the Spirit would send us without fear or dread, but we must make sure that God is sending us, that we are obeying Him in all that we do. Without the infilling of the Holy Spirit, we can do NOTHING! If God has called you to go to the most dangerous places on this earth, you can go without fear, for He is with you. As we obey Him nothing will injure us; that is His promise!

> But you will receive power when the Holy Spirit has come upon you; and you shall be My witnesses both in Jerusalem and in all Judea, and Samaria, and as far as the remotest part of the earth.
>
> –Acts 1:8 – NASB

God is calling His warriors to rise up and to tear the devil's kingdom down! If we are going to be effective against powers of darkness in this dark day and age, we are going to have to *war from a High Place* in Jesus. Many have gone forth in ignorance and tried, in the flesh or soulish realm, to *bring down* principalities in cities or nations and have come under great demonic attack. Everyone is called to pray but not all are called to be "generals" in the army of the Lord and to go into dark places where demonic powers are prevalent, for this requires much preparation.

> At Rephidim the Amalekites came and fought against the Israelites. So Moses said to Joshua, "Choose some men and go and fight the Amalekites tomorrow. I will stand on the top of the hill and watch you. I will be holding the walking stick God gave me." Joshua

obeyed Moses and went to fight the Amalekites the next day. At the same time Moses, Aaron, and Hur went to the top of the hill. Any time Moses held his hands in the air, the men of Israel would start winning the fight. But when Moses put his hands down, the men of Israel began to lose the fight. After some time, Moses' arms became tired. So they put a large rock under Moses for him to sit on. Then Aaron and Hur held Moses' hands in the air. Aaron was on one side of Moses and Hur was on the other side. They held his hands up like this until the sun went down. So Joshua and his men defeated the Amalekites in this battle.

–Exodus 17:8–13 – Easy-to-Read Version

Missionaries, God's ordained apostles, are a special group of warriors who have been trained and commissioned by the Spirit to go into dark places of the earth and to tear down *"rulers of darkness"* over regions. They live and war from a High Place in Jesus. They are strong in the Word and in the power of the Spirit. Like Moses they have intercessors that hold up their hands when they grow weary in their battles against forces of evil. Many are called to go to the nations, but few are chosen because few are willing to pay the cost in surrendering all to Jesus. (See Matthew 22:14.) If God has called you to go to the nations, your life must be *surrendered* and *prepared* in the Spirit. This *higher call* will require much time in the Word and in prayer. God wants every one of His children to walk in this High Place with Him, but it will require a life of sacrificial love and a full abandonment to God's will.

I have known, personally, those who have gone off to other nations in their own strength and will only to know utter defeat. In order to be God's *"vessel of honor,"* we must make sure that there is no opening in our hearts and lives where the enemy can enter and cause havoc. If there is fear, unbelief, bitterness, hate, unforgiveness, or unconfessed sin in our lives, there is danger of succumbing to the darkness that may come against us. We must be *fully* covered with God's presence and make sure we have our armor intact. Blessed are those who have gone to the nations in obedience to the Lord and have suffered martyrdom. Great will be their reward in Heaven, for they will receive a glorious martyr's crown.

Not only have missionaries been called to go to the High Place and war but God has a remnant in this hour that have been trained for years in the Word and in the "school of hard knocks" who war from the High Place. They are filled with the Spirit, and God has commissioned them to go *wherever* He would send them. They are His "living sacrifices," fully surrendered to His will in this dark hour. Like Moses they have climbed His Holy Hill and are praying and interceding in the Spirit to bring down evil rulers in cities and even nations. This *company* has known great spiritual warfare in their lives during their intense Spirit-training. Like the apostle Paul they have wrestled with "beasts," great opposition from the enemy, and have known great suffering. (See 1 Corinthians 15:32.) These *power houses* have not grown weary in well-doing. They continue to stand and to fight; they continue to walk with the Lord through *flood* and *fire*, and no man, no devil, can bring them down. These are God's true *apostles of faith*.

Through the many battles that these apostles have endured, there have been times when those around them have had to hold them up in prayer. These *battle-scared warriors* have their Aaron's and Hur's to hold up their arms during great and intense battles with dark powers. They know that they cannot pray against these *dark rulers* alone; they are humble and feel their need for others. No child of God can stand alone in this kind of *high warfare*, and this is the reason why God puts *teams together* to stand and to pray for one another.

Moses needed Aaron and Hur; he was not a *one-man* show. God's *guards* and *prophets* need others to stand with them in prayer as they bring down strong forces of evil in cities and nations. If prophets and guards grow weary and stop praying, the enemy may gain some ground, and this is not what God wants to happen. We must all undergird each other in prayer, especially those who are in the 5-fold ministry, for they are targeted by the evil one in order to attack them and to bring them down from the High Place that they are walking in. Moses sat on a large "rock," and we know that the "Rock" is Jesus. (See 1 Peter 2:4–8.) God gave Moses power and authority to sit on a *seat of authority,* and this was not something that Moses took lightly.

God's Ekklesia, His Church, God's *governing authority on earth,* is seated with Christ in heavenly places, and we have been given power and authority in the name of Jesus. God's desire is to bring all of His people up into a place of maturity in Him in order to rule and to reign with Him in power, but we must follow the pattern that is in the Word of God as we climb to the top of His Holy Hill. God's passion is to see *all* of His children come to the place where they, too, can have the strength and the power to bring down demonic forces. Jesus wants all of His children to rule and to reign with Him, but He will never *force* anyone to give themselves as a "living sacrifice" and abandon all for Him. The choice is ours, for no one can make that choice for another soul.

As I completed this section, the Lord gave me a powerful dream that I believe will bless you, for I know it was not only for me but for you! In this dream I was in a church, and I saw worshippers dancing in the Spirit. I went to the front *on the side* of the altar for personal prayer. Instead of being prayed for I prayed for a woman, and the power of God overwhelmed her as she fell to the floor. I believe she was one of the young women who was worshipping in the dance. I also saw a pastor friend of mine who is a missionary, and he was weeping.

Then there was a large room, and many were seated on different types of *chairs.* Some were metal, and some were flowered. There were many different styles and designs on these chairs. As I looked I noticed that not all of the chairs were occupied. I kept looking for *my chair* but couldn't find it. I was so frustrated looking for my chair because I knew that I had brought one with me. I finally found one that I thought was mine, but it had a *broken arm rest* on it. Others were trying to help me find my chair, but we couldn't find it.

In the next scene, I was looking for my car, and it was nowhere to be seen. I looked into a booklet and found out that it was in the *trash*. I was so upset! I found two workmen and asked them why it was in the trash because it was still in good shape. They didn't know why, but they said it was going to be destroyed! I then saw myself in my car, and it was close to a *ditch*. I was right on the edge of this ditch, and my car, along with me, was about to fall in. Then I pulled back hard on my steering-wheel and seat, and the car stopped moving forward. As I looked around I saw others pulling "stuff" out of my car. I remember seeing a beautiful *garment* that was sopping wet. I was upset because I knew that it was ruined.

What the Holy Spirit revealed to me concerning the meaning of this dream was amazing! The Lord showed me that none of those *chairs* were mine. The chairs represented "seats of authority," and the chair with the broken arm rest was no longer mine; it represented what God had accomplished through me in the past. God had new things in store for my life, and my past ministry was now fading away; it was now being *broken* off of me. The "arm rest" stood for a place of *rest,* and the Lord showed me that I will no longer find *rest* walking in my past anointing. This is also for God's people who are transitioning out of what they have operated in the past, their "old" ministries. There is something that is new and fresh in the Spirit on the horizon!

The *flowers* on the chairs represented God's glory. Jesus showed me that there is a *greater* glory coming to God's children and to the Church worldwide. I was *frustrated* as I looked for my *chair,* and the Lord showed me that I have been frustrated lately and unsettled in the place that I am in, spiritually. This is true for many in the Body of Christ. Many of God's people are frustrated and have been in a place of transition, spiritually. They haven't been able to find their *chair*, the place that God has ordained for their lives, but they are about to birth something new and fresh in the Spirit. They are undergoing great pressure and pain because of the *changes* that they are undergoing; this is all of the Lord. A greater power and anointing are now being released into my life and into yours. We have a <u>new</u> "seat of authority," a higher "seat of authority" then we have ever known. Great change is on the horizon!

The missionary pastor that was weeping in my dream represented my longing to go to the nations, and I know that God is going to give me the desire of my heart. Some of you are called to the nations, but this vision has not yet come to full fruition in the Spirit. The Lord is preparing you and me for our calling in the Spirit, and the fullness of it is about to come forth powerfully. Whatever God has placed in your heart know that it is about to be *birthed* in the Spirit. Don't give up! Keep praising Jesus and thanking Him for the full manifestation of your calling and destiny.

I went up to the front for prayer in this dream but went to the *side* of the altar. So many of God's children have been on the *sidelines* of ministry, not in the forefront, but this is about to change. God is about to take the unknowns, the forgotten ones, and make them the *head,* and they will see that they are not the *tail*. (See Deuteronomy 28:13.) This is the time of the *changing of the guards.*

I ended up not being prayed for but praying for others. What God revealed to me is that His children will no longer look to be prayed for and blessed. Their *cup* will be so full of His presence that they will pray for others in the power of His Spirit. They will be satisfied in God's love, and they will know that all of their needs are met in Him alone. In the overflow of the Spirit's presence in His people, they will pour *out* to others what He has poured *into* their hearts. This is the time of the *fullness* of the Spirit within us, and we will worship Jesus in a greater and more powerful anointing, and this will set many captive free.

My car was just about to fall into a *ditch,* but I *pulled back,* and the car stopped right on the edge. One of the meanings of ditch is: **to get rid of or give up.**[xxviii] God wants to ditch our past ministries, which the car represented, for something new and fresh in the Spirit, and we are on the *edge* of the greatest outpouring of the Spirit this world has ever known! This change in our lives and ministries will be so dramatic that the past ministries we have walked in will look like *trash* in comparison to what He has for us in this new era.

Thousands of God's children are still *pulling back* and *resisting* the *new things* that He has for them; they feel comfortable in what they have *always* walked in. I, for one, do *not* want to pull back or stay in what is fading away. I want to allow the Spirit to *ditch the old* for the *new things* that He has for my life. The old *garments* have been destroyed through the *floods* He has taken us through. Jesus has new and glorious *clothes* for us to wear, *new mantles* of power and glory. God has a *new vehicle* for us to ride in, even a *chariot of fire and glory.* God is telling us to let go of the old and enter into the new things that He has prepared for us in this very hour. Nothing in our past is *usable* any more, and we will not find comfort in them any longer. He is asking us to step out of the boat and onto *waves of glory* with Him. He wants us to come out of our comfort zone and into the new and exciting adventures that He has planned for our lives. God is taking us to places we have never been before, and we will take new territories for Jesus. We will take back what the enemy has stolen from us, and nothing will stop us from moving forward with the Lord! *Ditch* the past and embrace the new; it is time to walk in the High Place with the Lord your God!

Now, if anyone is enfolded into Christ, he has become an entirely new person. All that is related to the old order has vanished. Behold, everything is fresh and new.

–2 Corinthians 5:17 – TPT

Open your heart and hear the Spirit say:

"When I come this time it will not be as a meek and mild Savior, for I am coming in a way that will overturn tables of wickedness and will lift My people up to new heights of glory. This 'wave of glory' that is coming will be violent (powerful). It has a two-fold purpose: to lift My people up into heavenly places with Me and to deal with the wicked. Many of My children will rejoice as they behold this glorious wave, but others will run and try to hide from My glorious presence.

"My true children are crying out to Me in this hour to come and to show Myself strong to this generation, and I have heard their cries. Others believe that they are getting away with their evil schemes in your nation and in your government, but I see all that they are doing, and I say: 'This is judgment time!' Never has there been a day or an hour like the one you are living in right now. Rejoice that you have been found worthy to live in this generation and to walk with Me in 'white!' (See Revelation 3:4.) You will walk with Me in power as you yield fully to My Spirit. Full surrender is what I am asking for from each of My children. Some will respond while others will continue to go on their merry way.

"Not all of My children have opened their hearts fully to Me. I know those who have, and these are My remnant, those who will walk in the 'High Place' with Me. I have called and called these past years, but not

all of My children have responded. I will now turn up the heat, and those who have walked through the fire with Me, these will not be touched by what is coming. Those of My children who have ignored My warnings, these will feel My heat and fire along with the rest of this world.

"Make sure that you have your full armor on, children, for it is fireproof. These flames will not touch those who are abiding in Me, but those who are careless in their walk with Me, these very ones will be crying out to Me in great agony and tears of repentance. Do not try to shelter those who will feel this fire, for this is their salvation; I am dealing with them in mercy. Leave them in My hands, and I will save and deliver them. This goes for all of your loved ones who have refused to come to Me and to surrender their lives. Trust Me and rejoice, for even though you will see many suffer great afflictions, know that I am in full control and will save millions upon millions of souls in this generation. This is the time and the season for this to happen. Rejoice with Me, for I am coming soon—says your God!"

CHAPTER 7

God's Chariot Throne

Before we begin to study about *chariots* and their meaning in battle, let's start with one definition from Merriam-Webster: **a two-wheeled horse-drawn battle car of ancient times used also in processions and races.**[xxix]

As I began to study about the Ark and chariots, the Holy Spirit spoke to me and told me that He was going to give me a revelation concerning His throne and chariots. He began to put Scriptures together in a marvelous way, and one of the first things I found out was that the *first Jewish coin* actually had an imprint on it of a "Jewish deity upon a *winded chariot* as described in Ezekiel 10:16."[xxx]

When we think of chariots many people think of the Ben Hur movie and the *chariot race* he was in, but God wants to broaden our understanding in this hour to see that the chariot also represents Him coming to us on the *"wings of the wind."* Jesus wants us to see Him on His *chariot throne,* fighting our battles and delivering us from all evil.

> And when the servant of the man of God arose early and went out, there was an army, surrounding the city with horses and chariots. And his servant said to him, "Alas, my master! What shall we do?" So he answered, "Do not fear, for those who are with us

are more than those who are with them." And Elisha prayed, and said, "LORD, I pray, open his eyes that he may see." Then the LORD opened the eyes of the young man, and he saw. And behold, the mountain was full of horses and chariots of fire all around Elisha.

–2 Kings 6:15–17 – NKJV

My prayer is that the Spirit would open our eyes during the transformation we are going through in order to see that those who are with us in the battles are so much *more* and so much *greater* than the enemy's forces of Hell. May we see as we climb to the top of God's Holy Hill that this mountain is full of horses and chariots of fire all around us, even as they were around Elisha. As the Spirit opens our eyes and gives us revelation after revelation in His holy Word and visions of His splendor and glory, we are transformed more and more into His likeness. Without internal transformation we will never see into the Spirit-realm as God desires us to but will forever live in the *lowlands* of fear and unbelief.

The Lord then built on this revelation; He began to reveal to me the importance of *cherubim,* and their awesome place and position before Him. 1 Kings 6:23–28 tells us that King Solomon made 2 cherubim 10 cubits in size (15 feet tall), and he set them in the Holy of Holies. In doing research on this I discovered that the *narrow side* of the ark faced out toward the front of the curtain not the *broad side* facing out.[xxxi] This would make sense with the poles being on the side of the ark. Only in this position could the extended poles be seen in the Holy Place. (See 1 Kings 8:8.) The large cherubim were placed, one on each side of the Ark, and it looked like they were pulling the ark, the "Chariot of God."

> Look! The mighty chariots of God! Ten thousands upon ten thousands, more than anyone could ever

number. God is at the front, leading them all from Mount Sinai into His sanctuary with the radiance of holiness upon Him.

—Psalm 68:17 – TPT

These chariots are mighty, and God Himself is riding them! Now we will see in Scripture just how awesome these cherubim are and their part in doing battle as the Lord rides with them on His *chariot throne*.

> When the cherubim went, **the wheels went beside them;** and when the cherubim lifted their wings to mount up from the earth, *the same wheels* also did not turn from beside them.
>
> —Ezekiel 10:16 – NKJV, emphasis added

Here we see that the cherubim in Ezekiel coincide with the hammered gold cherubim angels that were on the ark along with the 2 that Solomon made for God's temple. The *wheels represent a chariot* according to 1 Chronicles 28:18 (AMP, emphasis added): "And for the altar of incense refined gold by weight; and gold **for the model of the chariot of the cherubim that spread their wings and covered the ark of the Lord's covenant.**"

> You shall make a veil [to divide the two rooms] of blue, purple, and scarlet fabric and fine twisted linen, skillfully worked with cherubim on it.
>
> —Exodus 26:31

Here we see the importance of the cherubim in that even the veil dividing the "Holy Place" from the "Holy of Holies" had cherubim embroidered onto it. Cherubim are beside and around God's throne in Heaven (see Revelation 4:6–10), and they sing: *"Holy, holy, holy is the Lord God Almighty, who was, and is, and is to come!"* (Revelation 4:8 – NIV). These cherubim are the "Chariot of God," the 4 cherubim that were displayed in the Holy of Holies.

The word "cherub" may come from a term "to guard." They are powerful guardians of God; these are God's *heavenly guards*. In Jewish folklore the "Throne Angels" are known as "Merkabah."[xxxii] In Hebrew "Merkabah" means a *chariot*.[xxxiii] I realized as I studied this that the "Living Creature" beside me in a dream I had years ago was actually a cherubim. This angel was huge and fearsome looking, but I had no fear in this dream. So much of this revelation is coming together for me now. I love the way God reveals His truths to us, little by little.

> Their faces looked like this: Each of the four had the face of a human being, and on the right side each had the face of a lion, and on the left the face of an ox; each also had the face of an eagle. Such were their faces. They each had two wings spreading out upward, each wing touching that of the creature on either side; and each had two other wings covering its body.
>
> –Ezekiel 1:10–11

In these verses we see that the cherubim are the "Living Creatures" that Scripture talks about. (See Revelation 4:6–9.) Ezekiel saw these awesome creatures in his glorious revelation of God's majesty and the throne of God. The glory of God was above these living creatures, and Ezekiel knew that they were cherubim.

> And **the cherubim lifted their wings and mounted up from the earth in my sight. When they went out, the wheels were beside them;** and they stood at the door of the east gate of the LORD's house, and the glory of the God of Israel was above them. This is the living creature I saw under the God of Israel by the River Chebar, and **I knew they were cherubim.**
>
> –Ezekiel 10:19–20 – NKJV, emphasis added

> When the Lord told the man in linen clothing to go between the Guardian Angels and take some burning coals from between the wheels, the man went in and stood beside one of the wheels, and one of the Guardian Angels reached out his hand (for each of the mighty Angels had, beneath his wings, what looked like human hands) and took some live coals from the flames between the Angels and put them into the hands of the man in linen clothes, who took them and went out.
>
> –Ezekiel 10:6–8 – TLB

> Then one of the seraphim flew to me with a burning coal in his hand, which he had taken from the altar with tongs. He touched my mouth with it and said, "Behold, this has touched your lips; and your guilt is taken away and atonement is made for your sin."
>
> –Isaiah 6:6–7 – NASB

While praying the Lord showed me that the *coals* in the above Scriptures have a two-fold purpose: they are used to bring judgment but also to bring purification to His people. Isaiah had his mouth touched by God's burning coal, and his life was forever changed! These coals represent God's fiery presence that burns up all that is not of Him. I believe the "man in linen" is the pre-existent One, Jesus. He went in between the cherubim, the Guardian Angels, and one of the angels put the coals into His hands. He then went to bring forth His righteous judgments. (See Psalm 11:6; Ezekiel 11:1–25.)

Jesus is the righteous Judge of all the earth; His judgments are True and Just. Jesus is the *"baptism of fire"* that cleanses us in the depths of our being. This is the fire that will transform us from the inside out; it will cleanse our hearts and lives fully. When this internal fire intensifies in our hearts and lives, we will cry out as Isaiah did when he said: *"Woe is me! for I am undone; because I am a man of unclean lips, and I dwell in the midst of a people of unclean lips: for mine eyes have seen the King, Jehovah of hosts."* (Isaiah 6:5b – ASV). Those who will ride with Jesus in His chariot of glory in this hour must experience this purifying fire! If we fall on Jesus we will be broken to pieces and know His purifying fire, but woe to those He falls on, for they will be crushed! (See Luke 20:18.)

> Moreover the word of the Lord came to me, saying, "Son of man, take up a lamentation for the king of Tyre, and say to him, 'Thus says the Lord God: "You were the seal of perfection, full of wisdom and perfect in beauty...You were the **anointed cherub who covers;** I established you; **you were on the holy mountain of God;** you walked back and forth in the midst of fiery stones. You were perfect in your ways from the day you were created, till iniquity was found in you. By the abundance of your trading you became filled with violence within, and you sinned; therefore **I cast you as a profane thing out of the mountain of God; and I destroyed you, O covering cherub,** from the midst of the fiery stones."'"
>
> —Ezekiel 28:11–12, 14–16 – NKJV, emphasis added

Just when I thought God was finished giving me revelation concerning the cherubim this revelation came to me concerning the king of Tyre who represents satan. When you study the passages in Ezekiel 28:11–19, you will see that this is describing our arch-enemy, satan. When he was created he was the *"seal of perfection"* and *"perfect in beauty."* He was an anointed cherub who "covered," and he was on the holy mountain of God *until* iniquity was found in him. He had a very high position before God, and great was his fall!

> I kept looking until thrones were set up, and the Ancient of Days (God) took His seat; His garment was white as snow and the hair of His head like pure wool. His throne was flames of fire; its wheels were a burning fire.
>
> —Daniel 7:9 – AMP, emphasis added

When I saw this in God's Word, I shouted! God's throne is actually a *moveable chariot.* Many Scriptures began to come together quickly, and I saw that our God is truly a "God of Judgment and War," and He rides upon the cherubim on the *"wings of the wind!"*

> He bowed the heavens also and came down; and thick darkness was under His feet. And **He rode upon a cherub (storm) and flew;** and He sped on the wings of the wind. He made darkness His hiding place (covering); His pavilion (canopy) around Him, the darkness of the waters, the thick clouds of the skies. Out of the brightness before Him passed His thick clouds, hailstones and **coals of fire.** The LORD also thundered in the heavens, and the Most High uttered His voice, hailstones and **coals of fire.**
>
> —Psalm 18:9–13, emphasis added

> You rode on the backs of flying creatures and swooped down with the wind as wings.
>
> —Psalm 18:10 – Contemporary English Version

> He rode a ·creature with wings [ᴸcherub; ᶜa mighty spiritual being/angel; Ezek. 1] and flew. ·He raced [...soaring] on the wings of the wind.
>
> —Psalm 18:10 – Expanded Bible

I love the expression in the Scriptures that says God rides "upon a cherub (storm)." God comes *in* and *as a storm,* and what we are seeing in our nation is definitely a storm of darkness and confusion. God rides **on top of it,** meaning that He is in full control of every storm in our nation and in our lives; He releases His judgment, His *"coals of fire"* upon the enemy. Our God comes in a *"dark cloud,"* and His glorious power and divine will are released in the midst of chaos and *darkness.* The darker the storm clouds the more glory we are about to see come forth. So, let's trust the Lord when we see darkness, for we know that the Lord our God is about to break through with His brilliance! (See Isaiah 60:1–2.) He is in full control of *all* that is happening in our nation and this world.

> And above the firmament over their heads was the **likeness of a throne,** in appearance like a **sapphire stone; on the likeness of the throne was a likeness with the appearance of a man high above it.** Also from the appearance of His waist and upward I saw, as it were, the **color of amber** with the appearance of fire all around within it; and from the appearance of His waist and downward I saw, as it were, the appearance of fire with brightness all around. Like the appearance of a rainbow in a cloud on a rainy day, so was the appearance of the brightness all around it. **This was the appearance of the likeness of the glory of the Lord.**
>
> –Ezekiel 1:26–28a – NKJV, emphasis added

> Then Moses went up, also Aaron, Nadab, and Abihu, and seventy of the elders of Israel, and **they saw the God of Israel. And there was under His feet as it were a paved work of sapphire stone, and it was like the very heavens in its clarity.**
>
> –Exodus 24:9–10, emphasis added

His body also was like beryl [with a golden luster], His face had the appearance of lightning, His eyes were like flaming torches, His arms and His feet like the gleam of burnished bronze, and **the sound of His words was like the noise of a multitude [of people or the roaring of the sea].**

–Daniel 10:6 – AMP, emphasis added

His feet were like burnished [white-hot] bronze, refined in a furnace, and **His voice was [powerful] like the sound of many waters.**

–Revelation 1:15, emphasis added

Then I looked, and behold, in the expanse (firmament) that was over the heads of the cherubim there appeared something [glorious and brilliant] above them looking like a [huge] **sapphire stone, formed to resemble a throne.**

–Ezekiel 10:1, emphasis added

We know from reading these Scriptures that the visions Ezekiel, Moses, and Daniel had were of a pre-incarnate "Living Word" of God, Jesus! How glorious these revelations of the throne of God must have been! Think about the power and the glory of our God: the Lord's face appearing as lightening, hearing His voice like the sound of many waters, seeing His glorious throne like a sapphire stone, and seeing His presence as fire with brightness all around as a glorious rainbow! I think about John on the Isle of Patmos and his glorious encounter with Jesus. The Lord's face was like the appearance of the sun, so bright, so glorious. The eyes of Jesus were as a blazing fire, and His feet like bronze, glowing in a furnace. His voice like the sound of rushing waters! (See Revelation 1:14–16.) How glorious is our God! Are you yearning to have deeper and more intimate encounters with your Savior? I am!

> Hezekiah prayed before the LORD and said, "O LORD, the God of Israel, who is enthroned above the cherubim [of the ark in the temple], You are the God, You alone, of all the kingdoms of the earth. You have made the heavens and the earth.
>
> –2 Kings 19:15

When we pray before the Lord, may we always see Him high and lifted up on a glorious throne that *moves* in power and justice. The Lord will come to us as He did to David in Psalm 18, ready to strengthen, deliver, and reveal His glory to us. Our God is on the *move,* and may we never see Him again as One who is not active in our lives or in this world. He is our Maker and our Creator, enthroned above the cherubim, and moving across the face of this earth in this dark hour. His throne is a *flame of fire,* and its *wheels a burning fire.* This was Daniel's vision, and I pray that it will become ours, too.

God gave me this revelation not only to encourage me but to encourage you, as well. He wants us to realize that His glory surrounds us and that He is working on our behalf to transform us, to *reverse the tables* in our lives, and to bring us to the pinnacle of His "Holy Mountain." God is at work in our nation and this world in ways that we cannot fully see in this hour, but soon it will be made plain to us as the knowledge of His glory fills the entire earth. May we always see our King Jesus enthroned above the darkness that surrounds us, and may His "chariot" and His "whirlwind" lift us high above this earth. I pray we will see and even experience the reality of being seated in the High Place with Him. Let's soar with Jesus on the *"wings of the wind"* and take our nation and the nations of this world for our King.

God's desire is to give us greater and stronger visions of who He is in this hour. So many of God's children believe that they could never have encounters with the living God as Ezekiel, Moses, John, and Daniel had, but nothing could be further from the Truth. Jesus loves us all the same, and the only reason some have greater encounters with God is that they spend time with Him in prayer, praise, and fellowship. They live a life of obedience, set apart to do the Father's will above all.

The Spirit gave me a prophecy at a recent prayer meeting and told us to get ready for *greater encounters* with Him. He was asking us to set more time apart with Him, waiting in His presence. Jesus told us to be still in His presence until we felt the Holy Spirit filling us with His Life and we could hear His still, small voice. The Spirit revealed to us that He is going to *unveil* what He is doing in our nation and this world as we spend time with Him. God told us that if we could see what He is doing right now in the Spirit-realm, we would not be able to take it in, that is how powerful the *movement* of God in our midst is!

That night I had some powerful dreams, and in one part of the dream, I saw and felt a powerful explosion. In this dream I was wearing a shirt with the American flag printed on it. The Lord showed me that there is a mighty explosion coming to our nation in this hour, and I believe God is about to deal with the deep root of evil in our government and the corruption that is all around us.

There is much on the horizon, and God is telling us to draw close to Him and to allow His Spirit to transform us and to fill us to overflowing with His presence so that we can ride His *glory wave*. Jesus is calling us to come and to ride with Him in His *chariot of fire*. He is calling you, and He is calling me. The question He asks us today is: *"Will you ride with Me and let go of the things of this world? Will you follow Me all the way and allow My Spirit to have His way in your life?* If you answer yes to His call, you are in for the *ride of your life!*

Listen to what Jesus is saying:

> *"I am coming to you in a 'chariot of fire' in order to lift you into the new place that I have for you. I am going*

to lift you up and into a spiritual 'portal of glory' that I have prepared for your life even before the foundation of this world. I am on the move, and I will not be stopped. See Me high and lifted up on My 'chariot throne' moving throughout this earth and releasing My glory in this very hour, and though it is dark, now you will see a bright Light hovering over your life and over your nation.

"Now, in this new era, you will see the impossible become possible. No more doubt and fear will cloud your life, for the days of gloom and darkness are lifting. Never look back, but know that this is a new day for you. You have been transformed, and you are now moving in My power and glory in new and glorious ways. These ways are new and exciting. You have not walked on this path before, and you will now experience the great turn-around that I have promised you. Never have you seen or known the things that you are walking into.

"Can you see a double-door before you? Can you see it beginning to open? Will you move into the fullness that I have for you? Never doubt what I have revealed to you in the past, for you are now entering into the full plan and destiny for your life.

"Where are your enemies now? Are you wondering why you feel such peace and rest in your soul? Does not My Word say that I will make even your enemies to be at peace with you? (See Proverbs 16:7.) This is the season that you have now entered into. It is a season of love, peace, and joy. This is your 'Solomon' season, a reign of peace for you, even though you will see and hear of much turmoil all around you. You have entered into the depths of My heart, and it is here that you will rule and reign with Me in great power!

> "So, come; move with Me in My 'chariot of fire,' for I am making 'all things new' in your life, in this very hour. I am lifting you; I am causing you to move with Me quickly now, and I will show you new and wondrous things, new things in My Spirit now—says your God!"

God's End-Time Horsemen

Who are God's end-time "horsemen"? Why is it necessary for the Lord to send them forth in our generation? Don't we live on a higher plane than the Old Testament saints? Aren't we more *enlightened?* Don't we have a *"better covenant"* than they had? The answer is yes to these questions, but we still need to learn the *ways of the Lord* and to have our *hearts cleansed deeply* by His holy fire. We still need to be *convicted of sin* and to learn to *follow the Father's will* in our lives. We need to *die daily, pick up our cross, and follow Jesus.* God is even stricter with us in the new covenant because we are walking on a higher plane: We have the very presence of God inside of our earthly "temples"! The Church needs true prophets and fathers in the faith who have been through fires and floods, and these men and women are God's end-time "horsemen." We will now see who these fiery *war horses* are as we continue on in this chapter.

> As they continued along and talked, behold, a chariot of fire with horses of fire [appeared suddenly and] separated the two of them, and Elijah went up to heaven in a whirlwind. Elisha saw it and cried out, "My father, my father, the chariot of Israel and its horsemen!"
>
> –2 Kings 2:11–12a

> When Elisha became sick with the illness of which he was to die, Joash the king of Israel came down to him, and wept over him and said, "My father, my father, the chariots of Israel and its horsemen!"
>
> –2 Kings 13:14 – NASB

When I read these Scriptures they came alive to me. I understood that the chariots, the horses, the whirlwinds, the ark, and the presence of God all fit together. As we have seen the "chariot" represents the throne of God and also God's *throne angels,* the cherubim, and now we will see why the "horsemen" are so important in God's Kingdom. As I studied this I realized that the Lord's prophets, Elijah and Elisha and all who are called to be God's pioneers, are called God's "horsemen."

In the above Scriptures we see that Elisha cried out the same words as King Joash did when Elijah was being taken up in a whirlwind. Joash called Elisha his *father,* for he knew that God's anointing rested mightily upon him. The Lord's "horsemen," Elijah and Elisha, walked in miracle power and moved kings and nations through their godly influence and the power of God's manifested presence. King Joash realized the power and influence that Elisha had over the nation and wept because he knew that Elisha was on his deathbed and that the loss would be great, to himself and also to the nation of Israel. Elisha was a true father and "horseman" of Israel, and now, in this generation, we will see God raise up His end-time "horses."

The "prophets," "pioneers," and "eagles" in this generation are God's "horsemen," the ones who ride with Jesus in His *chariot of fire* and experience the *zeal of the Lord.* They live to do the Father's will, and they walk in the power of the Spirit. These fiery leaders and pioneers have a powerful "breakthrough" anointing from the Holy Spirit. They walk in the Elijah and Elisha anointing in this new era. They are God's fiery prophets who, in the power of the Spirit, change the spiritual atmosphere over cities and nations and bring God's glory to the earth. Think about the power that Elijah walked in: When he prayed for the rain to stop, it did not rain for 3 years, and then when the time came for the rain to be released from the heavens, God travailed through His servant in order to release a deluge of rain. Elijah did not perform these miracles in himself but was always led by the Spirit of God, for he was fully submitted to Him.

> Behold, he shall come up like clouds, and his chariots like a whirlwind. His horses are swifter than eagles. Woe to us, for we are plundered!
>
> –Jeremiah 4:13 – NKJV

If you read Jeremiah chapters 4 and 5, you will see that this was God's judgment against Israel, His people, for their rebellion and wickedness and for their refusal to repent and to listen to the Lord's true prophets. Many believe that God will not judge His people in this hour, but God is the same yesterday, today, and forever. God is holy, and He will judge His people in righteousness. In the verse above it talks about God using the chariots of Nebuchadnezzar to bring judgment to Israel because of all the idolatry and wickedness in His people. Do we think that the Lord will not judge evil in His present-day Church?

God is sending forth His "horsemen" in this hour, prophets who will speak the whole Truth of God's Word. They are riding in the Lord's chariot and will be *"swifter than eagles"* as they soar with God to lands near and far. Jesus will cut through the hearts of His people with His holy Word, and millions will repent of their idolatry, fornication, and rebellion against the Father's will.

> O Lord, were You displeased with the rivers, was Your anger against the rivers, was Your wrath against the sea, that You rode on Your horses, your chariots of salvation?
>
> –Habakkuk 3:8

Our mighty King is coming not only to bring judgment but to save His people and to show them the *fullness* of His salvation. His "horsemen" will ride with Jesus in His chariot and bring freedom to millions of captive souls as they preach the Good News of His glorious salvation. They will release a fiery word of repentance, a two-edged sword that will convict of sin, and many will fall to their knees in deep repentance. Millions will come to know His full salvation through repentance, and as God breaks the chains of iniquity deep in their souls, they will praise the Lord with a loud voice of thanksgiving. Jesus desires that *all* would come to know His great salvation. He is merciful and kind, but He is also a God who judges the hearts of His people. Remember Ananias and Sapphira? (See Acts 5:1–11.)

> This is what the Lord says to me, "Go, station the lookout, let him report what he sees. When he sees a chariot, horsemen in pairs, a train of donkeys and a train of camels, let him pay attention and listen closely, very closely." And the lookout called like a lion, "O Lord, I stand continually on the watchtower by day, and I am stationed every night at my guard post. **Now look! Here comes a troop of riders, horse-men in pairs.**" And one said, "Fallen, fallen is Babylon; and all the carved images of her gods are shattered on the ground."
>
> –Isaiah 21:6–9 – AMP, emphasis added

Look around you, for in this very generation God's "horsemen" are beginning to rise and to come forth in power. They are a *company* that has been transformed in the glory of God, and they are walking in the High Place of holiness and power. They are crying out, as John the Baptist did, in this wilderness of darkness and spiritual depravity, and many are beginning to hear their voices. They walk in the anointing of Elisha and Elijah, and no *mask* will silence them. No governmental law will stop them from obeying and moving in the Spirit. Can you see them? Can you hear them? This is the Lord's end-time *troop*, and they are birthing God's end-time purposes in our nation and the nations of this earth. The idols in the Church, our nation, and this world are even now beginning to fall, for the Spirit of the Lord is on the move!

> Following Your word has kept me from wrong. Your ways have molded my footsteps, keeping me from going down the paths of the violent. My steps follow in the tracks of Your chariot wheels, always staying in their path, never straying from your way.
>
> —Psalm 17:4–5 – TPT

God's "horsemen" follow and obey God's Word, and it keeps them on His straight and narrow path of obedience. As *we* embrace God's ways we are daily being transformed and renewed in our deep hearts, and we will find our steps in the tracks of His *chariot wheels*. We will follow the Lord wherever He leads us, even as the cherubim followed the Spirit wherever He went. (See Ezekiel 1:12.) Living close to Jesus will keep us right on *track*, and we will never stray from His glorious presence.

> If you have run with the footmen, and they have wearied you, then how can you contend with horses? And if in the land of peace, in which you trusted, they wearied you, then how will you do in the floodplain of the Jordan?
>
> —Jeremiah 12:5 – NKJV

During this dark time in our nation and this world, God has been narrowing our interests and drawing us close to Him. We have been in a time of intense training, and God has narrowed our path. If we cannot learn to walk with Him in these lesser trials, how will we endure the greater fires and troubles that lie before us? The Lord's whole purpose in allowing these difficulties in our lives has been to strengthen us spiritually and to prepare us for the days ahead. This is what God was telling Jeremiah in the above Scripture. Jeremiah was in a time of despondency and was disheartened because so few were listening to his warnings from the Lord and because he was seeing so many of God's children living hypocritical lives. He was probably depressed because of the persecution he was suffering day after day. (See Jeremiah 12:1–4.) God wanted to strengthen His servant, even as He desires to strengthen us, in order to be able to *contend* with "horses," those who are strong, and to be able to stand in "floods," the overwhelming circumstances that try to bring us down. Jordan represents a place of *death*,[xxxiv] death to our flesh, and a call to pick up our cross daily and follow Jesus. Without the strength of a "horse,", which represents power, confidence, courage, and endurance,[xxxv] in our *inner man,* we will never survive the "floods" that our coming to our nation and this world.

I remember a dream that I had some years back about the house that I grew up in; I believe this was a *futuristic* dream. The whole house was made of solid, beautiful stones. As I looked, attached to the house were stalls and stalls of horses. I stopped by one of the horses and was frightened because it looked fierce; but the Lord told me not to be frightened of the horse. It was a powerful horse, and I knew that it belonged to Jesus. Some were *"dark but lovely,"* and I believe Jesus was showing me that these are the ones who have allowed the Spirit to work deep in their hearts and to bring up the *darkness* within them. God does not want us to fear the *dark side* that may lie deep within our souls. Jesus showed me that these are His *war horses* that have allowed the fire of His love to cleanse and to purify them deeply. The Lord also showed me that these were His end-time remnant, His pioneers, His strong and mighty warriors who have experienced His transforming power. These are His *miracle workers* who will walk the earth with Him and do exploits in His name.

I love the movie: *Secretariat!* Many people thought that Secretariat was a *speed horse* rather than a *distance horse*.[xxxvi] The crowd was shocked when they saw this outstanding horse win the American Triple Crown, for many couldn't believe that he could run the longer distance of 1 ½ miles in the 3rd race.[xxxvi] And yet this incredible horse won the 3rd race by 31 lengths.[xxxvi] I wept when I first watched this movie, for the Lord showed me that what happened at the Triple Crown's 3rd race is exactly what is going to happen with His true Church in the final days before His second coming. Right now the Church may look weak and powerless in the light of what is happening, but suddenly, all of this will change, for the Church is now entering into her finest hour! God's end-time "horsemen" will outrun the devil in a manner that will *shock* this whole world!

Secretariat was the greatest race horse of all times. He was inducted into the "National Museum of Racing and Hall of Fame" where he will be forever honored.[xxxvi] I think of God's "horsemen" who will be forever honored in God's "Hall of Fame" and never be forgotten. (See Hebrews 11:4–38.) The veterinarian that performed the necropsy on Secretariat estimated his heart to weigh between 21-22 lbs. A normal horse's heart weighs 8.5 lbs., so Secretariat's heart was 2.5 times larger.[xxxvi] In our earthly race as we overcome many obstacles and heartaches, I believe that our hearts will also be enlarged. The Lord's desire is to *stretch* our hearts so that we can embrace this whole world. God's powerful end-time warriors will bring in a *harvest of souls* too many to number in this final hour. They will finish their race strong and receive a triple-crown of glory!

Secretariat was said to have a *perfect heart,*[xxxvi] and our God is perfecting us day by day. He is calling us to be perfect, but what does this mean? (See Matthew 5:48; Genesis 17:1; Colossians 1:28.) Even though King David was not perfect, his whole heart was committed to the Lord. He was a true worshipper and wanted to please God. Yes, he failed miserably in the case of Bathsheba and Uriah, but he turned his heart back to the Lord and repented deeply for what he did. During his lifetime David did not turn to idols but trusted the Lord with his whole heart. David followed the path that God laid out before him and fulfilled God's will for his life. He truly was a man after God's own heart. (See Acts 13:22.)

> I saw heaven standing open and there before me was a white horse, whose Rider is called Faithful and True. With justice He judges and wages war. His eyes are like blazing fire, and on His head are many crowns. He has a name written on Him that no one knows but He Himself. He is dressed in a robe dipped in blood, and His name is the Word of God. The armies of heaven were following Him, riding on white horses and dressed in fine linen, white and clean.
>
> –Revelation 19:11–14 – NIV

In the end, these powerful warriors will ride with Jesus and will bring the final judgments into the earth. They are dressed in white, even now, and are being prepared for that awesome day when they will ride with Jesus on white horses in great power. The horses they will ride on represent what is in their *transformed natures:* God's anointing, endurance, and strength. They have the Holy Spirit's power pulsating through their whole being. These warriors have been made whole: spirit, soul, and body, and they are fully equipped to accomplish the will of their beloved, Jesus. Jesus is calling His bride to come and to *ride* with Him in His Spirit. His bride has been in intense training for this very time and season, and now we will see these mighty "horsemen" rise up, take the authority that Jesus has given them, and accomplish His whole will on this earth.

The Spirit says:

> *"All is coming together quickly now. My 'rescue mission' is underway, and I am sending out My ambassadors*

who will do My whole will. I am sending My end-time servants to the ends of the earth to rescue the diseased, forlorn, and weak ones who do not know My love and mercy.

"My 'harvesters' are fully prepared. They have all the 'tools' that they need to bring in this final harvest of souls. They are equipped with the 'power tools' that they need. They have My Word, My love, My glory, and above all, My presence dwelling deep in their souls. They have remarkable stamina and stability in My Spirit, and they will not succumb to the lies of the enemy or be caught in his deceptive traps.

"My prepared ones are beginning to stir; they are beginning to move to the forefront of the Spirit's activity in this hour. They have not given in to the enemy's lies neither will they pull back, for these are My 'horses,' My end-time strong ones who are moving forward. They are 'pulling' this movement forward in the strength of My Spirit. They have been 'groomed' for 'such a time as this.' (See Esther 4:14.) Their 'shoes' have been polished and strengthened in newness so that they can continue their present journey in Me and make it to the end. They have been 'fitted' with 'new shoes,' Gospel shoes, that will take them to the ends of the earth. These 'spiritual shoes' will not wear out. The old pattern, the old ways have been removed from their lives, and they are walking in newness of Life, the new Life and power that have been provided for them in My Spirit. This new group of warriors will now 'ride' with Me into the fullness that I have prepared for them. These strong 'horses' are My end-time prophets, My end-time 'harvesters' who will move with Me and will carry My presence to this generation. These are the ones who will pull My 'Chariot of Glory' and will release millions of souls.

> *I have called them; I will sustain them, and they will now run with Me in fearless zeal to complete the work that I have called them to accomplish.*
>
> *"Hear the sound of their 'hooves,' their feet shaking the ground and removing the works of the evil one. There is a thunderous sound that will not be silenced, for all will hear it, and millions will be released in this final hour—says your God!"*

The Jehu Company – The Zeal of God

One of the greatest "horsemen" that ever lived was *Jehu*. He walked in the power and strength of God to accomplish what the Lord had spoken years earlier. Elisha had one of the prophets take a flask of oil and anoint Jehu to be the king over Israel. God anointed him to be not only a king but one who would fulfill God's will in bringing His judgment to the house of Ahab.

> Meanwhile, Elisha the prophet had summoned a member of the group of prophets. "Get ready to travel," he told him, "and take this flask of olive oil with you. Go to Ramoth-gilead, and find Jehu son of Jehoshaphat, son of Nimshi. Call him into a private room away from his friends, and pour the oil over his head. Say to him, 'This is what the LORD says: I anoint you to be the king over Israel.' Then open the door and run for your life!"
>
> –2 Kings 9:1–3 – NLT

"**Jehu** was the tenth king of the northern Kingdom of Israel since Jeroboam I, noted for exterminating the house of Ahab. He was the son of Jehoshaphat, grandson of Nimshi, and possibly great-grandson of Omri...His reign lasted for 28 years."[xxxvii]

> "'Behold, I will bring calamity on you. I will take away your posterity, and will cut off from Ahab every male in Israel, both bond and free. I will make your house like the house of Jeroboam the son of Nebat, and like the house of Baasha the son of Ahijah, because of the provocation with which you have provoked Me to anger, and made Israel sin.' And concerning Jezebel the LORD also spoke, saying, 'The dogs shall eat Jezebel by the wall of Jezreel.' The dogs shall eat whoever belongs to Ahab and dies in the city, and the birds of the air shall eat whoever dies in the field."
>
> –1 Kings 21:21–24 – NKJV

Elijah spoke this word from the Lord in 1 Kings to King Ahab. I want to point out here that what God spoke to Elijah came to pass *years* later. God works in the same way today, for many prophetic words do not come to pass instantaneously. Many accuse true prophets of speaking false words when in reality they are true words from Heaven. I'm sure when others heard of this prophecy from Elijah concerning the house of Ahab many believed it would never happen. Years passed, and many, I believe, came against this man of God and mocked him.

Like those who mocked Elijah and Elisha so long ago, true prophets of the Lord are attacked and persecuted for speaking what they know they have heard from the Spirit. The 50 men from the *"company of the prophets"* knew what was going to happen to Elijah, for they told Elisha that his master was going to be taken away from him. (See 2 Kings 2:3.) Yet they *stood at a distance* watching Elijah and Elisha by the Jordan. (See 2 Kings 2:7.) Note here that they stood at a distance; they were *watching* to see what would happen, to see if what was spoken to them would truly come to pass. Many in this hour are just watching to see what will happen in our government and our nation. They do *not* truly believe that what the Lord has spoken concerning our nation will come to pass: God's judgment against evil and the 3rd Great Awakening.

Even after Elijah was taken up into Heaven, the *company of prophets* still wanted to go and search for him. Elisha told them not to, but they persisted until Elisha gave in to them. (See 2 Kings 2:15–18.) Because of unbelief, they wanted to search for Elijah; they did not believe the word of the Lord that was spoken to them.

This has been a time of great testing for the prophets, for God's "horsemen," but there are some who have stood firm in their prophetic decrees over our government and our nation. This, I believe, has been a time of separation between those who believe God's word and those who are filled with unbelief. Those who have stood firm in Truth will be placed in God's end-time Gideon army, and great will be their reward from Jesus for standing firm in the midst of this present darkness.

> Then Jehu got into a chariot and rode to Jezreel to find King Joram, who was lying there wounded. King Ahaziah of Judah was there, too, for he had gone to visit him. The watchman on the tower of Jezreel saw Jehu and his company approaching, so he shouted to Joram, **"I see a company of troops coming!"** "Send out a rider to ask if they are coming in peace," King Joram ordered. So a horseman went out to meet Jehu and said, "The king wants to know if you are coming in peace." **Jehu replied, "What do you know about peace?** Fall in behind me!" The watchman called out to the king, "The messenger has met them, but he's not returning."
>
> –2 Kings 9:16–18 – NLT, emphasis added

King Joram was the son of Ahab and Jezebel, and God was about to release His judgment upon the house of Ahab through Jehu. Jehu was fired up as he entered into his chariot which, I believe, was God's *chariot*. I believe that the angels of God rode with him and anointed him with the zeal of God. They saw *"a company of troops coming,"* and I know that in this very hour the Lord's end-time horsemen are riding forth in a *chariot of fire* to do the will of the Father. Jehu was not a man of words but one who was a *doer* of Gods' will. True *pioneers* have few words to say to *compromised* souls, for they are filled with the *zeal of the Lord*. They are not out to *reason* with the enemy or with anyone who would try to stop them from doing the full will of the Father.

> The watchman exclaimed, "The messenger has met them, but he isn't returning either! It must be Jehu son of Nimshi, for **he's driving like a madman.**" "Quick! Get my chariot ready!" King Joram commanded. Then King Joram of Israel and King Ahaziah of Judah rode out in their chariots to meet Jehu. They met him at **the plot of land that had belonged to Naboth of Jezreel.** King Joram demanded, "Do you come in peace, Jehu?" Jehu replied, "How can there be peace as long as the **idolatry and witchcraft of your mother, Jezebel, are all around us?**" Then King Joram turned the horses around and fled, shouting to King Ahaziah, "Treason, Ahaziah!" But Jehu drew his bow and shot Joram between the shoulders. **The arrow pierced his heart, and he sank down dead in his chariot.** Jehu said to Bidkar, his officer, "Throw him into the plot of land that belonged to Naboth of Jezreel. Do you remember when you and I were riding along behind his father, Ahab? The LORD pronounced this message against him: **'I solemnly swear that I will repay him here on this plot of land, says the LORD, for the murder of Naboth and his sons that I saw yesterday.' So throw him out on Naboth's property, just as the LORD said."**
>
> —2 Kings 9:20–26, emphasis added

God never forgets to "repay" the enemy for what he has stolen from us. It may take years and years, but our God is a *God of vengeance* who has seen all that the enemy of our soul has put us through. The Lord has *"worked together for good"* all of our pain and heartaches in order to transform us and to draw us close to His heart. (See Romans 8:28.) These are days of restoration, and we will *"crush the enemy under our feet"* in this very hour. The Lord's Jehu's will drive God's chariot like "madmen" and will not stop until the whole of God's will is accomplished on this earth. Some will not understand the passion and the zeal in the hearts of these fierce warriors. At times they may sound and look like *wild* men and women in the Spirit, but it will be the zeal and the passion of the Lord flowing through their lives. The devil's heart is about to be *pierced* as the fiery sword, the Truth of God's Word, pours through these uncompromising servants of God! The works of the enemy will be crushed, and the gates of Hell will come crashing down as God's Jehu's ride forth in a "breaker anointing," a power that this world has never seen! All of the promises that God has given us, even decades ago, will now come to pass speedily. Now we will see and experience the zeal and the passion of the Lord as we never have before!

> And the one who was in charge of the household, and the one who was in charge of the city, and the elders, and the guardians of the children, sent word to Jehu, saying, "We are your servants, and everything that you tell us we will do. We will not appoint any man king; do what is good in your sight."
>
> –2 Kings 10:5 – NASB

This powerful "troop" will have the respect of many, for all will see that they walk under an open Heaven and have an extraordinary anointing from the Spirit. People will be amazed at their teaching, for they will know they are teaching and preaching in the authority of Christ. (See Mark 1:22.) All will see that they have been with Jesus and that they are *not* ordinary men and women. (See Acts 4:13.) Many people will follow in their footsteps, for they will see that the love and grace of God rests upon them in a glorious way. Millions will follow them as they follow in Christ's footsteps. Leaders and kings will come to them for a word from the Lord, and they will listen to their godly counsel and direction. These powerful men and women of God have heard the sound of the trumpet, and they are ready to face any "giant" that would confront them. They have the "roar" of the Lion of Judah in them, the war cry of victory! The Scriptures below, from the Book of Job, describe these end-time *war horses* better than I could ever express.

> Do you give the horse his might? Do you clothe his neck with a mane? Do you make him leap like locusts? His majestic snorting is frightening. He paws in the valley, and rejoices in his strength; he goes out to meet the battle. He laughs at fear and is not dismayed; and he does not turn back from the sword. The quiver rattles against him, the flashing spear and javelin. He races over the ground with a roar and fury, and he does not stand still when he hears the sound of the trumpet. As often as the trumpet sounds he says, "Aha!" and he senses the battle from afar, and the thunder of the captains and the war cry.
>
> —Job 39:19–25

> "Know then that nothing of the word of the Lord, which the Lord spoke concerning the house of Ahab, shall fall to the earth, for the Lord has done what He spoke through His servant Elijah." So Jehu killed all who remained of the house of Ahab in Jezreel,

and all his great men, his acquaintances, and his priests, until he left him without a survivor.

–2 Kings 10:10–11

Not one Word of the Lord will fall to the ground, and I believe with all of my heart that what the Lord has spoken concerning our nation and this 3rd Great Awakening will surely come to pass. These *awakened* and *transformed reformers* will change the *climate* of this world as millions of souls run for shelter into the arms of Jesus. These Jehu's will not be violent against people but against the forces of hell that have kept millions of souls in bondage, for they know who their true enemy is! I believe that what Jesus desires to accomplish in this generation will be accomplished through His faithful children. They will "birth" His end-time purposes, and the glory of God will be released in a measure that this world has never seen.

> Then Jehu sent word throughout Israel, and all the worshipers of Baal came, so that there was not a person left who did not come. And when they entered the house of Baal, the house of Baal was filled from one end to the other…Then it came about, as soon as he had finished offering the burnt offering, that Jehu said to the guard and to the royal officers, "Go in, kill them; let none come out." So they killed them with the edge of the sword; and the guard and the royal officers threw them out, and went to the sanctuary of the house of Baal. They brought out the memorial stones of the house of Baal and burned them. They also tore down the memorial stone of Baal and tore down the house of Baal, and made it a latrine as it is to this day. So Jehu eradicated Baal from Israel.
>
> –2 Kings 10:21, 25–28

There are millions that are caught in the *web of idolatry* in our nation and this world. God is exposing and uncovering much in our nation, and these roots of evil have spread into the entire earth. In spite of what we see and hear, these demonic empires are now coming down, and all will see how our God deals with the evil designs of the devil. This has been a time of separating the wheat from the chaff, the light from the darkness, and the righteous from the unrighteous. Not one soul will escape the penetrating Light of the Spirit in this hour; every soul will be *examined*. Demonic a*ltars of compromise* will now be exposed in the hearts of God's people, and they will be torn down as we enter God's final showdown!

God's Final Showdown – The Fall of Jezebel

We have entered into a new decade, a new era, and we will now see the downfall of the *spirit of Jezebel*. This spirit of *perversion* and *compromise* is about to be exposed, and millions will see just how evil this demonic entity is. This Jezebel spirit is sly and works *undercover* thinking that no one will find her out. She dresses herself up like a true prophet of God, but underneath her *makeup* she is a devious and murderous demonic power.

As Elijah *confronted* the prophets of Baal and Asherah so is there a *final showdown* between *God's Truth* and the *lies of the enemy*. All the lying and deceiving *"prophets of Baal and Asherah"* will now be exposed in our nation, this world, and also in the Church worldwide. God's Jehu's are about to *demolish* this spirit under their "horses' hooves" as Gods' Spirit moves through them, Truth is spoken, and the deceit of the enemy is uncovered fully.

> When Jezebel, the queen mother, heard that Jehu had come to Jezreel, she painted her eyelids and fixed her hair and sat at a window. When Jehu entered the gate of the palace, she shouted at him,

"Have you come in peace, you murderer? You're just like Zimri, who murdered his master!"

–2 Kings 9:30–31 – NLT

The Jezebel spirit is one who *covers up* and sits at a "window" and prophesies. A window represents the prophetic, illumination, an opening, a portal, and an opening into the spirit-realm.[xxxviii] Jezebel represents all that is false and dark; she lives in the realm of lies and deceit. She disguises herself to be a *woman of peace and beauty,* but underneath she walks in perversion and a *compromising spirit of destruction* who allures her victims into a bed of fleshy pleasure and demonic compromise. This evil power comes against the true prophets with lies and will attack them mercilessly. This demon will lie and bring many false accusations against God's true prophets. It will whisper into the hearts of pastors and leaders and tell them that the true prophets are speaking lies and are nothing but trouble makers. She is confrontational and will try to intimidate the true servants of the Lord.

> Now Ahab told Jezebel everything that Elijah had done, and how he had killed all the prophets with the sword. Then Jezebel sent a messenger to Elijah, saying, "So may the gods do to me and more so, if by about this time tomorrow I do not make your life like the life of one of them." And he was afraid, and got up and ran for his life and came to Beersheba, which belongs to Judah; and he left his servant there.
>
> –1 Kings 19:1–3 – NASB

After Elijah experienced a glorious victory against the false prophets of Baal and Asherah and the fire from Heaven fell, Jezebel confronted Elijah and threatened to kill him. This mighty prophet of God was attacked by a *spirit of fear* and ran for his life. Elijah had just come down from the High Place of victory, and what came against him was an all-out attack from Jezebel to destroy his life. Many cannot understand how this mighty prophet of God could have feared this *woman,* but they do not understand the intensity of the attack that he was under. God was with His servant and restored him after his *ordeal* with Jezebel and gave him further instructions for his life. He overcame this demonic attack from the enemy, and so will every one of God's true prophets.

This *dark spirit* hates the true prophets of the Lord and will do anything to destroy their reputations, even threatening to kill them. This spirit of intimidation is still very active in this hour, but God's true prophets have nothing to fear, for the Lord is their Shelter. The Jezebel spirit will bring a very strong *spirit of fear* against God's true prophets, but as they allow the Holy Spirit to flood them, the perfect love of God will cast out all of their fear. (See 1 John 4:18.)

This spirit is so seductive, so sensual and pleasing to the flesh, that many have fallen prey to her alluring power, even in the Church. Many leaders and pastors have been caught in her *web of destruction,* but praise God, some of these leaders have truly repented. The Spirit has been convicting many souls concerning this *spirit of perversion,* but if they refuse to repent, they will now suffer great distress of soul, and some may even perish in their sin. Our God is holy, and His great *Light* is about to expose fully this demonic power that has destroyed countless souls.

> But I have this against you: you are forgiving that woman Jezebel, who calls herself a prophetess and is seducing my loving servants. **She is teaching that it is permissible to indulge in sexual immorality and to eat food sacrificed to idols.** I have waited for her to repent from her vile immorality, but she willingly refuses to do so. Now I will lay her low with terrible distress along with all her adulterous partners if they do not repent. And I will strike down

her followers with a deadly plague. Then all the congregations will realize that I am the one who thoroughly searches the most secret thought and the innermost being. I will give to each one what their works deserve.

–Revelation 2:20–23 – TPT, emphasis added

But I have a few things against you, because you have some there who hold the teaching of Balaam, who kept teaching Balak to put a stumbling block before the sons of Israel, **to eat things sacrificed to idols and to commit sexual immorality.**

–Revelation 2:14 – NASB, emphasis added

The Jezebel spirit lures her victims into her *web* through *adultery, pornography, and fornication,* and these demonic forces are rampant in the Church. This is the season when God is *thoroughly* searching the deep hearts and minds of His people, for the Lord sees all that is being done *under cover.* Everything that is hidden in darkness will now be uncovered by His glorious Light.

God has dealt with false prophet's time and time again, but many of them have refused to repent. Not only will these false prophets be dealt with in this hour but all who have listened to them and have embraced their deception will now come under swift judgment. The Lord will give to each one what they deserve; it is a fearful thing to fall into the hands of the living God. (See Hebrews 10:31.)

There have been some who have sneaked in among you unnoticed. They are depraved people whose judgment was prophesied in Scripture a long time ago. They have perverted the message of God's grace into a license to commit immorality and turn against our only absolute Master, our Lord Jesus Christ.

–Jude 1:4 – TPT

Millions pride themselves that they are faithful spouses and have overcome lust in their lives, but few realize that they are *"eating the food sacrificed to idols."* So many people in the Church do not understand what this means, and they can't see that they are committing *spiritual adultery* before the Lord. These Scriptures below show us what *spiritual adultery* is in His sight.

> You adulteresses [disloyal sinners—flirting with the world and breaking your vow to God]! Do you not know that being the world's friend [that is, loving the things of the world] is being God's enemy? So whoever chooses to be a friend of the world makes himself an enemy of God.
>
> –James 4:4 – AMP

Millions are eating *"food sacrificed to idols,"* but what is this *food?* God's Word tells us that those who are *"flirting with the world"* and being the *"world's friend"* is likened to adultery in the sight of God. If we love the things of this world (idolatry), the Word tells us that we are God's enemy. You may think or say: **"Not me! I love God; I go to church and read my Bible. I do good works, and I'm trying hard to change my life."** This may look well and good to all those around you. Many may believe that you are living a life that is pleasing to God, but hear what the Lord requires:

> For if you offered him thousands of rams and ten thousands of rivers of olive oil—would that please Him? Would He be satisfied? If you sacrificed your oldest child, would that make Him glad? Then would He forgive your sins? Of course not! No, He has told

you what He wants, and this is all it is: to be fair, just, merciful, and to walk humbly with your God.

–Micah 6:7–8 – TLB

God is looking for *internal change* in our hearts; He is looking for *obedient* hearts. The Spirit desires to bring internal transformation deep in our hearts so that we can be fair, just, and merciful. Jesus wants us to walk humbly with Him and to feel our desperate need for Him. Our Father wants us to cling to Him and not to the idols of this world. So many people cling to sex, money, sports, and the pleasures and ungodly entertainments of this world; they "eat" these idols and satisfy their souls with them instead of with the presence of God and doing His will. Some of these idols look innocent enough, but this is how the *spirit of compromise* enters the hearts of Jezebels *victims*. She doesn't care if people go to church and accomplish good works; she doesn't even care if they read the Bible, for as long as she can keep them "eating" the idols of the world, she knows that she has them captive. Jesus wants to live His Life *through* us, and this can only come as we are *crucified with Him*. We cannot *fix* ourselves in our own strength; only through total surrender to His will and a deep, internal, transforming work in our hearts will we be made whole.

> You cannot drink from the cup of the Lord and from the cup of demons, too. You cannot eat at the Lord's Table and at the table of demons, too.
>
> –1 Corinthians 10:21 – NLT

> Do not love the world or the things in the world. If anyone loves the world, the love of the Father is not in him. For everything in the world—the lust of the flesh, the lust of the eyes, and the pride in one's possessions—is not from the Father, but is

from the world. And the world with its lust is passing away, but the one who does the will of God remains forever.

—1 John 2:15–17 – CSB

We are called to love others and to be Christ's witnesses on this earth. Those who *eat* demonic *idols of lust* and covet *things* more than souls are caught in Jezebel's *trap,* whether they realize it or not. They are walking in false peace and are *willfully ignorant* of what God requires of them. Only as we do the Father's will can we be freed from the entanglements of this world. If we live for ourselves and our own pleasures, to please ourselves and not God, we will forever walk in deception and compromise.

Now these things took place as examples for us, so that we will not desire evil things as they did. Don't become idolaters as some of them were; as it is written, **The people sat down to eat and drink, and got up to party.**

—1 Corinthians 10:6–7

Therefore, put to death what belongs to your earthly nature: sexual immorality, impurity, lust, evil desire, and greed, which is idolatry.

—Colossians 3:5

God is calling the Church to repentance concerning compromise and idolatry as well as adultery and fornication. We are the ones who are to put these things to death in our lives through the power of the Holy Spirit. In our own power we can't, but we can do *all things through Christ* who strengthens us. (See Philippians 4:13.)

Little children, guard yourselves from idols.

—1 John 5:21

As *guardians of the ark* we are called to guard our hearts from idols and the evil influence of Jezebel. The Holy Spirit will give us all the grace that we need to stand firm against the Jezebel spirit that desires to not only bind our lives but destroy us.

> Jehu looked up and saw her at the window and shouted, "Who is on my side?" And two or three eunuchs looked out at him. "Throw her down!" Jehu yelled. So they threw her out the window, and her blood spattered against the wall and on the horses. And Jehu trampled her body under his horses' hooves.
>
> —2 Kings 9:32–33 – NLT

I had a dream years ago about a man who was in a bedroom, and in this room there were many demonic faces on the walls. This man was in bed with a woman that was *hideous* looking! As he turned away from the woman and looked at me, he said with a smile: *"It is worth it!"* The Lord showed me that this was a Jezebel spirit that had seduced him.

The *walls* in my dream represented the *walls of deception* that have been built up in the hearts of God's children through years of *compromise*. Jezebel hides *behind* these walls, but when we are determined to be free from her control, we will allow the Holy Spirit to tear down these *walls* and to *expose* her lies in our lives. As we uncover our deep heart before the Lord in Truth, the Spirit of God will free us completely from her control, and we will no longer live *compromised* lives. We will see Jezebel's *blood* spattered as the *walls* in the hearts and lives of millions of God's children are torn down. She will be trampled under the *"horses' hooves,"* the Lord's Jehu's, in this very hour.

This demonic power strips souls of their dignity and their identity in Christ. Never have we seen such a confused and perverse generation that has been trapped and deceived into believing her lies. Millions do not even know if they are male or female in this hour so great is this demonic influence in *blinded* souls. Jezebel has *castrated* millions of souls, and this has kept them spiritually barren and fruitless. Countless souls have been bound with chains and have become *spiritual eunuchs* under her demonic control. Only in the power of the Spirit will these souls be released and come to know their true identity in Christ.

> Then Jehu went into the palace and ate and drank. Afterward he said, "Someone go and bury this cursed woman, for she is the daughter of a king." But when they went out to bury her, they found only her skull, her feet, and her hands.
>
> –2 Kings 9:34–35

Here we see that her greatest influence has been in the *minds* of countless souls. Her *deceptive lies* have been listened to and embraced by millions. This *mind control* of Jezebel has been effective and has controlled the actions and works of millions on this planet. Jezebel's demonic influence has been greater than most have realized because of the subtlety of her ways. She has worked through *religious spirits* and the *natural reasoning* of man, and these spirits are rampant in the Church. Because of these religious spirit's and man-made doctrines, the Spirit's power has been kept at bay in millions of churches across the earth, but praise God, this is about to change dramatically and suddenly. Our Father in Heaven has a plan that will awaken deadened hearts and release controlled minds, and all will know that it is not by might or by man's power that this is accomplished but by the power of the Holy Spirit! (See Zechariah 4:6.)

> When they returned and told Jehu, he stated, **"This fulfills the message from the LORD,** which He spoke through His servant Elijah from Tishbe: 'At the plot of land in Jezreel, dogs will eat Jezebel's body. Her

remains will be scattered like dung on the plot of land in Jezreel, so that no one will be able to recognize her.'"

–2 Kings 9:36–37, emphasis added

I believe with my whole heart that this is the season of fulfillment; the season when we will see the influence of Jezebel in the Church and in this world come down. When God's mighty hand of judgment is released against this demonic power, we will see and experience a freedom in the Spirit to preach and to teach God's Word to a people who will not only *hear* the Truth but will be able to *receive* the deliverance that they have longed for. Divine healings and incredible demonic deliverances will break forth as loud cries are heard, not only in the Church but in stadiums and buildings across our nation and this world. This demonic power that has held so many people captive is now *coming down,* and the freedom and liberty of the Spirit will be released in a measure we have never seen before. What a glorious day we live in, for we are the generation that will see the fulfillment of all that God has promised us! We will, at last, see this final harvest of souls come into the Kingdom and will rejoice as we see the *whole earth filled with the knowledge of the glory of God!* (See Habakkuk 2:14.)

King Jesus says:

> *"I am coming with a 'flaming sword' to bring My judgment and My glory to My people. Much is about to be revealed, and your nation will be stunned. The enemy can no longer withhold Truth, for the time of 'unveiling' has come.*
>
> *"My 'flaming sword' will bring vengeance against your enemies, My people, and the last cord of bondage that has held you captive is now being 'snapped.' In this freedom you will be released to do and to say all that I have placed in your heart and mind. Now you*

will see and know My plans more fully, for your life, for this nation, and for the world.

"There are 'spiritual connections' that are now coming together very quickly. I am organizing My 'teams' that will go forth together in oneness and unity. There will be no division in these groups, for they are My end-time 'troops,' My 'horsemen,' that I have called to take this land and these nations for Me. The teams will pull great 'loads' for Me in the Spirit: My power, gifts, and glory. They will pull My 'chariot' along with My angels and bring great deliverance to many souls in this generation. They will be able to 'handle' the devils that come against them, that try to stop them, and with one word, one swift movement of their hand, the 'webs of deceit' and the lies of the enemy will be removed, for they (the enemy) will be as nothing in their sight.

"These strong leaders walk in My presence and will experience the zeal of My heart for this world, for the lost and the dying. The 'spirit of Jezebel' will now be removed: her influence and control over countless millions of souls will be broken. My Jehu's will bring her down, and she will now fall to the ground, for My 'horsemen' will crush her. She will no longer hide behind a 'wall of deception and deceit,' but she will show herself as she truly is: an evil, wicked, deplorable, and disgusting entity that has controlled not only this world but the Church for too long. Watch her fall now as she is exposed in the eyes of millions.

"What a day for you to live in. What a great and glorious day that you have entered into. Rejoice, children, for I am on My way, and now you will see what I will do—says your God!"

CONCLUSION

There's nothing greater than the Spirit's transforming power in our lives! As we daily embrace our cross and follow Jesus all the way into the power of His resurrection, we will stand in awe and be amazed at what Jesus will accomplish *in* and *through* us in this generation that so desperately needs Jesus.

When all of the havoc was coming forth after the 2020 election, I prayed and asked the Lord about what was happening because we were confident that God was going to move powerfully in the election and that we would see a different outcome. But God's ways are not our ways. Jesus has something greater in store for us, for this nation, and for the world than we could ever dream or imagine. As I prayed and sought the Lord concerning all the darkness and the chaos we were seeing, the Spirit gave me the following Scripture in 1 Corinthians. This Word from the Lord came alive in my heart and encouraged me greatly. It was a *now* word for me, and it brought me great peace. I no longer struggle, wondering what is happening in the earth, for I know that God is in full control, and in His perfect timing He will work in ways that will astound us!

> So resist the temptation to pronounce premature judgment on anything before the appointed time when all will be fully revealed. Instead, wait until the Lord makes His appearance, for He will bring all that is hidden in darkness to light and unveil every secret motive of everyone's heart. Then, when

the whole truth is known, each will receive praise from God.

–1 Corinthians 4:5 – TPT

Another Scripture that I have been reading and clinging to is from Psalm 103:19 (NKJV) which states: *"The LORD has established His throne in heaven, and His kingdom rules over all."* When we not only read this Scripture but truly believe it, nothing can disturb our faith or cause us to tremble in this hour. God is over ALL, and nothing can, or will, stop what the Spirit is accomplishing in this very hour.

As I pondered on how to conclude this book, these Scriptures came to mind, and I feel that they convey the heart of Jesus beautifully to His end-time pioneers and warriors, His transformed ones.

> Then the angel said to her, "Do not be afraid, Mary, for you have found favor with God. And behold, you will **conceive in your womb and bring forth a Son, and shall call His name JESUS.** He will be great, and will be called the Son of the Highest; and the Lord God will give Him the throne of His father David. And He will reign over the house of Jacob forever, and of His kingdom there will be no end." Then Mary said to the angel, "How can this be, since I do not know a man?" And the angel answered and said to her, **"The Holy Spirit will come upon you, and the power of the Highest will overshadow you; therefore, also, that Holy One who is to be born will be called the Son of God.** Now indeed, Elizabeth your relative has also conceived a son in her old age; and this is now the sixth month for her who was called barren. **For with God nothing will be impossible."** Then Mary said, "Behold the maidservant of the Lord! **Let it be to me according to**

your word." And the angel departed from her...Then she (Elizabeth) spoke out with a loud voice and said, **"Blessed are you among women, and blessed is the fruit of your womb!** But why is this granted to me, that the mother of my Lord should come to me? For indeed, as soon as the voice of your greeting sounded in my ears, the babe leaped in my womb for joy. **Blessed is she who believed, for there will be a fulfillment of those things which were told her from the Lord."** And Mary said: "My soul magnifies the Lord, and my spirit has rejoiced in God my Savior. For He has regarded the lowly state of His maidservant; for behold, henceforth all generations will call me blessed. For **He who is mighty has done great things for me, and holy is His name."**

–Luke 1:30–38, 42–49, emphasis added

We are the generation that has found favor with God, and we are bringing forth God's Son to a generation that desperately needs Him. The Holy Spirit has come and "overshadowed" us and planted His "seed," His Word, deep into our spiritual womb. God has a remnant that has believed and received His "implanted" Word, and what is coming forth from our lives will be the very Life and essence of our King Jesus. (See James 1:21.) Nothing is impossible with God, and even as Mary was favored to bring forth Jesus from her natural womb so are God's chosen ones "birthing" His Son, and they will fulfill His end-time purposes in the earth.

For those who have said with Mary: *"Behold the maidservant of the Lord!* ***Let it be to me according to your word,"*** you will now be empowered to walk in the High Place of miracles, signs, and wonders beyond what you have dared to dream! Those who have allowed the Spirit to transform them into the image of His Son, these very ones will now be empowered to bring down forces of evil in this nation and even the world. You are blessed because *you have believed that there would be a fulfillment of what God has spoken to you,* even if the promise came decades ago. Know that God has regarded your lowly estate, and all will now call you blessed! The Spirit has done a mighty work in you, and now He will do exploits through you. Blessed is the "fruit" of your spiritual womb! You have yet to see the full glory and power that the Lord desires to release through your life!

> Now it will come to pass that in the last days the mountain of the house of the Lord will be [firmly] established as the highest of the mountains, and will be exalted above the hills; and all the nations will stream to it.
>
> —Isaiah 2:2 – AMP

God is firmly establishing His people on His Holy Mountain, and they will never be removed or shaken by Hell again! The Lord is lifting His true children up to the highest mountain peak of glory in this hour, and many souls will come to them and ask: *"What must I do to be saved?"* This is harvest time, and the nations will come to Jesus, the Lord of all! We will be "beacons of light" to the lost and dying. I pray you will be filled with the fullness of His presence in this very hour.

> But we have this treasure in earthen vessels, that the excellence of the power may be of God and not of us. We are hard-pressed on every side, yet not crushed; we are perplexed, but not in despair; persecuted, but not forsaken; struck down, but not destroyed—always carrying about in the body the dying of the Lord Jesus, that the life of Jesus also may be manifested in our body. For we who live are always delivered to death for Jesus' sake, that the life of Jesus also may be manifested in our mortal flesh.
>
> —2 Corinthians 4:7–11 – NKJV

What a treasure we have in these earthen vessels! All of the glory and the power that will be released from our lives will be from the Spirit alone! As we experience the transforming power of the Spirit in our lives, His life will be manifested in our mortal flesh even in the hardest situations. As we carry about in our bodies the dying of the Lord Jesus, His life will be manifested in and through us. It is the power of the cross and His resurrection that we will experience as we walk in full abandonment to our God in this very generation. I pray that as we are hidden in His cross all the glory, honor, and praise will go to Him and Him alone for what *He* will accomplish in this hour!

As I bring this book to its conclusion, I wanted to add a powerful revelation that the Lord recently gave me. During a time of fasting and after an anointed time of prayer, the prophetic word below came forth from the Holy Spirit. As I wrote God reminded me of a prophecy that William Seymour released over 100 years ago. He was the one that God used to "birth" the Azusa Street revival. He prophesied that what was coming in about 100 years would be greater and more far-reaching than what they experienced during the Azusa Street revival and that the Shekinah glory of God would be greater in this last great outpouring![xxxix] I encourage you to read about the glorious power and miracles that came forth at that time. I believe the revelation that William Seymour, and others, released so long ago is for this very generation. Other prophets have been given dreams and have spoken about the year 2022 recently, and they believe that the year 2022 will be the beginning of a Great Awakening, even the 3rd Great Awakening!

Some believed that this 3rd Great Awakening would come forth in the year 2006 or 2009, but the Lord had me look up the date when William Seymour graduated into glory, and it was: SEPTEMBER 28, 1922! I shouted out loud because soon we will enter into the year 2022. God gave me several confirmations confirming that the year 2022 is going to be glorious: The word from the Lord below was the 222 prophecy saved in my computer, the #22 also lines up with Isaiah 22:22 concerning the authority Jesus has given His true Church in receiving the "key of David," and, of course, the year 2022 and the 100-year prophecy from William Seymour. I am thrilled that God is having this book released in 2022, for I believe it is prophetically showing that God's people will experience a greater fullness and transformation in the days ahead. I believe this 2022 book is for "such a time as this!" This is the time for the "manifestation of the sons of God!" (See Romans 8:19.)

All who have truly given their lives to Jesus have been given "the Keys of the Kingdom," His authority, but I believe in this new, glorious season there will be a far greater release of power and authority from on High...far greater than what any other generation has experienced in the past. Those who have been prepared and transformed for this spectacular season will be robed, filled, and anointed with a double portion of power and authority from the Lord. They will be the ones who will walk in the High place with Jesus, transformed in His glory and walking in miracles, signs, and wonders.

> So Samuel grew, and the LORD was with him and let none of his words fall to the ground.
>
> −1 Samuel 3:19

The Lord also showed me that what these true prophets of old spoke of, these very promises, will now come to pass. Not one of the words they have prophesied in the Spirit will fall to the ground. God holds the time and the season for these prophetic utterances to come forth, and I believe they are coming forth soon!

Sister Woodworth Etter, who God used to release a powerful revival in Chicago during this same time period, also prophesied that what would come forth in 100 years will far exceed what they experienced, and that we, our generation, would see an untold number of souls come into the Kingdom![xxxix] Those who have "ears to hear" have been hearing these very things in this hour. I believe the former and the latter rain together has been saved for this generation!

> Be glad then, you children of Zion, and rejoice in the Lord your God; for He has given you the former rain faithfully, and He will cause the rain to come down for you—the former rain, and the latter rain in the first month.
>
> –Joel 2:23

> Tell them therefore, "Thus says the Lord God: 'I will lay this proverb to rest, and they shall no more use it as a proverb in Israel.'" But say to them, **"The days are at hand, and the fulfillment of every vision."**
>
> –Ezekiel 12:23, emphasis added

> Therefore say to them, "Thus says the Lord God: **'None of My words will be postponed any more, but the word which I speak will be done,'** says the Lord God."
>
> –Ezekiel 12:28, emphasis added

> Then the Lord said to me, **"You have seen well, for I am ready to perform My word."**
>
> –Jeremiah 1:12, emphasis added

I believe that we are in this very time and season and that God is ready to perform His Word. I believe the time of delay has ended and that His promises to us, our nation, and this world will no longer be postponed. Get ready, saints of God, for now we will see the fulfillment of every vision that the Lord has given us!

I pray that this prophetic word will bless you and encourage you to move into the next glory that God has prepared for your life! To God be the glory!

Hear what the Lord would say:

> *"I am coming soon. Get ready to move with Me, for there will be no more delay. What I have promised to your forefathers is now coming to pass. Not one word, not one prophecy, has fallen to the ground, for now you will see the fulfillment of what has been prophesied for this very generation. (See 1 Samuel 3:19.) Trust Me and know that you have not stood in faith in vain.*
>
> *"It was prophesied, even 100 years ago, that this 3rd Great Awakening would come forth, and now it is time! (Prophesied by William Seymour – Azusa Street Revival, and others.[xxxix]) This is a Rhema season, a NOW time, for My promises and this 3rd Great Awakening to come forth.*
>
> *"The 'wretched' ones, those who have grieved and been bound by evil forces, will now be released. Those in the 'catacombs' of fear and unbelief will now come forth in resurrection power. Those who have known demonic control and bondage will now look up into My face, and their chains will fall off!*
>
> *"I have kept a people hidden in 'caves,' prophets in hiding who will now come forth in great power to shatter the plans of the enemy. They have been in the 'dark' for years and have 'feasted' on Me, My presence, and My love and are now filled to overflowing. There will be a great unveiling of these prophets, these 'John the Baptists' who will preach and teach concerning My soon coming. They will prepare the way quickly, and miracles, signs, healings, and deliverances will follow their preaching. These prophets are not quiet and*

unassuming but will preach and speak prophetically in great power and authority. You have not seen them yet, but they are here NOW! These prophets and apostles will shake the whole earth with My Word and power. You have never seen, and neither have you heard, of the things that will now come forth. Miracles without number, signs in the heavens and the earth, and healings that no one could ever dream of will come forth quickly now! (See 1 Corinthians 2:9.)

"*I have kept these 'things' hidden from the fearful, disobedient, and rebellious ones. Those living in compromise and idolatry do not believe that I am going to move in unprecedented ways. Their eyes have grown dim, and their ears have closed to Truth, but I have a people, a believing remnant, that is about to 'explode' on the scene. They will not come forth quietly but with a loud 'trumpet' sound that will awaken a 'sleeping' Church...a Church that has grown 'dull' because of demonic control, religious tradition, and the fear of man.*

"*Now you will see explosive moves of My Spirit that will not stop until I come. Continual revivals and glory will be released in the coming years until the last of these souls come into My Kingdom. Every soul that cries out to Me and is destined for glory will now come home to Me from the North, South, East, and West, and not one of them will be lost—says your God!*"

BIBLIOGRAPHY

i. "6310. peh." *BibleHub.com*, Bible Hub, https://Biblehub.com/hebrew/6310.htm. Accessed 9 September 2021.

ii "Transform."*Merriam-Webster.com Dictionary,* Merriam-Webster, https://www.merriam-webster.com/dictionary/transform. Accessed 22 April 2021.

iii. "Victims of Sexual Violence: Statistics." *Rainn.org*, National Sexual Assault Hotline, https://www.rainn.org/statistics/victims-sexual-violence. Accessed 22 April 2021.

iv. "Mountaineering." *Wikipedia.org,* Wikipedia, https://en.wikipedia.org/w/index.php?title=Mountaineerng&oldid=1017239041. Accessed 22 April 2021.

v. "Numbers in Scripture." *BibleStudyForLife.com*, Bible Study For Life, https://Biblestudyforlife.com/numbers.htm. Accessed 13 September 2021.

vi. "Purpose and Types of Guardianship." *FamilyLawSelfHelpCenter.org*, Family Law Self-Help Center, https://www.familylawselfhelpcenter.org/self-help/guardianship/overview/purpose-and-types-of-a-guardianship. Accessed 6 June 2021.

vii. "Guardian." *Dictionary.com*, Dictionary, https://www.dictionary.com/browse/guardian. Accessed 6 June 2021.

viii. "Guardian." *Etymonline.com*, Online Etymology Dictionary, https://www.etymonline.com/word/gu

ix. ardian#etymonline_v_33834. Accessed 6 June 2021.
"Guardian." *Merriam-Webster.com Dictionary*, Merriam-Webster, https://www.merriam-webster.com/dictionary/guardian. Accessed 6 June 2021.

x. Browning, David. "Take Me In." *SongLyrics.com*, Song Lyrics, http://www.songlyrics.com/dave-browning/take-me-in-lyrics/. Accessed 6 June 2021.

xi. "Spiritual Meaning of Thighs." *ThankGodForJesus.org*, Thank God for Jesus, https://www.thankGodforJesus.org/spiritual-meaning-of-thighs/. Accessed 3 November 2021.

xii. "Watchman." *Merriam-Webster.com Dictionary*, Merriam-Webster, https://www.merriam-webster.com/dictionary/watchman. Accessed 13 August 2021.

xiii. "Watchman." *Dictionary.com*, Dictionary, https://www.dictionary.com/browse/watchman. Accessed 13 August 2021.

xiv. "Gap." *Merriam-Webster.com Dictionary*, Merriam-Webster, https://www.merriam-webster.com/dictionary/gap. Accessed 13 August 2021.

xv. "Set One's Teeth on Edge." *Dictionary.com, Dictionary*, https://www.dictionary.com/browse/set-one-s-teeth-on-edge. Accessed 17 August 2021.

xvi. "107 Inspiring Joyce Meyer Quotes about Love, Patience & Motivation." *InternetPillar.com*, Internet Pillar, https://www.internetpillar.com/joyce-meyer-quotes/. Accessed 6 November 2021.

xvii. Klein, Stephen. "Tiger Dream Meaning and Interpretations." *DreamStop.com*, Dream Stop, http://dreamstop.com/tiger-dream-symbol/comment-page-3/. Accessed 13 December 2021.

xviii. Carrie. "Mice Dream Interpretation and Meaning." *SleepCulture.com*, Sleep Culture, https://sleepculture.com/mice-dream-interpretation-meaning/. Accessed 13 December 2021.

xix.	Ballenger, Mark. "What Is the Glory of God According to the Bible?" *ApplyGodsWord.com*, Apply God's Word, https://applyGodsword.com/what-is-the-glory-of-God-according-to-the-bible/. Accessed 8 September 2021.
xx.	"Dress rehearsal." *Merriam-Webster.com Dictionary*, Merriam-Webster, https://www.merriam-webster.com/dictionary/dress%20rehearsal. Accessed 12 September 2021.
xxi.	"The Number 40." *Aish.com*, Aish, https://www.aish.com/atr/The_Number_40.html. Accessed 12 September 2021.
xxii.	"Changing of the Guard." *Wiktionary.org*, Wiktionary, https://en.wiktionary.org/wiki/changing_of_the_guard. Accessed 13 September 2021.
xxiii.	"Why did the Magi bring gold, frankincense, and myrrh to Jesus?" *GotQuestions.org*, Got Questions, https://www.gotquestions.org/gold-frankincense-myrrh.html. Accessed 13 December 2021.
xxiv.	Parkin, Raelynn S. "What is Soaking?" *BrideSong.Blog*, Bride Song's Blog, https://bridesong.blog/what-is-soaking/. Accessed 13 December 2021.
xxv.	Conner, Bobby. "Awestruck by What We Behold!" *BobbyConner.org*, Bobby Conner, https://www.bobbyconner.org/articles/Awestruck-by-What-We-Behold!. Accessed 5 November 2021.
xxvi.	"Moriah." *EastonsBibleDictionary.org*, Easton's Bible Dictionary, https://www.eastonsBibledictionary.org/2598-Moriah.php. Accessed 23 October 2021.
xxvii.	"Ron Kenoly–We're Going Up to the High Places Lyrics." *SongLyrics.com*, Song Lyrics, http://www.songlyrics.com/ron-kenoly/we-re-going-up-to-the-high-places-lyrics/. Accessed 23 October 2021.
xxviii.	"Ditch." *EnAcademic.com*, English Terms Dictionary, https://terms_en.enacademic.com/12912/ditch. Accessed 26 October 2021.

xxix. "Chariot." *Merriam-Webster.com Dictionary*, Merriam-Webster, https://www.merriam-webster.com/dictionary/chariot. Accessed 26 October 2021.

xxx. "¼ Shekel Judea." *Numista.com*, Numista, https://en.numista.com/catalogue/pieces90465.html. Accessed 26 October 2021.

xxxi. Badillo, Tony. "The Floor Plan: Does it Reveal a Temple with a Human Form?" *TempleSecrets.info*, Temple Secrets, http://www.templesecrets.info/. Accessed 14 December, 2021.

xxxii. "Seraphim, Cherubim & The Four Living Creatures." *WhyAngels?.com*, Why Angels?, https://www.whyangels.com/seraphim_cherubim_creatures.html. Accessed 26 October 2021.

xxxiii. "4818. Merkabah." *BibleHub.com*, Strong's Concordance, https://Biblehub.com/hebrew/4818.htm. Accessed 26 October 2021.

xxxiv. "The Passage of Jordan the Symbol of Death." *Biblehub.com*, Bible Hub, https://Biblehub.com/sermons/auth/pressense/the_passage_of_jordan_the_symbol_of_death.htm. Accessed 3 November 2021.

xxxv. Henry, Miles. "What do Horses Symbolize Spiritually in Dreams and the Bible?" *HorseRacingSense.com*, Horse Racing Sense, https://horseracingsense.com/what-do-horses-symbolize-art-dreams-bible/. Accessed 6 November 2021.

xxxvi. "Secretariat (horse)." *Wikipedia.org*, Wikipedia, https://en.wikipedia.org/wiki/Secretariat_(horse). Accessed 1 November 2021.

xxxvii. "Jehu." *Wikipedia.org*, Wikipedia. https://en.wikipedia.org/wiki/Jehu. Accessed 2 November 2021.

xxxviii. Barnes, Deana. "What Windows Mean in Dreams." *NeWinePouring.com*, NeWine, https://newinepouring.com/what-windows-mean-dreams/. Accessed 6 November 2021.

xxxix. Edds, Michael. "100 Year Old Prophecies of Revival are Coming to Pass!" *GreatAwakening.Blogspot.com*, Encouragement for the Last Days, https://greatawakening.blogspot.com/2012/03/100-year-old-prophecies-of-revival-is.html. Accessed 6 November 2021.

ACKNOWLEDGMENTS

First of all I would like to thank Jessica Hallmark for all of her hard work in editing this book. Her help was invaluable. I am blessed to be your spiritual "grandma." Jessie, you are a gift from Heaven, and *"for such a time as this"* you have been brought into the Kingdom to be a blessing, not only to me, but to many. I love you!

I want to acknowledge my family at Oak Creek Assembly of God church, especially all of those who have enriched and blessed my life in love and friendship and specifically Pastor Brooks and Sherry. I love you all! I thank God for the day that Jesus made Oak Creek Assembly my home. The best is ahead, and God is about to pour out His fire and glory in our midst in a measure that will astound us!

I pray God's blessings upon Darlene and Son Rise Ministries in North Carolina. My heart is always with you. I believe that God has so much more for you. Keep pressing in; Jesus has untold blessings in store for you.

Holy Spirit, I acknowledge that You have been the Inspiration for the writing of this book. Without Your anointing I know that this book would never have been written. You have given me glorious revelations in Your Word, and I thank you from the bottom of my heart.

ABOUT THE AUTHOR

Theresa Reyna lives in Cudahy, Wisconsin with her husband Ron. She has three grown children and eight grandchildren. She has a master's degree in Biblical studies and was ordained by Son Rise Ministries in November of 2009. Her earnest desire is to do the will of the Father and accomplish her calling and destiny in Christ. Her passion is to reveal the full Truth of God's Word in order to see captive souls set free and God's children walking in the "High Place" with Jesus. This is Theresa's 5th book.

You can connect with her at www.lovecallsministry.com.

Theresa Reyna's Books:
    Unbelief: The Deadly Sin
    Called to Travail
    Prepare the Way of the Lord
    The God of War